FOOTBALL ON TRIAL

*Spectator violence and development
in the football world*

PATRICK MURPHY,

JOHN WILLIAMS
and

ERIC DUNNING

LONDON AND NEW YORK

First published 1990
by Routledge
11 New Fetter Lane, London EC4P 4EE

Simultaneously published in the USA and Canada
by Routledge
a division of Routledge, Chapman and Hall, Inc.
29 West 35th Street, New York, NY 10001

© 1990 Patrick Murphy, John Williams and Eric Dunning

Phototypeset in 10pt Baskerville by
Mews Photosetting, Beckenham, Kent
Printed in Great Britain by
Richard Clay Ltd, Bungay, Suffolk

British Library Cataloguing in Publication Data

Murphy, Patrick, *1943–*
Football on trial.
1. Western Europe. English association football
supporters. Crowds. Anti-social behaviour
I. Title II. Williams, John, *1954–* III. Dunning, Eric,
1936–
306.483

Library of Congress Cataloging in Publication Data also available

ISBN 0-415-05023-5

CONTENTS

CONTENTS

ILLUSTRATIONS

vii

FOREWORD

I am delighted to have been asked to write the Foreword for *Football on Trial*. It is the third book on football and its various problems by the Leicester team, and it is specially fitting as we look forward to the World Cup in Italy this year, and beyond to the United States in 1994, that this collection of essays has an *international* flavour. English football has no monopoly over complex and deep-seated difficulties. *Football on Trial* successfully identifies some of the more important defining elements of the 'English condition' while locating our own game firmly on the international stage. It is, as a consequence, a challenging and provocative read and a considerable and convincing achievement.

Nor is this collection concerned only with issues of violence and indiscipline on and off the field of play, though that is its main organizing theme. It also poses a number of exciting questions and possibilities about the game's future, for example, about the development of soccer in the United States, hosts of the World Cup Finals in 1994. In addition, the Leicester team considers the implications of developing European integration for football and examines the competition between soccer and the 'gridiron' game.

The Football Trust has provided financial support for research at Leicester University since 1982. In 1987, the Trust provided the funds for the establishment there of the Sir Norman Chester Centre for Football Research. Since that time, the Centre's work has spread from a central interest in problems of hooliganism to looking at, among other things: the community functions of clubs; women and football; the concept of 'membership'; football and education; and football, safety and spectator facilities. It is a wider-ranging brief, and the Centre receives and deals with hundreds of enquiries every year from students, academics, the police, professionals within the game and, of course, the media. It plays an invaluable role in disseminating research-based information about a sport which has been tempted in the past to take important decisions without properly consulting the facts. In a climate which was not wholly hospitable to research, I am pleased to say that the Football Trust has been able through its support for the Sir Norman Chester Centre to perform a vital function in bringing together the academic world and the world of football. It is a marriage which deserves to last, and we are sure it will.

Football in Britain faces many problems, but its overall future is far from bleak. Crowds have been rising again over the past few years. The post-Hillsborough climate has provided fresh possibilities for new relationships between clubs and their supporters. It also provides a challenge for the Football Trust, the Football Grounds Improvement Trust and other bodies to meet the demands of clubs and their fans for safer, more comfortable spectator facilities. On the international stage, the promise of Italy and the feast of entertainment which is in prospect will bring together once again, via television and live attendance, hundreds of millions of spectators in celebration of a game which, as *Football on Trial* demonstrates, spans the globe like no other. Despite its difficulties, the game will never lack an audience, nor young boys and (increasingly) girls who want to play it. The future health of the game requires high quality research about its strengths and weaknesses. *Football on Trial* gives those of us with the interests of the game at heart cause for deep thought about its problems but also for great optimism about its continuing capacity to engage the passions.

Richard Faulkner
Deputy Chairman of the Football Trust

PREFACE

In June 1990, footballers representing the twenty-four nations whose teams have won through the preliminary rounds will meet in Italy to contest the fourteenth World Cup Finals. Not for the first time in the history of the world's most popular sport, they will be competing in an atmosphere which can be realistically described as embattled and beleaguered. 'There is tension in our national game as there has never been before – on the pitch, off the pitch, in the boardrooms and in the corridors of power. Goodness knows where it will all lead.'[1] These were the words of Aston Villa manager, Graham Taylor, written in November 1989. Shortly afterwards, similar sentiments were expressed by the Swiss General Secretary of FIFA (the Fédération Internationale de Football Associations), Joseph Blatter. Speaking specifically of spectator hooliganism as a spreading international problem, he is reported to have said: 'We want to defend the popularity of this great game . . . If we don't, hooliganism will indeed destroy it.'[2]

The essays in *Football on Trial* are concerned mainly with aspects of soccer's 'hooligan crisis'. They build in a variety of ways on the analyses in our *Hooligans Abroad* (1984; 1989) and *The Roots of Football Hooliganism* (1988), and are offered in the hope that they may make a small contribution to the 'defence' of which Joseph Blatter spoke.

Only two of the essays in *Football on Trial* have been published previously. The particular issues dealt with include: the roots of player indiscipline and violence, the social history of spectator hooliganism in Britain, and the part played by the mass media in the generation of the latter. There is a degree of overlap and repetition in these historical essays. We hope the reader will bear with us in this. We have not attempted to edit out all repetitions in these essays because we want each of them to be readable on its own.

Also included are an essay on soccer hooliganism as a European phenomenon and a case study of some participant observation research carried out on a group of English soccer hooligans in the early 1980s. The former is based on some collaborative, cross-cultural research we are currently engaged in with a number of continental colleagues. In the latter, a group of hooligans are allowed, as it were, 'to speak for themselves'. Despite the fact that football hooliganism has changed in specific ways since this research was carried out – some of them are documented in the social history chapters – the case study nevertheless reveals a number of underlying attitudes, values and motivations which have persisted. There is also a chapter based on what one might call 'grounded speculation' which addresses, in a preliminary and provisional way, the complex issue of why no direct equivalents of European-style soccer hooliganism appear to have arisen in the United States. This is offered in the hope that it may help to stimulate policy-relevant comparative research and was written with the fact very much in mind that the 1994 World Cup Finals are to be played in the USA. Finally, we have included an essay on the sorts of policy strategies which seem to us to take more account of research findings and the complexities of the phenomenon. We think they are strategies which might stand a better chance of reducing the incidence of soccer hooliganism than those which have been applied – and which have, on balance, failed – over the past thirty years.

Although most of the essays in *Football on Trial* are based on our research into football hooliganism, we have also addressed a number of other aspects of the overall crisis which currently faces the game. Central in this connection are the prospects for soccer of the intensifying process of competition between different national sport forms which appears to be accompanying the current trend towards greater world integration. We have singled out the competition between soccer and American or 'gridiron' football for special attention in this regard. Also considered are the implications for the Association game of the accelerating trend towards greater European integration, and the frequency with which spectator tragedies seem to have struck the English game in recent years.

Many people have helped us in our research on football and football spectators. Special thanks are due to Margaret Milsom and Ann Ketnor for undertaking the onerous task of typing the manuscript. Ivan Waddington and Adrian Goldberg read through some of the chapters and offered valuable comments. Tom Bucke was in charge of the computations which are central to the discussion of English fans at the 1988 European Championships. Finally, thanks are due to the Football Trust, not only for their financial assistance over the years, but also for the invaluable support they have given to our research in so many non-financial ways.

NOTES

1 *Today*, 24 Nov. 1989.
2 *The Times*, 8 Dec. 1989. Mr Blatter reports that FIFA is proposing to use its leverage to get major soccer clubs, world-wide, to convert their stadia into all-seaters as a means of dealing with the hooligan threat. While such stadia may be desirable in themselves, we have to reiterate that our research suggests that it is wrong to see them as a panacea. Hooliganism is a deeply rooted *social* phenomenon, and will only respond to appropriate *social* measures. Changes to the 'built environment' are by and large irrelevant in that regard. See our *All-Seated Football Grounds and Hooliganism: the Coventry City Experience*, Sir Norman Chester Centre for Football Research, University of Leicester, 1984.

Chapter One

FOOTBALL ON TRIAL:
Reflections on the future of soccer as a world game

Soccer is, without any shadow of doubt, the world's most popular sport. It is, as Lawrence Kitchin put it as long ago as 1966, the only 'global idiom' apart from science.[1] Some idea of the game's development towards its premier world position is provided by the fact that, when FIFA started life in 1904, it had only seven national associations as members, all of them European. By 1986, however, it had a membership of 150 drawn from every quarter of the globe.[2] In short, soccer as an organized game is now played in the majority of the world's nations at a level sufficiently high for their national teams to be recognized by FIFA as qualifying for entrance to the World Cup.

Of course, soccer is not only popular as a participant sport but as a spectator sport as well. A measure of its popularity in the latter regard is provided by the fact that some 1.75 million people are recorded as having attended the World Cup Finals in Spain in 1982.[3] As a television spectacle, the game's global appeal is even greater. More particularly, a staggering figure of no less than 200 million people are estimated to have watched the 1986 World Cup Finals on TV. If recent trends continue, an even greater number will watch the 1990 Finals in Italy and an even greater number still, the 1994 Finals in the United States. What are the principal sources of soccer's global appeal?

The late Bill Shankly, a former manager of Liverpool FC, was certainly exaggerating when he suggested that football is a 'more important matter than life or death'. Nevertheless, in making such a suggestion, he came close to capturing the quasi-religious character of the support that the game manages to attract in countries all over the world. The sociologists Stephen Edgell and David Jary were elaborating on the basic idea articulated by Shankly when they postulated in 1975 that soccer is what they called an 'evolutionary

1

universal', similar, they contended, to science, industrialism, jazz and rhythm and blues in what they described as its 'capacity to optimize biological gratifications and social ends'.[4] That may be a bit of a mouthful of jargon but the underlying idea appears to be basically sound. Arthur Hopcraft expressed something similar both more circumspectly than Shankly and more elegantly than Edgell and Jary when he wrote that:' What happens on the football field matters, not in the way that food matters but as poetry does to some people and alcohol does to others; it engages the personality'.[5] In short, there appears to be something about the structure of soccer that gives it a very wide appeal in the modern world, an appeal that appears to be relatively independent of the level of development of countries, the socio-political character of the regimes by which they are ruled, their allegiances and the alliances that they are involved in. The rapid development of women's football in many countries in recent years suggests that the appeal of the game may also be in a certain sense relatively independent of gender. However, as we shall argue later on, the continued stress on football as a 'man's game' may well lie at the roots of many of its current problems. It is, for example, perhaps more than a coincidence that in England, where hooliganism has been entrenched as a serious social problem for some time, women's football has a rather low status, with few participants or spectators. But let us enquire a little more closely into the sources of soccer's appeal.

Part of the wide appeal of soccer – or of 'Association football', to give the game its proper name[6] – undoubtedly stems from the fact that it does not require much equipment and is thus comparatively cheap to play. It can also be played informally with less – and sometimes more – than the full complement of players. It is also playable on the streets, on school playgrounds and in open fields; Ferenc Puskas, the captain of the famous 1950s Hungarian side, described vividly how he taught himself the rudiments of the game in a goose pasture using a bundle of rags instead of a ball![7] Ideally, though, the game does require a properly levelled pitch,[8] together with goal-posts and nets, and providing such equipment and a levelled surface can be initially expensive. However, similar requirements are necessary for practically every sport, so it remains true to say that soccer is comparatively cheap. Nevertheless, we think that relative cheapness is only one aspect of a broader constellation of characteristics that account for soccer's wide appeal.

Many of the features we shall identify in the discussion that follows

2

are, of course, not peculiar to soccer but shared by other sports as well. If we are right, though, it is *only* soccer that possesses the *whole* constellation. In attempting to show how that is so, we shall start by looking at aspects of the basic structure of the game.

The rules of soccer and its overall structure are both comparatively simple. For example, it started out with only fourteen basic rules compared with fifty-nine in rugby.[9] As a result, soccer has always been easier to understand and learn, whether from a playing or a spectating point of view. Furthermore, the basic rules of soccer have remained virtually unchanged since 1863 when the game as we now know it was first invented. This has imparted a degree of stability and continuity which must have facilitated its diffusion around the world. However, whilst the rules of soccer have remained remarkably stable over time, they have nevertheless involved a fine balance between what one might call 'fixity' and 'elasticity'. What we mean by this is that, whilst the rules of soccer have permitted the unambiguous communication of what is and what is not permitted in the game – despite the existence of characteristically different national football styles, including different national styles of fouling, there can be few human activities on which there exists such a near-universal consensus globally as that regarding the rules of soccer – they have simultaneously provided endless scope for tactical innovation in the quest for playing success. Think only of the last four decades. Since the 1950s, we have witnessed the demise of 2-3-5 and its replacement by the 4-2-4 and 4-3-3 systems. We have also seen the 'push and run' and the 'long ball' games, the use of 'sweepers' and 'liberos', to say nothing of the concept of 'total football' which is said to have originated in the Netherlands in the 1970s.

The tactical evolution of football and the merits of different ways of organizing the disposition of players on the field are subjects that provide ample scope for discussion and debate among soccer *cognoscenti*. We think, though, that the basic appeal of the game runs considerably deeper. Even for its 'intellectuals', that is to say, soccer's appeal is more than intellectual. It is visceral as well. To paraphrase Arthur Hopcraft, there is something about it that 'engages the passions'.

It is, of course, possible to derive forms of aesthetic satisfaction from watching a game of football. The skills of individual players in controlling and striking the ball and the execution of skilful manoeuvres by the members of a team provide plenty of scope in this regard, particularly at the highest levels of the game. The excitement of a match

3

can also be enhanced by spectacular presentation. The very fact of being a member of a large, expectant crowd can be exciting as well. Then there is the question of the way in which competitions are organized: for example, whether in the form of 'cups' or 'leagues' or some combination of the two. Long-term competitions of these kinds add spice to particular matches for players and spectators alike.[10] However, there is also reason for believing that the very structure of the game has evolved in such a way that it is intrinsically conducive to the regular generation of excitement.

As they have come down to us since 1863, the rules of soccer have developed so as to involve a fine balance between a number of inter-dependent polarities.[11] We have already mentioned the balance between fixity and elasticity of rules. Others are the polarity between force and skill, that between providing scope for physical challenge and controlling it, that between individual and team play, and that between attack and defence. As early as 1863, the game can be said to have developed in these regards into what Norbert Elias calls a 'mature' sport.[12] As such, its structure permits the recurrent genera-tion of levels of tension-excitement that are enjoyable for players and spectators alike. At the heart of this tension-excitement is the fact that matches are 'mock battles' played with a ball, physical struggles between two groups governed by rules which serve to allow the passions to rise yet keep them – most of the time – in check. To the extent that they are enforced and/or voluntarily obeyed, the rules of soccer also limit the risk of serious injury to players.

Given such a structure, at a football match one is able to experience in a controlled and socially acceptable manner and in a short and concentrated period of time a whole gamut of strong feelings: hope when one's team looks close to scoring and elation when they do; fear when the opponents threaten to score and disappointment when they succeed. During a closely fought match, the spectators flit constantly from one feeling-state to another until the issue has finally been decided. Then, the supporters of the winning side experience triumph and jubilation, those of the losers dejection and despair. If the match has ended in a draw, the supporters of both sides are liable to experience a mixture of emotions.

Soccer matches are, of course, by no means invariably closely fought encounters. Unlike, say, 'classical' concerts and theatre, sports performances are unscripted and this gives them an element of greater spontaneity and uncertainty.[13] In attending a football match or other sport one is, as it were, taking a greater risk with one's emotions. Perhaps this constitutes part of sport's appeal? However, the unscripted character of soccer also means that matches can fail to come up to expectations and be experienced as monotonous and dull. Nevertheless, in a properly organized competitive framework,[14] playing in or watching a game of football is, more often than not, emotionally arousing. Indeed, a match which, for the neutral spectator, may be dull or monotonous, may be experienced by the committed fan as highly arousing especially if it produces the 'right' result. This structural capacity for generating excitement enables matches to serve as a counter to the emotional staleness and monotony that are liable to be engendered by the normal routines of everyday life.[15] But, of course, to experience excitement at a soccer match one has to *care*. In order, as it were, for the 'gears' of one's passions to engage, one has to be *committed*, to *identify* with one or another of the teams and to *want* to see it win. The question of identification is an issue of critical importance both for the routine functioning of soccer and for some of the problems generated in connection with the game. Because of its importance, identification is a subject to which we shall return later on. Before we do, we want first of all briefly to discuss some aspects of the development of the modern game.

As we have said, the soccer form of football dates from 1863. That was the year when the English Football Association, the first national football ruling body in the world and the progenitor of the modern game, was founded. Games called 'football', of course, can be reliably traced back to the fourteenth century.[16] In the Middle Ages, however, 'football' was just one of a variety of names applied in Britain to a class of 'folk games' – games of the 'common people' – that were, comparatively speaking, unregulated, rough and wild. Other names were 'camp ball', 'hurling' and 'knappan'. Continental variants included 'la soule' in France, 'rouler la boule' and 'la souile'[17] in Belgium and the 'gioco della pugna' in Italy. It was in England in the nineteenth century, however, that the development of recognizably modern forms of football began to take place. This process appears to have started in the public schools around the 1840s and to have been continued and consolidated by adult members of the upper and middle classes in the 1850s and 1860s. It was, in a very important respect, a 'civilizing' development in that it involved the increasing abandonment of mass games played by unrestricted numbers of people according to local, customary rules and their increasing replacement by games characterized by limited numbers that were equalized between the contending sides and which involved written, national rules which demanded from the players the exercise of strict self-control over physical contact and the use of physical force.

Two main forms of football emerged in conjunction with this process: soccer and rugby. Of the two, and perhaps for the sorts of reasons we identified earlier, soccer proved by far the more successful. It diffused to every corner of the globe whilst, with one or two notable exceptions such as France and more recently Italy, Romania, the USSR and Japan, rugby has remained restricted mainly to countries of the former British Empire. However, with its successful diffusion, problems for soccer began to accrue. Whilst the game was restricted to the English upper and middle classes, it was possible to rely for order on the field of play on the fact that, as 'English gentlemen', the players could be expected to abide voluntarily by the rules, to control themselves and to settle disputes by means of discussion. As the game spread to wider social circles, however, it became necessary to add more formal mechanisms of control. It was largely in this way, for example, that referees and linesmen and the regulations concerning penalty kicks were introduced. Problems of control were further exacerbated as the game spread internationally and, above all, as soccer at the highest levels began to attract large crowds and to be commercialized and spectacularized.[18]

In this developing situation, players – many of them, of course, not British – who were not familiar with the 'gentlemanly code' began to participate more and more, players who were not restrained by the ethos of 'fairness' or by ideas such as the notion that 'taking part is more important than winning'. Forms of class, regional and national – latterly, increasingly ethnic and racial – hostility and rivalry began to be superimposed on the intrinsic tension of matches, heteronomous forms of tension generated in the wider society and unrelated to the football match *per se*. At the same time, players at the highest levels began to be seen more and more as representatives of the cities, towns and countries whose populations paid to see them play and, in this context, they began to experience growing pressure for success in what was becoming an increasingly competitive field. Such pressure came not only from the crowds but from the media as well. Most directly of all, it came from the whole panoply of managers, coaches, club officials and directors who began to be employed more and more as top-level clubs began, to a degree, to develop into bureaucratically run business enterprises. In this situation, players found themselves competing for finite – though, of course, over time generally expanding – prestige and monetary rewards. Given this, together with the mounting pressures to which they were subject to fulfil the expectations of a multiplicity of others, it is hardly surprising that, besides attempting to improve their individual and team skills and to develop new tactics and tactical team-formations, more and more responded by bending and breaking the rules and by using forms of cheating and intimidatory violence that contravene not only the 'laws' of the game but its 'spirit' as well.

In recent years, commentators on soccer have sometimes spoken of a trend towards increasing violence in the game. Some of them seem convinced that football is on the slippery downwards slope towards 'barbarization', that it is experiencing a kind of 'civilizing process' in reverse as far as the behaviour of players is concerned. However, we are not so sure. We have no wish to deny that a problem of player violence exists, though it takes different forms in different countries and is more serious in some than in others. Yet, by contrast, say, with rugby or American football, both of which are focused more centrally on muscularity and physical power (though in the latter case more formally than in the former), soccer still seems intrinsically to be an exemplar of a relatively highly civilized and at least potentially non-violent sport. That is to say, to the extent that it occurs – and there are obviously differences between clubs, countries, periods and even particular individual players in this regard – the violence of soccer appears to be less a function of the rules *per se* and more a function of (for example) the ethos and values of the players and the pressures they are under.

The impression that soccer is, in fact, a relatively non-violent game is reinforced when one takes account of the very great speed at which the modern game is played (perhaps especially in Britain), the intense pressure to win that is placed on top-level players, and the competition for rewards in which they are involved. Given all of that, one might perhaps expect much higher rates of foul and dirty play and of serious injuries than seem currently to occur.[19]

However, whilst the evidence for a 'reverse civilizing process' as far as player violence is concerned may be problematic, the situation regarding *crowd* violence would appear, at least superficially, to be different. As far as Britain, more specifically mainly England, is concerned, the press, with its frequent references to 'thugs', 'savages', 'lunatics', 'louts' and 'mindless morons' whenever the subject of football hooliganism raises its head, certainly contributes to the widely held impression that fan behaviour has grown considerably less civilized in recent years. What are the facts in that connection? It is to the subject of spectator violence, more specifically of football hooliganism, that we shall turn our attention now. We shall start by returning to the question of identification and by considering some basic facts.

From the start to the finish of their lives, human beings are orientated towards and interdependent with fellow humans.[20] They need to form close affective bonds, whether directly with other people or indirectly through some symbolic medium such as a flag. (In football, whether or not it is exploited for purposes of commercial gain, such symbolic bonding can be with a club and its emblems.) Such bonds, however, tend to be simultaneously inclusive and exclusive. That is to say, the membership of any 'we-group' tends to imply generally positive feelings towards other members of the group and pre-fixed attitudes of competitiveness, hostility and exclusiveness towards the members of one or more 'they-groups'.[21] Although such a pattern can be modified – for example, via education – it is easy to observe how frequently the very constitution and continuation over time of 'we-groups' seems to depend on the regular expression of hostility towards and even actual combat with the members of 'they-groups'. That is to say, specific patterns of conflict appear to arise out of this basic form of human bonding and simultaneously to form a focus for the reinforcement of 'we-group' bonds. Such a pattern is one of the things that seem to be at work – at different levels and in complex ways – in football hooliganism. Let us elaborate on this.

The majority of people who go to watch a football match – we are thinking primarily of top-level, professional football in this connection – go because they have some form of bond or identification with the team. It may be that they have learned to identify with it because it represents the town or city where they were born. Or perhaps it just represents a part of it such as a particular social stratum, a local community or district or a religious or ethnic group. Whatever is the case in this regard, these people will have had to be introduced to the game via exposure to what one might call the 'subculture of football'.[22] Such an introduction will have probably come initially via the agency of a 'significant other' such as a parent and will have been sustained through, for example, membership of a football-orientated peer group. That is the case because not all members of, say, the working class in a particular town or city are 'football people'. However, the 'significant other' who introduces a person to football and to more or less continuous bonding or identification with a particular club might also be a cousin, an uncle, an aunt, a neighbour, a teacher, or one or more members of a peer group. Increasingly in modern society, of course, the role of 'significant other' in this regard can be played by television. That, together with the fact of geographical mobility, helps to explain why the support for top-level teams tends to be more than simply local.

Although some people go to football matches on their own, the majority of spectators tend to go in the company of family members and/or friends. At a match, that is to say, members of the crowd are bonded both directly to small groups in their immediate vicinity and, less directly, to one or another of the teams. At a more abstract level, they are bonded to the club and, at a more abstract level still, to the game *per se*. It is common to think of a large crowd as an anonymous, amorphous and unorganized mass. In fact, as one can see, a football crowd is an aggregate of small, tightly knit groups united in their more or less strong interest in, identification with and knowledge of the game, but simultaneously divided, among other things, over whether they support one or another of the two contending teams.

This basic line of cleavage represents an axis of potential conflict at any football match. Such conflict is likely to be most intense when and where one of the following conditions or a combination of them holds. More particularly, intense conflict in connection with a football match is more likely when and where: (1) the teams represent groups that are in some kind of serious conflict with each other in the wider society; (2) the rival supporters are strongly committed to victory for their sides, but where this commitment is not tempered by a 'fair play' ethic based on a notion of sport as playful and friendly competition rather than serious rivalry; and (3) where the groups involved, measured on what one might call a 'localism–cosmopolitanism' scale, stand towards the 'localism' end of the continuum and hence have a learned difficulty in tolerating 'difference' or 'strangeness'. Such 'localistic' groups represent the general human tendency towards 'we-group' inclusion and 'they-group' exclusion in a particularly stark and extreme form.

In British society – and perhaps in others, too (at the moment we are not sure) – each of these three conditions tends to prevail most frequently in the working class, particularly at the lower levels. Since, moreover, football in Britain is primarily a working-class sport, this means that the game has had a history of violent crowd disorderliness stretching back to the origins of professional football at the end of the nineteenth century.[23] However, this is not the place for an analysis of the history of football hooliganism in the United Kingdom. Other chapters in this volume touch upon this issue. Rather, what we want to do is to look more closely at the different forms of football hooliganism that are currently observable.

It is common for people to think of football hooliganism as a simple and unidimensional phenomenon. In fact, however, it is complex and multifaceted. It also takes a number of different forms. More particularly, it varies along a complex of separable but partly overlapping continua. Central among these continua are: (1) the degree to which the hooliganism is match-related; (2) the degree to which violence is involved and, when it is, the forms that it takes; (3) the degree to which the hooligan groups are organized and to which their disruptive behaviour is planned before the match; and (4) the degree to which heteronomous values, values entirely unconnected with the ideal of football as a 'sport', are expressed. Let us elaborate on this.

Behaviour of the kind that is liable to be labelled as 'football hooliganism' officially and by the media can take the form of a 'pitch invasion' by a single individual or a small group. It can also take the form of a mass encroachment on to the field of play. Whatever their scale, pitch invasions and encroachments can be for such purposes as celebrating the scoring of a goal. They can also be an act of defiance to the authorities and to 'respectable' society and its values. Mass encroachments, however, are often indicative of a concerted and possibly – though not necessarily – pre-planned attempt by a group of fans to secure the suspension of a match which their side is losing and which involves a vital issue such as relegation to a lower division. The hope is that, by behaving in this way, they will be able to force the authorities to arrange a replay and thus give the side with which they identify and with whose League status their self-esteem is bound up another chance. Whatever their kind and scale, it is important to note that pitch invasions do not always involve physical violence. However, *reactive* violence by the 'invading' fans can be provoked if they are injudiciously handled by the authorities.

Violent match-related football hooliganism can take the form of a physical attack on a referee or linesman who is perceived, whether rightly or not, as having made a decision biased against the team which the fans involved in the attack support. It can also take the form of an attack on a player or players of the opposing side who are, again rightly or wrongly, perceived as having engaged in foul or unfair play. Alternatively, it can take the form of an attack on fans of the rival team; for example, because their mode of expressing support for *their* team involves denigration of the opponents and is thus experienced as a threat to the self-image of the attacking fans and to their identification with and support for their team.

The number of fans who take part in such match-related violence varies. It can also involve the use simply of fists or feet, or, alternatively, weapons such as knives or missiles of various kinds can be used. Where weapons are employed – unless they have simply been picked up or fashioned on the spot – the probability is high that a degree of premeditation and pre-planning will have been involved. In such cases, that is to say, the fans will have come to the match with the knowledge that they might be involved in a fight. However, it might have been the intention of some of them to fight only defensively and not to initiate attacks. Their interest in football, in other words, might have been greater than their interest in fighting.

In England, especially since the mid-1960s, a certain kind of person has been attracted to football primarily because they see it as an attractive context in which to fight. In a football context, a ready-made group of opponents is available: the supporters of the opposing team. At a football match, too, given the large crowds, it is comparatively easy to act disruptively and escape detection and arrest. For such groups, football serves as a focus for a kind of 'war games'. They attack opposing supporters because they see them as 'invaders', and they attack them in pubs, city centres and on public transport as well as in and around the football ground itself. Related to this is the fact that groups of this kind see travel to away matches as providing an opportunity for 'invading' the territory of others and for attempting to establish control over it for a while.

Behaviour of this latter kind can be entirely unrelated to football, and some members of the groups involved can have little or no interest in or knowledge of the game *per se*. What attracts them fundamentally is the opportunity for fighting, for demonstrating their masculine prowess in terms of a set of values that stress as signs of being a 'real man' such things as fighting, being loyal to friends in a fight, and not 'backing down'; that is, not running away and refusing to fight. Also likely to be involved is a strong measure of local identification and local pride, together with an equally strong measure of hostility and contempt towards outsiders. A degree of pre-planning and organization is likely to be involved as well. Such groups can also vary in terms of whether they are interested in fighting for its own sake – for example, because they find it pleasurably exciting and because being present at or taking part in a fight serves as a means of enhancing their prestige among their peers – or whether they are involved in disturbances at football for politically motivated reasons. In England, again since the mid-1960s, both these forms of football hooliganism – they are often closely interrelated – have become increasingly common. In fact, one can say that they constitute the currently dominant forms of English football hooligan behaviour.

Politically motivated groups, particularly groups associated with far right political parties such as the National Front and the British National Party, have been attracted to football partly because they see football hooligans as potential recruits to their cause and partly because, as 'white supremacists', they are opposed to the increasing numbers of black players who have become prominent in the British game in recent years. One of the things they find attractive about football in this regard is the frequent expression of racist sentiments not only by many of the football hooligans but also by far larger sections of British crowds.

Whether more or less overtly politically motivated or not, what these wholly or relatively non-football-related forms of hooliganism in conjunction with football have in common is the fact that they involve the expression of values asociated with concepts of violently aggressive masculinity. The people who engage in such behaviour come over-whelmingly from around the bottom of the social scale.[24] However, some of the 'generals', the organizers and orchestrators of these aggressive and socially disruptive acts in a football context, come from the lower middle classes and, in a few cases, members even of the higher professional strata are known to have been involved.

As one can see, in Britain at any rate, perhaps especially in England, football hooliganism is related in a complex way to the class structure. It is not, as is commonly believed, a simple consequence of short-term phenomena such as unemployment (the favoured left-wing explana-tion) or 'permissiveness' (the thesis favoured by the political right). Of course, such short-term phenomena[25] and the political and socio-cultural reactions and adjustments to them inevitably have some effects on football hooliganism and similar problems. However, such effects are for the most part epiphenomenal. That is to say, they affect the surface manifestations of football hooliganism far more than they affect its core. At its roots, if we are right, football hooliganism is the consequence of a deep-rooted complex or configuration of socio-cultural traits, more specifically of a long-established subculture of aggressive masculinity that is predominantly but by no means solely lower class. It is a subculture that celebrates very narrow, rigid and exclusive notions of locality, community and nation, notions that involve an ambivalent mixture of contempt for and fear of anything or anybody that is 'different', 'foreign', 'strange'. As such, again at least in England, it receives substantial reinforcement from a popular press which, although it regularly condemns the hooligans as 'louts' or 'scum', equally regularly celebrates the superiority of the English over 'Krauts', 'Frogs', 'Argies' and other national groups described using similarly derogatory terms. In this way, the popular press in England contributes to the perpetuation of a cultural climate in which the extreme expressions of nationalism and racialism by the football hooligans are able to flourish. At the least, the 'tabloid' press fails to provide regular counters to sentiments of this kind.

In this and other ways, the popular press in England can be said to constitute part of the problem of football hooliganism. This fact may help in part to explain why English football hooligans have engaged in hooliganism abroad more frequently than their counterparts from other countries. So, too, may the fact that extreme nationalist political parties became involved in football hooliganism in England at least as early as the late 1970s. They were attracted to football, not only as a potentially fruitful context for recruiting to their cause but also because travel to matches abroad provides regular opportunities for celebrating their ideas of 'English supremacy' by fighting 'foreign foes'.

Together with a class structure which plays a part in regularly producing and reproducing a culture of aggressive masculinity, Britain's chauvinistic popular press and the regular generation in Britain of support for extreme right white supremacist groups constitute important parts of the configuration of cultural and behavioural traits that combine to make up the distinctively English variant of football hooliganism. Any policy designed to reduce the incidence of hooliganism in a football context will require the authorities to approach the problem, not simply by means of the common 'knee-jerk' imposition of severer punishments and stricter controls, but also by social and educational measures aimed at attracting people to milder, less destructively aggressive and chauvinistic forms of masculine behaviour and at weaning them away from a crudely xenophobic popular press.

But let us begin to bring this chapter to a close. If our arguments have any substance, football is threatened at the moment not so much by a problem of growing violence on the field of play – there *is* such a problem, but it is, in our opinion, overblown both by the press and in the popular imagination[26] – as by the twin scourge of spectator hooliganism and, in Britain at least, a sensationalizing and crudely xenophobic popular press. Action is urgently needed currently on both these scores. It is needed, however, not only on account of the intrinsic threat posed by such problems but also because we appear to be living at the moment at a critical historical conjuncture. More particularly, we are passing through a period of rapid, profound and widespread social change, a period when many old forms of social integration are breaking down and new forms are emerging. Such processes are bound to have multiple implications for and repercussions on the playing and organization of football. Let us elaborate on this.

Whilst it would be naïve to think that Europe is on the brink of quickly becoming some kind of single, federated super-state – a kind of United States of Europe – it is clear nevertheless that the nation-states of at least the western parts of the European continent are at present becoming more integrated with one another, more inter-dependent and mutually attuned, and hence more subject to pressures and controls centralized at the European level.[27] These processes necessarily involve, to a degree, the disintegration of specific institu-tions at the level of particular nation-states. At the same time, developments especially in the spheres of transport and communication are making world society as a whole more integrated in specific respects. These disintegration and reintegration processes are creating a whole host of opportunities for some groups and disadvantages for others. They are also leading to the emergence of new focuses of competition and conflict, or perhaps just contributing to the intensification of lines of cleavage that have already been in evidence for some time.

As far as soccer is concerned, it may be that these processes, coupled with the growing influence of multinational companies in the finance of European clubs and the overtones of television, are creating the conditions which will enhance the likelihood of the formation of a European Football League. The creation of such a League, however, is bound to involve conflict, dissension and resentment as some groups strive to take advantage of the opportunities thus presented and others – for example, some of the current representatives of football's national ruling bodies and the representatives of clubs which just miss being included in the new European competition – fight against their anticipated or actual loss of 'perks', autonomy and status.

It is not possible to predict either the precise form that such a European League would take or how serious the conflicts associated with its formation are likely to be. One can, however, say that an as yet little-noticed aspect of the development towards greater European integration consists of the fact that soccer hooliganism is beginning to become an increasingly European problem rather than one restricted simply to particular nations. We are thinking in this connection not only of the growing numbers of continentals who are beginning to ape the English and engage in hooliganism abroad but also of the evidence that there are definite, albeit currently small, linkages between the hooligans of different countries, perhaps especially between hooligans with far-right political affiliations.[28] Given this, in order to tackle the problem of football hooliganism effectively, co-ordinated action *at a European level* is going to be required and not just action in particular countries independently. However, if the balance between conflict and consensus in the emergent development towards a more integrated framework for European football veers too strongly towards the conflict pole, it may prove even more difficult to secure the necessary co-ordination than it has done in the past and the scourge of hooliganism may continue to grow with serious repercussions for what is, in many ways, an already beleaguered game.

The development towards greater world integration that we spoke of, whilst not devoid of opportunities for soccer, at the same time has implications which could intensify the threats to which the game is currently subject. We are thinking particularly of the fact that North American sport forms, particularly 'gridiron' football, are currently being vigorously marketed in Europe, backed by American capital and media 'know-how'. That is to say, a process of intensifying competition is beginning to occur on a world scale between sports such as soccer, which developed in the 'first industrial nation', Britain, and sports such as gridiron football, which developed in the principal 'second-wave' industrial country, the USA. The media-supported idea that American sports are entirely free from spectator violence is perhaps an important weapon on their side.[29]

It is again too early to predict what the outcome of this competition is going to be. Since it involves deeply rooted cultural preferences, the process is unlikely to be quick. It is, moreover, a two-way process, one that is taking place on both sides of the Atlantic. That is to say, not only does gridiron football constitute a threat to soccer in the lands where the latter first originated and took root, but soccer is a threat to gridiron football in the country of its origin, too. Data adequate for reaching a definitive judgement on this issue are not available at the moment, but let us look at some of the facts that are currently at hand.

The first British gridiron team, the 'London Ravens', was formed as recently as 1983. By 1983, however, the 'Budweiser League', sponsored by the American brewing combine, Anheuser-Busch, had a membership of 105 teams and the rival 'British Gridiron Football League' a membership of 72. Similarly, although there is a widespread feeling that the British TV audience for National Football League (NFL) football may have reached a peak – whether temporary or not it is impossible at present to say – Channel 4's audience for its coverage of gridiron matches in the USA rose from 1.1 million in 1982–83 to 3.7 million in 1987–88.[30] Market research suggests that the majority of Britons who are attracted to the TV-watching of American football are younger male professionals and male members of the lower middle classes, a fact which may be further contracting the social range from which British soccer draws its spectating clientele at a time when a concerted attempt is being made to take the game 'up market'. It is perhaps also worth pointing out in this connection that very few people some twenty or thirty years ago would have envisaged that the American game had any future whatsoever outside its native shores.

The converse of this transatlantic spread of the gridiron game is the fact that, although professional soccer has virtually collapsed in the United States, Association football has been spreading there rapidly at the grass-roots level. Thus, some eight million players are currently registered with the US Soccer Federation. Perhaps just as significantly, whereas there were only seventeen women's collegiate soccer leagues in the USA in 1977, today the figure is nearer 400 and the US women's team ranks among the top ten in the world.[31] It seems likely that the fact that the 1994 World Cup Finals are going to be staged in the United States may well give a further boost to soccer in that country, perhaps helping in the revival there of the professional game. This time, the fact that a far larger number of native Americans will have had playing experience of soccer may help it to take firmer root.

Whether or not there will be hooliganism in the context of the 1994 World Cup Finals is another eventuality which it is impossible to predict. It is, however, possible to offer some grounded speculation on the comparative success of soccer as a participant sport in the USA. Even in what is probably still the world's most affluent society, the game's relative cheapness is obviously a factor of some importance in this connection. Probably more important, however, is the fact that, as a game, soccer does not place such a premium as gridiron football does on sheer size and strength. In that sense, soccer is potentially more 'democratic': a greater proportion of any population is physically equipped to play it. It is perhaps also reasonable to describe soccer as intrinsically more 'civilized', at least when it is played according to the rules. That is to say, while it, too, is a mock battle played with a ball, in soccer the warlike element is less obvious, more muted and controlled. It is, for example, a more open game in the sense that scrimmages and mêlées are not a central feature. That, together with the smaller number and greater simplicity of its rules, makes it easier to control. Nor is tackling off the ball a legitimate tactic, and the players do not dress up in a form of armour in some ways reminiscent of that worn by medieval knights. The protective clothing of gridiron players is even referred to as 'armament' in a recent book describing American football for British TV viewers.[32] Finally, although some forms of illegitimate soccer violence are perhaps difficult for the match officials to detect and control – for example, the use of elbows when climbing to head the ball or the apparently accidental trip – they are, as far as we can tell, fewer in number than those available to gridiron players. At least that appears to be the case if one takes account of the following repertoire of violent practices which are, or at least once were, apparently legitimate in the gridiron game: 'blind-side hitting'; 'chop-blocking'; 'clubbing' or 'bouncer's wallop'; 'crackback block'; 'ear-holing'; 'head-butting'; 'leg-whipping'; 'rake-blocking'; and 'spearing'.[33] In short, or so it seems reasonable to believe, soccer is neither so intrinsically expressive nor so intrinsically supportive and reinforcing of an ethos of male aggressiveness. That is to say, even though a form of aggressive masculinity has come to be operative, perhaps especially in the English game, the basic rules of soccer are less dependent on that fact. By contrast, gridiron football is essentially an embodiment and display of male aggressiveness and power. It is also marketed as such.[34]

Of course, with its emphasis on such matters as the precise

measurement of time, distance and the measurable aspects of individual performance, American football is also reflective of such things as the high level of rationalization reached by capitalism in the United States, the dependency of the game there on privately owned and market-orientated mass media of communication, and the fact that the ownership and control of American professional football clubs are more overtly capitalistic than is the case with most professional sports in Western Europe. Nevertheless, it also seems reasonable to suppose that gridiron football is a game which could only have grown up and taken root in a society where there is considerable support for ideals of masculinity which celebrate or at least tolerate a greater amount of overt physical violence than is considered desirable by the dominant and majority groups in the societies of Western Europe.

If this line of reasoning has any substance, it suggests that the recent success of soccer in the USA may be attributable in part to the trajectory of that country's civilizing process. The fact that, so far as we can tell, the game there has spread mainly among the middle classes and the recent success of soccer among women in the USA would both seem to be consistent with this hypothesis. Also possibly consistent with it may be the fact that gridiron football seems to have increased in popularity precisely when the United States was at the height of its de-civilizing involvement in the Vietnam War.[35] We are thinking in this connection, not only of the death, injury and brutalization of so many American conscripts in Vietnam and the ramifications of this brutalization when they got back home but also of the consequences for the American public of repeated exposure to war rhetoric from politicians and the media. That is to say, those conditions may have been conducive to the creation of an 'atmosphere' or environment which favoured the successful marketing of an aggressive, 'masculinistic' sport. By contrast, the conditions that have been emerging in the United States more recently may have been conducive to the spread of soccer, a sport that is arguably at least potentially more civilized and civilizing.

Soccer, of course, is not always played according to the formal, written rules. Like any social activity, it can be conducted in terms of a 'spirit' or ethos which condones rule-infractions to a greater or lesser degree. In Britain at least, such an ethos appears to be currently widespread if not entirely dominant in the game. More particularly, soccer in Britain tends to be organized and played in terms of a set of masculine values which, although perhaps less extreme than those which govern American football, nevertheless place equal or greater stress on strength, stamina and physical challenge than they do on skill with the ball. Whilst these values may help in part to explain the relative lack of success of England teams at the highest levels of international competition, they cannot be said in any meaningful sense to be a 'cause' of football hooliganism. However, true though this may be, neither can this masculine ethos be said to work as a counter to the hooligan problem. On the contrary, it appears to play a part of some significance in helping to construct and perpetuate an atmosphere at soccer matches where hooliganism is allowed to flourish.

It is clear that decisive action – not only at a national level but at a European level, too – needs to be taken urgently regarding the multiple aspects of soccer's current crisis. More particularly, action is required in relation to player violence and cheating. However, it is needed much more urgently regarding spectator violence and a pattern of media reporting that frequently leads to distorted views of what such violence actually entails. Without effective action in these spheres, what is arguably one of humanity's most civilized and, when properly organized and played according to the rules, potentially *civilizing* social inventions will be hampered in its competition with its intrinsically more violent, but capital-backed and superbly media-packaged, North American rival.

POSTSCRIPT: HILLSBOROUGH, HOOLIGANISM AND ENGLISH FOOTBALL

We cannot close this chapter without drawing attention to the spectator tragedies which have bedevilled the British game in recent years, culminating in the deaths of ninety-five spectators at the Hillsborough Stadium, Sheffield, in April 1989. It seems unlikely to be purely coincidence that all, or almost all, the major sporting disasters that have taken place in First World countries since the Second World War have, to our knowledge, firstly occurred at soccer, and secondly involved British, usually English, fans. These incidents have, between them, led to almost 300 deaths since 1945, nearly 200 in the past five years alone. Some of these fatalities have resulted from hooliganism combined with inadequate and unsafe spectator facilities (as at the Heysel Stadium, Brussels, in 1985, for example). But most of them have been the product of large crowds being herded into aged and outdated facilities which are palpably ill-equipped to deal with occasions of emergency, misjudgements in the management of crowds or spectator panic. American football may be more intrinsically violent, more obviously a 'war game' and, in that sense, less civilized than British soccer, but it is certainly watched in more civilized surroundings. The physical condition of English stadia cannot be said to be a 'cause' of spectator hooliganism, any more than player violence can. It can, however, be said to be a mark of the relative decline of the country which gave soccer to the world. It should also be pointed out that many of the factors which contributed to the tragedy at Hillsborough – the perceived necessity for the strict segregation of spectators; the closure of specific turnstiles; the penning of spectators and the use of perimeter fences; the misinterpretation by police officers of what was actually happening on the terraces – were all predicated on the expectation of hooliganism and the need to prevent it. In this and other ways, recent British soccer tragedies cannot be fully understood without reference to the wider social context and the game's spectating traditions.

In the national outcry which followed Hillsborough, the point was repeatedly made by Government spokespersons and members of the political left that the conditions and locations of many English football stadia are wholly unsuited to the staging of a spectator sport in a modern industrialised society and that to treat spectators with apparent contempt and brutality is to invite disasters of a violent or accidental kind. There is much in this observation. But such statements also imply that the condition of English football grounds is somehow alien to the character and condition of public facilities and public space in Britain more generally: that they have been, as it were, 'left behind' as other public facilities have been successfully developed and modernised, to an extent which makes English football and the 'neo-tribal' rivalries it helps to sustain and reinforce seem archaic and misplaced. Claims of this kind are rather more difficult to substantiate. For one thing, social indicators in Britain point to an increasing polarity between the lifestyles and circumstances of those who are most reliant for a reasonable standard of living on public-sector support and those better placed to take advantage of prevailing market forces.[36] For another, connections can be made between the spate of recent *non-footballing* disasters in Britain – at the King's Cross tube station and Clapham railway junction, for example – and those at our major football grounds. Here, the underlying link appears to be the relative neglect of such public facilities and their safety in favour of financial expediency, and the requirements of short-term profit.[37] Finally, it is perhaps also significant that, in a number of recent European surveys which have used a variety of social, economic and cultural indicators to measure the health, attractiveness and quality of life on offer in major European cities, those in Britain – particularly those in England – seem to lag far behind their Northern European equivalents on many counts.[38] The same could certainly be said about most English football grounds when compared with what is on offer on the Continent. Any recent visitor to 'the island' from the more affluent cities of Northern Europe would probably find in the ethnically divided and crime-ridden inner city areas of urban Britain; or late at night in most provincial English city centres with their male- and drink-dominated streets, pubs and clubs; or in the isolated and isolating, run-down, high-unemployment public housing estates in many locales, much which is in keeping with the general tenor and character of English football support. These reflections of residual resistance to processes of modernization – exhibited by football, for example, in the poor condition and facilities of many English stadia; in the near exclusion of women from the game as players and spectators; in the aggressive parochialism, racism and hooliganism now routinely associated with the behaviour of some young English fans; and in aspects of the way in which the game itself is coached and played in England – may seem out of place in the context of a more highly integrated, more egalitarian First World society of the 1990s. They are manifestly not out of character, however, with the anti-intellectual, non-cosmopolitan and divided Britain of today.

NOTES AND REFERENCES

1   Lawrence Kitchin, 'The Contenders', the *Listener*; 27 Oct. 1966.
2   Alan Tomlinson, 'Going Global: the FIFA Story', in Alan Tomlinson and Gary Whannel (eds) *Off the Ball: the Football World Cup*, London: Pluto, 1986, p. 85.
3   Tomlinson, 'Going Global', p. 91.
4   Stephen Edgell and David Jary, 'Football: a Sociological Eulogy', in Michael Smith, Stanley Parker and Cyril Smith, (eds) *Leisure and Society in Britain*, Harmondsworth: Penguin, 1972, pp. 214–29.
5   Arthur Hopcraft, *The Football Man*, Harmondsworth: Penguin, 1968, p. 12.
6   The word 'soccer' is derived from an abbreviation of 'Association'.
7   Ferenc Puskas, *Captain of Hungary*, London: Naldret, 1954.
8   The term 'pitch' is used in Britain for a 'playing field'. Thus,

'soccer pitch', 'cricket pitch', 'rugby pitch', 'hockey pitch', etc.

9   By contrast, American football is governed by more than 1,800 rules which fill a book that runs to 210 pages. See Richard Saul Wurman, *American Football: TV Viewers Guide*, Newton Abbot: David and Charles (Access Press), 1982, p. 20.

10 It is common to think of leagues and cups as intrinsic to modern sport. However, they were anathema to the pristine English ideology of amateurism and were resisted in top-level Rugby Union Football up to the 1970s.

11 Norbert Elias and Eric Dunning, 'Dynamics of Sport Groups with Special Reference to Football', in Norbert Elias and Eric Dunning, *Quest for Excitement: Sport and Leisure in the Civilizing Process*, Oxford: Basil Blackwell, 1986, pp. 191–204.

12 Norbert Elias, 'An Essay on Sport and Violence', in Elias and Dunning, *Quest for Excitement*, pp. 155ff.

13 This is also true, of course, of improvised jazz and improvised theatre. Conversely, much of modern professional wrestling consists of performances which, if not exactly scripted, are subject to pre-planning to a high degree. Indeed, one is almost tempted to use the term 'choreography' in this connection.

14 We are thinking here primarily of the way in which the league and cup forms of organization combine with the structure of the game as such to maximize the likelihood that soccer matches will be experienced as exciting. Of course, this is always a question also of individual and culturally defined meanings. Given that, fans are often able to derive a degree of satisfaction even from intrinsically dull matches if their team wins. But that raises the issue of identification which is dealt with later in this chapter.

15 See Norbert Elias and Eric Dunning, 'The Quest for Excitement in Leisure' and 'Leisure in the Sparetime Spectrum' in their *Quest for Excitement*.

16 The analysis here is based on that in Eric Dunning and Kenneth Sheard, *Barbarians, Gentlemen and Players: a Sociological Study of the Development of Rugby Football*, Oxford: Martin Robertson, 1979.

17 Roland Renson, 'Folk Football: Sport and/or Ritual', *Proceedings of the IX HISPAA Congress: Sport and Religion*, Lisbon: 1982, p. 275–84.

18 See Chapter 2 of this volume, 'The Roots of Player Violence in Football in Socio-historical perspective', pp. 26–36.

19 Ibid. This is an area where precise quantitative data are lacking, especially data that would enable one to establish trends and historical and cross-cultural variations in this regard.

20 The following analysis is based primarily on the theoretical discussion provided by Norbert Elias in his *What Is Sociology?* London: Hutchinson, 1978. See especially, Chapter 5, pp. 134ff.

21 Ibid.

22 See Ian Taylor, 'Soccer Consciousness and Soccer Hooliganism', in Stanley Cohen (ed.), *Images of Deviance*, Harmondsworth: Penguin,

1971, pp. 134–64.

23 See the analysis in Eric Dunning, Patrick Murphy and John Williams, *The Roots of Football Hooliganism: an Historical and Sociological Study*, London: Routledge & Kegan Paul, 1988. See also Chapter 2 in the present volume.

24 Dunning, Murphy and Williams, *The Roots of Football Hooliganism*, especially pp. 184ff.

25 The experience of being unemployed for, say, one year or five years is likely to be experienced as long-term by the people directly involved. Official definitions of 'long-term' unemployment also tend to be based on such relatively short time-periods. However, fundamental social processes tend to be 'trans-generational' in character, to take place over stretches of time that are considerably longer. It is such longer-term processes that we have in mind when referring to the deep-seated socio-cultural traits which, if we are right, are most fundamentally involved in the recurrent production and reproduction of football hooliganism.

26 See Chapter 2 in the present volume, 'The roots of player violence in socio-historical perspective'.

27 At the same time, the structures associated with Russian domination in the East are rapidly crumbling. It is difficult to believe that the two sets of processes – those in the West and those in the East – are not fundamentally connected. More particularly, it seems, the post-Second World War settlement is beginning to unfreeze, in large part as the hitherto relatively undisputed dominance of the two 'super-powers', the United States and Soviet Union, is coming under challenge. In short, we are living through a period of *fundamental* social change, a period when the international balance of power and the contours of international relations are altering in a way that involves the 'lid being taken off' intra-national processes that were previously suppressed.

28 See, for example, the findings of Kris Van Limbergen and his colleagues of the Catholic University of Leuven, especially their two-part report on 'The Societal and Psycho-sociological Backgrounds of Hooliganism in Belgium', 1989 (unpublished).

29 See Chapter 8 in this volume, 'Why are there no equivalents of soccer hooliganism in the United States?', pp. 194–212, for a review of the currently available evidence on this subject.

30 See J. A. Maguire, 'More Than a Sporting "Touchdown": the Making of American Football in Britain, 1982–1989', University of Loughborough (unpublished), 1989, p. 12.

31 Anton Rippon, 'Missionaries Who Sell the World Game', *Independent*, 22 Sept. 1989.

32 Wurman, *American Football*, pp. 2–9.

33 Wurman, *American Football*, p. 13. These practices are defined by Wurman as follows:

'*Blind-side hit*' – used on quarterbacks in the act of completing a throw – and on a tailback receiving an option-play pass from the quarterback and unable to see the onrushing tackler.

'Chop-blacking' – vicious blocking down to the knees when a man is held by a teammate and is in a rigid or off-balance position.

'Clubbing' or *'bouncer's wallop'* –illegal, jawbreaker delivered via a smash of arm and fists to neck. Use of it against receiver Lynn Swann of Pittsburgh led Coach Chuck Nell to charge that a 'criminal element' was loose in the sport.

'Crackback block' – illegal since 1976 in college play and since 1979 in NFL play, this is a clip delivered at or near the scrimmage line by an end slanting back in from the outside.

'Ear-holing' – aiming the crown of the head at a player's ear with devastating result.

'Head-butting' – illegal since 1979, but still common. Grabbing jersey, pulling forward and following with a sharp blow to the head.

'Leg-whipping' – offensive lineman, having failed on a block, reaches back with his legs and flails them across a man's shins.

'Rake-blocking' – ramming opponent's chest, then whipping the face mask up to the chin.

'Spearing' – outlawed by colleges in 1970. This is the deliberate use of the helmet to punish a man, whether stopped or not. Example: in a notorious 1978 incident, Jack 'Black Death' Tatum (Oakland) stuck it to Darryl Stingley (New England receiver). Stingley was left permanently paralysed.

34 Again, see Wurman, *American Football*, where, for example, we are told (p. 20), that a veteran NFL referee described his duties as 'trying to maintain order during a legalized gang brawl involving 80 toughs with a little whistle, a hanky and a ton of prayer'.

35 See, for example, the findings of Richard Sipes who found that the popularity of the 'combative' sports of football and hunting rose in the United States during the Second World War, the Korean War and the Vietnam War, whilst the popularity of baseball, defined by Sipes as a 'non-combative' sport, declined ('War, Sports and Aggression', *American Anthropologist 75*, (1973) pp. 64–86.

36 See, for example, Frank Field, *Losing Out*, Oxford: Basil Blackwell, 1989.

37 See, 'Britain's Drift Towards Recurring Disaster', Peter Jenkins, *Independent*, 18 April 1989.

38 A recent example comes from the French magazine *Le Point*. *Le Point* drew up forty five criteria divided into seven headings – quality of life, culture, welfare, transport, dynamism, environment and public safety. When all these factors were compared and weighted for each city, the first British city to be mentioned in a list of fifty large European cities was London – in twenty-eighth place. Birmingham

fared even worse, ranking forty-ninth most desirable. Commenting on these and similar findings from a survey conducted by the University of Reading, the *Guardian* observed that, 'Our cities are northern in geographical position, but southern in terms of their quality of life. Next stop the Third World?' ('Cities in Swill', *Guardian*, 15 June 1989).

Chapter Two

THE ROOTS OF PLAYER VIOLENCE IN FOOTBALL IN SOCIO-HISTORICAL PERSPECTIVE

It is all too easy in one's enthusiasm for the world's most popular sport to forget that football is a social product with a whole series of social ramifications. It is also easy to forget the converse: namely, that the social context in which the game is played has a whole series of ramifications on football *per se*. The relationship is mutual. It is with some aspects of this mutuality – of this interrelationship or interdependency between soccer and society – that we shall concern ourselves in this chapter. In particular, we are going to concern ourselves with the roots of player violence in the game and we are going to address the issues involved historically as well as sociologically.

The subject of soccer violence is, of course, a very timely one. That is the case not least because, as we are repeatedly told by the media these days, the game's reputation has been tarnished in a number of countries in recent years by the 'hooligan' behaviour, not only of spectators but also of players. Indeed some commentators have written as if the game is caught up in a self-destructive trend towards spectator indiscipline and violence. But let us become more concrete.

The first thing worthy of note in this connection is the fact that it is not only in soccer or, indeed, sport more generally, where it is widely believed that violence is currently increasing. There is a pervasive belief that we are living today in one of the most violent periods of history. Indeed, it is probably fair to say that, not only in Britain but in Western societies more generally and perhaps in non-Western societies, too, the fear that we are currently undergoing a process of 'decivilization', especially but not solely with regard to physical violence, is deeply imprinted in the contemporary *Zeitgeist*, one of the dominant beliefs of our time. The psychologists Eysenck and Nias, for example, refer to what they call 'a number of acknowledged facts' which, they claim,

26

'have helped to persuade many people that the civilization in which we live may be in danger of being submerged under a deluge of crime and violence'.[1] Arguing from a different perspective and with soccer much more centrally in mind, another psychologist, Peter Marsh, contends that recent developments have led to a decline in the opportunities for 'socially constructive ritual violence' – what he calls 'aggro' – with the consequence that uncontrolled and destructive violence has increased. Implicitly using a variation of Erich Fromm's distinction between 'benign' and 'malignant' aggression,[2] Marsh argues that there has been 'a drift from "good" violence into "bad" violence'. People, he says, are 'about as aggressive as they always were but aggression, as its expression becomes less orderly, has more blood as its consequence'.[3]

We have no wish to deny the very great dangers that threaten us in the modern world. Nuclear war is an obvious possibility, though many people think that its likelihood has diminished as a result of recent events in Eastern Europe. Another possibility is ecological catastrophe on a global scale. The latter may involve physical violence in a non-metaphorical sense but, if it does occur, a factual increase in violence in and among human groups is a highly likely accompaniment. Nor do we wish to deny that the modern world has been *extremely* violent in one particular respect; we are thinking of the violence and destructiveness of modern war. There have been more than 100 wars since 1945 and, between them, they have claimed in excess of 30 million victims. It is not our wish to discount or minimize the seriousness of problems such as these. We do, however, want to suggest that the sorts of diagnoses offered by Marsh and Eysenck and Nias need to be placed in proper historical perspective. If one does that, what the historical record strongly suggests is that, whilst wars have grown more violent and destructive as the twentieth century has progressed, largely in conjunction with the increasing destructive power of armaments, and whilst violence is probably increasing in many countries at the moment,[4] the majority at least of Western societies are today considerably more 'civilized' internally, considerably less violent than they used to be, say, 100 or more years ago. The history of soccer offers a prime illustration of the long-term trend in this regard. More specifically, the evidence suggests that the modern game developed as part of a 'civilizing process'[5] and that it is far less violent, far less rough and wild than its antecedents in the Middle Ages and the early modern period. Let us look at some of the evidence for this.

Modern soccer is descended from a class of medieval folk games which, in Britain, went by a variety of names such as 'football', 'camp-ball', 'hurling' and 'knappan'. Continental variants included *la soule* in France and the *gioco della pugna* in Italy. The ball in such games was carried and thrown and hit by sticks as well as kicked, and matches were played through the streets of towns as well as over open country. They were played by variable, unrestricted numbers of people, sometimes in excess of 1,000. There was no equalization of numbers between the contending sides, and the rules were oral and locally specific rather than written, standardized and enforced by a central controlling body. However, despite such local variation, the games in this folk tradition shared at least one common feature: they were all play-struggles which involved the customary toleration of forms of physical violence that have now been tabooed, together with a general level of violence that was considerably higher than is permitted in soccer today. In order to illustrate that this was so, we shall have to restrict ourselves in the present context to one British and one Italian example.

Take the following extract from the seventeenth century account by Sir George Owen of the Welsh game of 'knappan'. The number who took part in this game sometimes exceeded 2,000 and some of the participants played on horseback. The horsemen, said Owen, 'have monstrouse cudgells, of iii foote and halfe longe, as bigge as the partie is well able to wild (wield)'. He continued:

> at this playe privatt grudges are revendged, soe that for everye small occasion they fall by the eares, wch beinge but once kindled betweene two, all persons on both sides become parties, soe that sometymes you shall see fyve or vi hundred naked men, beatinge in a clusture together, . . . and there parte most be taken everyman with his companie, soe that you shall see two brothers the on beatinge the other, the man the maister, and frinde against frinde, they now alsoe will not stick to take upp stones and there with in theire fistes beate their fellowes, the horsemen will intrude and ryde into the footemens troupes, the horseman choseth the greatest cudgell he can get, and the same of oke, ashe, blackthorne or crab-tree and soe huge as it were able to strike downe an oxe or horse . . . when on blowe is geven, all falleth by the eares, eche assaultinge other with their unreasonable cudgells sparinge neyther heade, face, nor anye part of the bodie, the footemen fall soe close to it, beinge once kindled with furie as they wholey forgett the playe,

and fall to beatinge, till they be out of breathe . . . . Neyther may there be anye looker on at this game, but all must be actours, for soe is the custome and curtesye of the playe, for if one that cometh with a purpose onlye to see the game, . . . beinge in the middest of the troupe is made a player, by giveinge him a *Bastonado* or two, if he be on a horse, and by lending him halffe a dozen cuffs if he be on foote, this much may a stranger have of curtesye, althoughe he expect noethinge at their handes.[6]

That the continental variants of this folk tradition were as wild and rowdy as their counterparts in Britain is suggested by Alan Guttman's description of the *gioco della pugna*. It was played in Northern Italy, mainly with the fists, and it was, according to Guttman:

often little better than a pitched battle, a tournament fought with weapons provided by nature. An even rougher version . . . occurred when the 'players' hurled rocks at each other, a pastime honoured by Savanarola's condemnation. In Perugia, a thousand or more men and women joined in the annual stone fight, which became so violent that the authorities attempted to moderate the bloodshed in 1273 by threatening that those who killed their opponents would henceforth be tried for murder.[7]

There may be a degree of exaggeration in these accounts but, by and large, the wildness of this folk tradition is confirmed by other sources.[8] Indeed, it was entirely consistent with the overall ferocity of such games that, in some parts of Britain, the participants played in iron-tipped boots.[9] But let us look at the modern game.

By contrast with its folk-antecedents, modern soccer exemplifies a sport that is more 'civilized' in at least seven senses that were lacking in the ancestral forms. More particularly, modern soccer is more 'civilized' in the sense that it involves:

1 numerical equality between the contending sides and the restriction of each side to eleven players on the field at any given time;
2 a strict and clear-cut demarcation of the roles of players and spectators;
3 specialization around the practices of kicking, 'chesting' and heading, and, for the goalkeeper, catching, kicking and throwing. It also involves the elimination of the use of sticks for purposes of striking either other players or the ball. Similarly, all the players play on

foot. In other words, practices that were often indiscriminately and, seen from a modern standpoint, dangerously intermixed in the old folk tradition have come nowadays to be separately institutionalized to form a set of specific and differentiated games which, together, form a cognate class. Soccer is one of this class of games. Others are rugby, hockey, American football, Australian football, and polo;
4 centralized rule-making and administrative bodies, the Football Associations of the different countries. They are nowadays, of course, ultimately subject to the jurisdiction of such international bodies as UEFA (the Union of European Football Associations) and FIFA (the Fédération Internationale de Football Associations);
5 a set of written rules which demand from players the exercise of strict self-control over physical contact and the use of physical force, and which prohibit force in certain forms;
6 clearly defined sanctions such as 'free kicks' and 'penalties' which can be brought to bear on those who break the rules and, as the ultimate sanction for serious and persistent violation of the rules, the possibility of excluding players from the game, suspending them for a period and/or levying on them monetary fines; and
7 the institutionalization of specific roles which have the task of overseeing and controlling the game, that is, the roles of 'referee' and 'linesman'.

The early development of soccer in this 'civilizing' direction – that is, towards a type of game characterized by the above constellation of characteristics – occurred as part of a continuous social process. One significant 'moment' in this process consisted of the formation in 1863 of the Football Association. Among the rules accepted by the newly formed Association in December 1863, the following two are especially interesting for present purposes:

Rule 10: Neither tripping nor hacking shall be allowed and no player shall use his hands to hold an adversary.

Rule 14: No player shall be allowed to wear projecting nails, iron plates, or gutta-percha on the soles or heels of his boots.

'Hacking' was defined as 'kicking an opponent intentionally' and 'tripping' was defined as 'throwing an adversary by the use of the legs'.[10]

At first, these and the other rules of the new Association were enforced simply by means of 'on-the-spot' negotiations between the captains of the contending sides.[11] Such an arrangement clearly depended on the following complex of social elements: the social homogeneity of the players (that is, the fact that they were recruited solely from the upper and upper middle classes); the fact that, as such, they were all adherents to the social code of 'gentlemen' and that they would not deliberately infringe the rules. If they unintentionally did so, they were expected immediately to admit their guilt. Those who deliberately persisted in 'trying to gain 'unfair' advantage by breaking the rules would have been ostracized and branded as 'cheats', 'bounders' or 'bad sports'. Such a method of control also depended on the fact that matches at that early stage were 'one-off' affairs which promised no reward other than the intrinsic satisfactions of taking part in the game and of winning rather than losing. That is to say, such matches did not form part of a long-term struggle to win a league or cup and did not hold out the promise of medals or monetary rewards. However, as the game spread socially and geographically and the social homogeneity of the players was reduced, as more formal forms of competition began to be introduced, and as the game began to become increasingly professionalized and commercialized, so the competitive pressures grew more intense, leading to the necessity of abandoning aspects of the old 'gentlemanly' ethos with its emphasis on self-control and to supplement it more and more with external and formalized controls such as referees and linesmen, disciplinary committees and tribunals, game-specific penalties, suspensions and monetary fines. Let us look at the issue of player violence in this modern, highly competitive game.

If one looks simply at the data on recent trends of player indiscipline and violence, it is easy to come up with a picture of ongoing and progressive deterioration. Take, for example, the figures in Table 1, which reports the sendings-off and cautions given in first-team matches in the English Football League from 1970–1 to 1987–8. Since these figures are based only on incidents seen by referees and linesmen and recorded by them, they do not provide a complete and entirely accurate picture of violence in the game. Their accuracy is further compromised by inconsistencies among referees in their application of the rules and by the changing policies of the Football Association in this regard.

The figures also reflect the incidence of verbal indiscipline and simple cheating and not simply violent conduct *per se*. Information from Scotland may provide a clue as to relative proportions in this regard.

Whereas overall numbers of recorded player offences 'north of the border' between 1980–81 and 1987–88 show an increase of just over one-third, offences that did not obviously involve violence or foul play increased by 60 per cent.[12] Moreover, there is little doubt that a not inconsiderable part of the increase in player misbehaviour shown by the figures in Table 1 reflects the way in which fouling has found a more central place in the prevailing ideologies and values of how football 'should be played'. As the technocratic vocabulary of the 'professional' and the 'job' has come more and more to supplant the traditional language of 'sport' and 'virility', so more 'instrumental' forms of indiscipline appear to have become more commonplace.[13] Similarly, as the pressures in the modern game have increased, so more managers, players and coaches seem compelled to accept – and in some cases to recommend – that intentional fouling and the associated strategy of attempting to gain an advantage by deception is an appropriate and, indeed, 'professional' response. A number of well-known professional footballers in England have recently confirmed this view in books about their experiences as players.[14] But this elevation of the goal of winning at the expense of the rules, regulations and 'spirit' of the game is world-wide. Recent examples include Maradonna's 'hand of God' goal against England in the 1986 World Cup Finals (which helped to win the trophy) and the feigned injury of the Chilean goalkeeper in his country's match against Brazil in the qualifying tournament for the 1990 World Cup (which led to Chile being expelled from the competition). Examples such as these presumably help to explain why some football administrators in England claim that the game is no 'harder' than it used to be, but that it is certainly more 'cynical' in its instrumental use of violence and deception.[15]

However, let us look more closely at the figures in Table 1. On the face of it, these figures appear to be indicative of the occurrence of a more or less continuous and approximately four- to five-fold increase in undisciplined and violent player behaviour over the seasons 1970–1 to 1987–8. On the rough but not unrealistic assumption that the figures relate to 4,000 matches every season, the rise from 37 to 210 sendings-off amounts to an increase from one sending-off in every 108 matches to one sending-off in every 19. Another way of expressing it would be to say that, whilst in 1970–1 there was one sending-off in every 3,564 player-hours, in 1987–8 there was one in every 627. Thus, in whatever way one measures it, one cannot deny that the increase has been substantial. There are, however, at least two reasons for believing that the seriousness of this increase should not be exaggerated at least as far specifically as violent offences are concerned. Let us elaborate on this.

Table 1 Sendings-off and cautions for field offences, first-team matches in the English Football League, 1970/1 – 1987/8*

	Sendings-off	Cautions	Totals		Sendings-off	Cautions	Totals
1970/71	37	905	942	1979/80	114	3,520	3,634
1971/72	41	1,685	1,726	1980/81	120	3,333	3,453
1972/73	82	2,320	2,402	1981/82	147	3,821	3,968
1973/74	77	2,241	2,318	1982/83	229	3,748	3,977
1974/75	94	2,412	2,506	1983/84	163	4,067	4,230
1975/76	100	2,519	2,619	1984/85	174	4,101	4,275
1976/77	96	2,669	2,765	1985/86	206	4,140	4,346
1977/78	106	2,998	3,104	1986/87	215	4,037	4,252
1978/79	117	3,266	3,383	1987/88	210	4,001	4,211

Adapted from: Digest of Football Statistics, 1988, Table 4.4, p. 64. Prepared for the Football Trust by the Sir Norman Chester Centre for Football Research, University of Leicester.
* The figures are for all League, League Cup, FA Cup and Welsh Cup matches played by English Football League clubs. Figures for the four Welsh member-clubs in the Football League are not included. From 1984–5, the figures also include matches played for the Freight Rover/Sherpa Van Trophy.

Close scrutiny of the figures in Table 1 reveals an especially substantial increase of players sent off in the 1972–3 season, when the number exactly doubled. And ten years later, in 1982–3, a smaller but still substantial jump of around 18 per cent occurred. Each of these rises can be accounted for, at least in part, by changes in the approach of the authorities to violent and foul play. In 1972, a campaign to outlaw the 'tackle from behind' was launched by the Football Association, which provided referees with increased powers to punish offending players. In 1982, referees were instructed to 'get tough' with players who used the so-called 'professional foul'. On both occasions, these changes in strategy contributed to the larger-than-usual increases in sendings-off. On both occasions, too, there were media campaigns which highlighted problems of player indiscipline and its consequences for the image and general well-being of the game.

These observations do not involve a denial of the significance of the increases in offences recorded in Table 1. They do, however, sensitize one to the fact that figures such as these are not simple and

objective measures of player behaviour but the results of complex inter-
actions between such behaviour and judgements about it by administrators and officials at various levels who are, themselves, subject to
more or less intense pressures and constraints.

The second reason for approaching the increase in player violence
suggested by Table 1 with caution becomes apparent if one looks at
the latest figures – those for 1987–8 – on their own. In that year, there
were 210 sendings-off in around 4,000 matches. As we said, this
amounts to one sending-off in around every 19 matches or one in
around every 627 player-hours. That hardly represents a massive
amount of violent and undisciplined behaviour. Such a judgement is
strengthened if one takes account of the fact that the figures refer to
the participation of fit, highly trained young male atheletes in a fast,
highly competitive and robust physical game in which they are competing at the highest level for prestige and monetary rewards. Given
that, such figures could be argued to represent a very high level of
effective official control and of equally effective self-control or self-
restraint exercised by the players on themselves.[16] In short, even
though, in England at least, the levels of violence and indiscipline in
soccer appear to have increased over the last two decades – and this
applies as much, if not more, to the non-professional levels of football
– the game still remains a much more 'civilized' activity than the
antecedents out of which it grew. One indication of the fact that this
is probably the case is provided by a newspaper report from 1898 that
we came across in the course of our researches. The report in question reads:

> Herbert Carter has died at Carlisle from injuries received while
> playing football last week, when he was acidentally kicked in the
> abdomen. Two other football players also died on Saturday from
> injuries received in the course of play, vis. Ellam of Sheffield, and
> Parks of Woodsley. These, together with the case of Partington,
> who died on Wednesday last, make a total of four deaths during
> the past week.[17]

It could, of course, have been simply a chance set of circumstances
that led to the deaths of four soccer players being reported in a single
week. However, that it was probably indicative of a game and a wider
society that were both considerably more violent than England is today
is suggested by the figures regarding rugby football in the 1890s that
are set out in Table 2. Rugby, of course, was and remains a rougher

game than soccer but, assuming these figures to be at least reasonably accurate, they do reveal rates of injury that were considerably higher than would be tolerated in any game today:

Table 2 Deaths and injuries in Yorkshire rugby, 1890/1–1892/3

	Deaths, etc.	Broken legs etc.	Arms	Collar bones	Other injuries
1890/91	23	30	9	11	27
1891/92	22	52	12	18	56
1892/93	26	39	12	25	75

Source: *Wakefield Express*, 8 April 1893. Quoted in Eric Dunning and Kenneth Sheard, *Barbarians, Gentlemen and Players: a Sociological Study of the Development of Rugby Football*, Oxford, Martin Robertson, 1979

It is, accordingly, reasonable to suppose that, despite the increase in player violence that has undoubtedly occurred in recent years, the modern game has developed as part of a long-term 'civilizing process'.

NOTES AND REFERENCES

1 H.J. Eysenck and D.K.B. Nias, *Sex, Violence and the Media*. London: Maurice Temple Smith, 1978, p. 17.
2 Erich Fromm, *The Anatomy of Human Destructiveness*. Harmondsworth: Penguin, 1977.
3 Peter Marsh, *Aggro: the Illusion of Violence*. London: Dent, 1979, p. 142.
4 E.G. Dunning, P.J. Murphy, W.H.T. Newburn and I. Waddington, 'Violent Disorders in Twentieth Century Britain', in G. Gaskell and R. Benewick (eds) *The Crowd in Contemporary Britain*. London: Sage, 1987.
5 Norbert Elias, *Uber den Prozess der Zivilisation* (2 vols), Berne: Verlag zum Falken, 1939; second edition, Berne and Munich: Francke Verlag, 1969. English translation vol. 1, *The Civilizing Process: the History of Manners*, Oxford: Basil Blackwell, 1978; vol. 2, *The Civilizing Process: State-Formation and Civilization*, Oxford: Basil Blackwell, 1982.
6 Quoted in Eric Dunning and Kenneth Sheard, *Barbarians, Gentlemen and Players: a Sociological Study of the Development of Rugby Football*. Oxford: Martin Robertson, 1979, pp. 27–8.
7 Allen Guttmann, *Sports Spectators*. New York: Columbia University Press, 1986, p. 52.
8 See Dunning and Sheard, *Barbarians, Gentlemen and Players*, pp. 21–45.
9 Ibid.

10 Geoffrey Green, *The History of the Football Association*, London, Naldrett, 1953, p. 38.

11 ibid., p. 558.

12 The Football Trust, *Digest of Football Statistics, 1988*, Table 5.5, p. 82.

13 See Stephen Wagg, *The Football World: a Contemporary Social History.* Brighton: Harvester, 1984, p. 151.

14 A recent example is provided in a biography of the Manchester United and England full back, Viv Anderson. He is reported to have defended the 'professional foul' by declaring, 'If someone is through and likely to score, then I will definitely up end him. That's part and parcel of the game. I'd do that without thinking. I'd commit a professional foul, if need be, if it was the right thing at the time.' See 'Professional foul is fair play in Anderson's book', *The Times*, 15 Nov. 1988.

15 See, for example, the remarks of Gordon Taylor, Secretary of the Professional Footballers Association, as reported in the *Sun*, 30 Nov. 1987.

16 This exercise of self-control by players is not solely an individual phenomenon and does not take place in a social vacuum. More particularly, they operate informal norms among themselves which, in the case of professional players, reflect their common interest in keeping injurious physical contact under control because their livelihoods depend on what is, for most of them, a short period in the game. Of course, such norms are contradicted by other norms which reflect the pressure to win for prestige and financial reasons.

17 *Leicester Daily Mercury*, 15 Nov. 1898.

Chapter Three

FOOTBALL HOOLIGANISM IN BRITAIN BEFORE THE FIRST WORLD WAR*

Over the past two decades, football hooliganism has come to be regarded as one of Britain's more serious 'social problems'. It has been the subject of an enduring moral panic and has recurrently drawn forth demands from the media, politicians and a variety of self-appointed 'moral entrepreneurs' for 'tough action'. A number of attempts have also been made to explain it but, so far, popular 'theories' on the subject have tended to outnumber their academic counterparts. In fact, despite a widespread feeling in official and media circles that football hooliganism has been 'over-researched', it is probably fair to say that the rigorous academic explanations so far on offer boil down to only three: the social psychological explanation of Marsh, Rosser and Harré (1978), and the sociological explanations of Taylor (1971)[1] and Clarke (1978).

It is consideration of the theories of Taylor and Clarke that forms the starting point of this chapter. Discussion of what they have written will show why we regard an analysis of football hooligan violence before the First World War as an important precondition for moving towards an adequate sociological understanding of the present-day phenomenon. We shall outline some of the common features of their theories first and then summarize what we take their central arguments to be. After that, and before discussing some of our own research findings, we shall examine the work of three historians who, without claiming to make a direct contribution to the understanding of football hooliganism today, have begun to undertake work on its late nineteenth and early twentieth century counterparts. Finally, we shall offer some preliminary reflections on the sociological significance of the historical part of our research.

* J. Maguire of the University of Loughborough was a co-author of an earlier version of this chapter.

SOCIOLOGICAL THEORIES OF FOOTBALL HOOLIGANISM

A feature common to the explanations of football hooliganism offered by Taylor and Clarke is the assumption that the *perception* of football crowd behaviour in Britain as socially problematic is largely or entirely new. Similarly, what one might call the 'factual' as opposed to the 'perceptual' dimension of the problem – that is, disorderly spectator behaviour *per se*[2] – is held by them to have occurred on a substantial scale in this country for the first time in the 1960s. Neither of them attempts to hide the occurrence of football-related violence in Britain in the past. It is simply their contention that present-day football hooliganism is a social phenomenon that is unprecedented as far as its central characteristics are concerned. This contention, however, is *a priori*, based neither on systematic diachronic studies nor on research-based comparisons of present-day crowd behaviour with its counterparts in the past.[3] It is also accompanied by cognate forms of explanation. More particularly, Taylor and Clarke have searched for explanations of football hooliganism solely or mainly in terms of recent changes either in British football and/or in the British working class. Let us, very briefly, examine the explanations that they offer.

According to Taylor, 'there are empirical differences between the violence in football in the 1960s and the violence which characterized earlier stages in the game's development'. 'Most obviously of all', he writes, 'the invasion of the playing pitch by the spectator is quite clearly . . . new'. Taylor attributes this and other 'new' aspects of present-day football hooliganism to the effects on what he calls a 'subcultural rump' of working-class fans of the 'bourgeoisification' and 'internationalization' of the game. By the term 'bourgeoisification' he is referring partly to the attempt by the football authorities from the late 1950s onwards to attract a middle-class and 'affluent' working-class audience to the game. However, he is also referring partly to the transformation in the life-chances and lifestyles of top players that followed the abolition of the maximum wage in 1961. By the term 'internationalization' he is referring to the parallel attempt to develop new, more international focuses of competition for the game. Taylor sees these processes as having begun in the 1950s and 1960s in conjunction with the emergence of Britain as an 'affluent society', a process which made available a wider range of leisure opportunities to the working class and which, even at that early stage, led attendance at Football League matches to begin to decline.

As far as fans specifically are concerned, Taylor argues that traditional working-class supporters are deeply imbued with 'soccer consciousness'. Part of this consists in the belief – sometimes Taylor seems to assert it as a fact – that the game used to be a 'participatory democracy'. That is, taking the 'weaker' version of his thesis to constitute what he 'really' meant, working-class fans, according to Taylor, believe that they were able in the past to exert a degree of control over the policies of their clubs. However, they were not consulted over the changes associated with 'bourgeoisification', and experience the increasing orientation of the game to a middle-class audience as a usurpation. They also resent the fact that players seem to have severed their links with the working class. Football hooliganism has arisen in this situation, he suggests, as an attempt by young working-class fans, in the face of changes that have been externally imposed, to assert a form of control that they believe members of their class were able formerly to exert. In short, according to Taylor, football hooliganism is best understood as a working class 'resistance movement'. 'Bourgeoisification' and 'internationalization', the processes against which this resistance is directed, also help to explain the football authorities' concern. Football hooligan behaviour is necessarily problematic from their standpoint since it offers a basic challenge to their perception of the game and the way in which they want to see it develop.

Clarke's analysis is not dissimilar. 'Football's history', he argues, 'has always been marked by violence both on the pitch and off it', but present-day inter-fan-group violence is a 'new extension of the traditional forms of spectatorship'. Clarke attributes this new development to the conjuncture in the 1960s between, on the one hand, what he calls the 'professionalization' and 'spectacularization' of the game, and, on the other, changes in the social situation of working-class youth. These changes, as he puts it, 'have had the combined effect of fracturing some of the ties of family and neighbourhood which bound the young and the old together in a particular relationship in pre-war working class life'. That is, according to Clarke, working-class boys before the Second World War typically went to football matches with their fathers, uncles and older brothers or as part of generationally mixed neighbourhood groups. In that context, their behaviour was subject to relatively effective external control but when, from the 1960s onwards, they began increasingly to go to matches in the company solely of their age peers, control by older relatives and neighbours could no longer operate. At the same time, as a result of 'professionalization', 'spectacularization' and the correlative emphasis on the game as a commodity to be passively consumed, they found themselves, as far as their football involvement was concerned, in a context that was growing more and more alien to the culture of their class. The net result was football hooliganism. Centrally involved – and new – in this connection was inter-fan-group fighting. However, as part of 'the process of making the game safe for its supposed new, quiescent, middle class, family audience', pushing, jostling, crowd surges and swearing, the first three previously accepted as an inevitable consequence of crowd density, the fourth as 'part of the "man's world" of the football subculture', came to be seen as 'things that only the hooligan fringe does'. In that way, the problem of football hooliganism was perceptually amplified out of proportion to the increase in violence that had 'really' occurred.

The research reported in this chapter is based on assumptions that are in many ways radically different from those of Taylor and Clarke. More particularly, we knew prior to starting the research that spectator disorderliness at football matches had occurred on a substantial scale in the three and a half decades before the First World War. We also knew that such behaviour was regarded, at least in certain quarters, as a problem requiring remedial action. However, at that stage, our knowledge was rudimentary and we wanted to discover more about a number of aspects of the problem. More specifically, we wanted to find out:

(a) in as much detail and, given the inevitable limitations of historical research, as precisely as possible, what the rate of spectator disorderliness in the 1880s, 1890s and early 1900s was;
(b) the forms that such disorderliness took, whether physical violence was involved and, if so, how serious it was, where it took place and who the targets were;
(c) how such disorderliness was perceived by interested groups, what kinds of remedial action, if any, were taken in an attempt to curb it, and with what success. In particular, we were interested in discovering whether there was a parallel in that period to the largely media-generated moral panic of our own time, a panic which appears to have contributed to forms of official intervention which seem, on the whole, to have reinforced and even exacerbated the problem;
(d) whether spectator disorderliness on any scale occurred during

the inter-war years and in the decade or so immediately following the end of the Second World War.

Answers to such questions are not simply intrinsically interesting but vital to an adequate understanding of present-day football hooliganism. More particularly, an historical analysis is crucial in order, firstly, to provide a comparative frame of reference which highlights what, if any, the distinctive features of the contemporary phenomenon really are, and secondly, to ensure that an adequate conceptual apparatus is employed in developing an explanation. The second of these points is the most difficult and probably requires a degree of elaboration. Expressed very briefly, what we basically mean is that only theoretically guided diachronic research can enable one to determine what the 'periodicity' of a social phenomenon such as football hooliganism is. Theoretically a number of possibilities appear to exist in this connection. Here are a few of the more obvious among them. The phenomenon may, for example, be relatively constant over time or it may follow a cyclical pattern – that is, it may recurrently rise and fall. Alternatively, it may evolve slowly and gradually, perhaps at a pace which quickens until a conjuncture is reached at which its character is more or less radically transformed. It is also possible that a social phenomenon may be unique to a particular era, rooted in historically specific conditions and totally lacking in precedents of any kind. Since these are not mutually exclusive alternatives, it is also, of course, possible that a social phenomenon may evolve according to a cyclical pattern and that it may, at any particular point in time, display continuity with the past and contain historically novel elements. The reason why we have introduced these distinctions is that, although it is not by any means the only factor that has to be taken into account, the form of explanation one adopts in relation to a phenomenon such as football hooliganism is clearly crucially dependent upon the pattern uncovered by diachronic research.

Limited space restricts us in the present context to a discussion of our findings relevant to the first and second sets of questions raised above. In addition, the fact that we are concerned here solely with data about the period before the First World War means that, whilst we can provide a comparative frame of reference for the analysis of present-day football hooliganism, we are unable to look at what one might call the 'long-term periodicity' of fan disorderliness at or in conjunction with the game. But let us become more concrete and examine the work of the historians we referred to earlier.

HISTORICAL RESEARCH ON FOOTBALL HOOLIGANISM

Although Taylor and Clarke theorized about football hooliganism as if it were almost a uniquely present-day phenomenon, the historians, Mason (1980), Hutchinson (1975) and Vamplew (1979), have recently undertaken research into football crowd disorderliness in the late nineteenth and early twentieth centuries. Since their work sheds light on to the diachronic aspects of the problem, a review of the adequacy of their analyses will provide a framework around which the data we have collected on football hooliganism before the First World War can be organized.

Mason recounts seventeen examples of spectator disorderliness at football between 1863 and 1915. The first occurred in 1883, the last in 1909. Eleven of them involved physical violence. He uses these examples as a basis for constructing a rough typology. Disorders at football matches before 1915, he says, can be placed into three main categories. The first and largest number resulted from anger at the decisions of the referee or the attitudes of opposing players; friction between rival supporters, he claims, seems to have almost always been sparked off by activity of this sort on the field. The second category resulted from terrace overcrowding, and the third from crowd dissatisfaction over decisions taken by the clubs. On this basis, Mason concludes that order was the norm at football matches in this period and that, when it did break down, serious disturbances were very much the exception rather than the rule. However, whilst he is able to form a judgement concerning the types of disorder which, he admits, did occur, and whilst he provides a rough assessment of the relative frequency of the different types, he makes no attempt to identify the occurrence of trends. In this respect at least, the work of Hutchinson is superior.

According to Hutchinson (1975: 11), 'riots, unruly behaviour, violence, assault and vandalism, appear to have been a well-established, but not necessarily dominant pattern of crowd behaviour at football matches, at least from the 1870s'. However, within this broad generalization, he claims to have detected a curvilinear trend. More specifically, he argues, crowds in the 1870s were small and relatively well behaved. They became more disorderly towards the end of the 1870s and in the 1880s as the game spread geographically and down the social scale and as, correlatively, the number of spectators increased. By the 1890s, however, despite the continuing increase in their size, crowds, according to Hutchinson, had begun to grow more orderly once again. This view is based on the presentation of reports of thirteen crowd disorders, nine of them involving physical violence. Three occurred in the 1870s, three in the 1880s, four in the 1890s, and only one in the 1900s. Additional support is provided by reference to contemporary opinion. Thus Hutchinson (1975: 5) relates that, 'by the 1890s, references were continually made to the respectable nature of the spectators, their enthusiastic and controlled behaviour'. This putative tendency for the rate of football crowd disorder to decline from about 1890 was attributed by Hutchinson largely to the processes of professionalization and regularization that accompanied the formation of the Football League. More particularly, the supposed reduction in crowd disorderliness was accomplished, he claims, largely by means of a policy of levying admission charges and, in the case of some clubs, by moving to 'better' areas of a town. In short, behaviour improved as crowds grew more 'respectable' and this was achieved, according to Hutchinson, by means of various stratagems designed to remove, or which had the unintended consequence of removing, the 'rowdier' spectators. Direct control measures were used as well. In particular, the number of police at matches was increased and free admission was granted to soldiers and sailors in uniform in the hope that, when necessary, they would aid the police.

Vamplew's contribution consists largely in an application to the problem of the categorization of sports crowd disorders developed by the social psychologists Mann and Pearce (1978). They distinguish between what they call 'frustration', 'outlawry', 'remonstrance', 'confrontation' and 'expressive' disorders. The first occurs 'when spectators' expectations of access to the game and the way it will be played or adjudicated are thwarted'. The second takes place 'when groups of violence-prone spectators use sports events to act out their anti-social activities by attacking officials, fighting with rival fans, and destroying property'. The third involves the use of the sports arena for political protest. The fourth 'breaks out when spectators from rival religious, geographic, ethnic or national groups come into conflict'. And finally, 'in expressive disorder the intense emotional arousal which accompanies victory or defeat, particularly if it is exciting or unexpected, triggers uninhibited behaviour in which members of the crowd become completely abandoned' (Vamplew 1979, 1–4). According to Vamplew (pp. 2f.), 'of these five types . . . all but remonstrance can be found at soccer grounds in the nineteenth and early twentieth centuries, though the majority of incidents appear to have been of the frustration or confrontation varieties'. He supports this conclusion by reference to six examples of 'frustration' disorder and one each of the 'outlawry', 'confrontation' and 'expressive' types. Later, he adds two unclassified examples, making a total of eleven in all. One is from the 1880s, seven are from the 1890s, and three from the period 1900–14. Further support is provided by figures that Vamplew has culled from the FA (Football Association) Minute Books and which he presents in tabular form (See Table 3):

Table 3 Clubs punished for crowd misbehaviour

	Closures	*Cautions*
1895	4	8
1896	10	13
1897	6	2
1910	–	3
1911	3	1
1912	1	1

Source: Vamplew 1980

These findings, Vamplew suggests, tend to support Hutchinson's conclusion regarding a curvilinear trend. He accounts for this ostensible pattern by reference to the variety of measures taken by the FA, the Football League and particular clubs. More specifically, according to Vamplew, although crowd control was not always their primary objective, such measures had consequences for spectator behaviour. He writes:

> Improvements in the organization and conduct of . . . matches reduced the stimuli to frustration and confrontation disorders; the fencing off of pitches, the segregation of various sectors of the crowd, and the exclusion of specific spectators lessened the dangers of confrontation and outlawry disturbance; and the stricter controls on betting and the deterrent effects of control agents reduced the likelihood of all kinds of disorder. When trouble did occur both the segregation of the crowd, and especially the presence of the police, acted to weaken the contagion dynamics of disorder and to contain the disturbance.
>
> (Vamplew 1979: 15 and 16)

PRELIMINARY QUANTITATIVE FINDINGS

Before presenting a summary of our own data, we shall briefly develop a critique of the work of these historians. The first thing worthy of note is the small number of cases on which they base their generalizations. There are also discrepancies between the interpretations that they offer. Most obvious is the difference between Mason, who regards the incidence of spectator disorderliness in this period as having been minimal, and the other two, who regard it as having been relatively substantial. There are, moreover, considerable discrepancies between their estimates of the incidence of disorderliness in particular decades, most notably, perhaps, between the estimates of Hutchinson and Vamplew. Thus, although Vamplew thinks his analysis supports Hutchinson's conclusions, the latter argues that a decline in the rate of crowd disorderliness began in the 1890s whilst the former's data show the highest incidence in that decade and a decline only in the 1900s. This discrepancy is probably a consequence of the relatively small amounts of data on which they base their claims. Let us, accordingly, present some of the results of our own researches as a test of their conclusions. We shall start by discussing our replication of Vamplew's approach to the problem via FA data. Our results are summarized in Table 4.

The figures in this table are in many respects at variance with those offered by Vamplew (See Table 3). There are, we think, three possible reasons for such discrepancies. The first is the fact that Vamplew did not break his figures down between clubs inside and outside the Football League. Indeed, we suspect that they refer solely or mainly to Football League clubs. However, the Football League was not founded until 1888, which means that in the 1890s it was still a new organization and did not enjoy its currently elevated status. Given that, we have recorded actions against both categories of clubs in our table, a fact which presumably helps to explain why our overall figures are so much higher than those of Vamplew. On the other hand, our figures for Football League clubs are in all cases lower than Vamplew's totals. This may stem from the fact that there are occasional ambiguities in the FA Minute Books and that we decided to exclude all ambiguous cases. A further possibility is that Vamplew was mistaken regarding membership of the Football League around the turn of the century and included clubs which only joined it later. But, however these discrepancies are to be explained, it remains the case that both

Vamplew's figures and our own point to a fall in the number of incidents felt to warrant FA action after 1897. Let us enquire into the matter a little more closely.

Table 4 Action taken by the FA in an attempt to curb spectator misconduct and disorderliness, 1895–1915

Year	Football League		Outside Football League		Annual totals		
	Closure	Caution	Closure	Caution	FL	Others	Combined
1895	2	1	7	8 (1)	3	16	19
1896	1	1	13	10 (2)	2	25	27
1897	1	1	8	4 (1)	2	13	15
1898	0	0	1	1	0	2	2
1899	0	2	4	0	2	4	6
1900	0	2	2	1	2	3	5
1901	0	0	0	7 (1)	0	8	8
(1902) (1903)			Records missing				
1904	0	0	0	1 (1)	0	2	2
1905	0	0 (1)	0	0	1	0	1
1906	2	2	0	4	4	4	8
1907	1	1	0	4	2	4	6
1908	0	1	0	1	1	1	2
1909	0	1	1	1	1	2	3
1910	0	0	0	4	0	4	4
1911	2	1	0	1	3	1	4
1912	0	1	1	0	1	1	2
1913	0	0	0	0	0	0	0
1914	0	2	0	0	2	0	2
1915	0	0	0	1	0	1	1
Totals	9	16 (1)	37	48 (6)	26	91	117

Source: FA Minute Books, 1895–1915. (The figures in brackets refer to forms of FA action other than closure or caution, e.g. the banning of a single spectator.)

Vamplew's analysis of the FA records takes the form of a comparison between two three-year periods, 1895–7, and 1910–12. He then, in effect, invites the reader to link the sets of figures thus obtained by means of a gradually declining downwards slope. Our own more detailed researches, however, suggest that such an imaginary downwards line is purely and simply a function of the way in which Vamplew has approached the problem and the way in which he presents the figures. That is, judging the FA records on a year-by-year basis, the number of actionable disturbances in this period at football grounds over which the FA claimed jurisdiction did not undergo a gradual decline; there was a sharp, once-and-for-all drop after 1897. Then, between 1898 and 1915, although there were quite marked fluctuations from year to year, the number only once rose above half the 1897 level – in 1906, when there were eight recorded cases – and in two years, 1905 and 1913, there were no recorded instances at all. More crucially, Vamplew fails to treat the reliability of the FA records as problematic. Research in other areas sensitizes one to the possibility that a sharp change in officially recorded statistics in a single year may be more a consequence of changes in recording procedures or of administrative organization and practice than of changes in the phenomenon that the statistics are designed to measure. That is particularly the case when the statistically recorded rise or fall is followed by relative stabilization at the new level (Hood and Sparks 1974). In our view, we are probably dealing with such a statistical artefact in this case. Geoffrey Green has shown how membership of the FA grew rapidly in the last quarter of the nineteenth century, placing great strain on the central organization, among other things, as far as matters of discipline were concerned (Green 1953: 144f.). As a result, the power to deal with problems such as spectator disorderliness was, to a considerable extent, devolved to local Associations. According to Green, the years 1895 to 1897 were crucial as far as this process of decentralization was concerned, that is, precisely those years when our FA data suggest that a significant decline in crowd disorderliness occurred.

If the decline suggested in Table 4 was a consequence of this change of administrative organization and practice, and assuming that the number of cases of crowd disorderliness known to FA officers in that period either remained relatively stable or increased, the number of incidents treated by local FAs should have grown. We were unable to obtain relevant information from the Leicestershire and Birmingham FAs. As a result, the test of our supposition had to rely more heavily on the analysis of newspaper reports. We undertook a survey of national, local London and Birmingham papers but our most intensive study was of the *Leicester Daily Mercury*. The base year for the general survey was 1880 but, for the Leicester part of the research, we chose 1894, partly because it was the year in which Leicester Fosse – later to become Leicester City – gained entry to the Second Division of the Football League, and partly in order to match as closely as possible the time-series obtained from the FA records. As far as these are concerned, it is impossible to go back any further since only their records from 1895 have been preserved. Table 5 shows the number of spectator disorders reported in the *Mercury* in the period 1894–1914:

Table 5 Incidents of spectator misconduct and disorderliness reported in the *Leicester Daily Mercury*, 1895–1914

Year	Filbert Street	Elsewhere in Leicester or Leicestershire	Overall Leicestershire totals	Elsewhere in England	Elsewhere in UK	Annual totals
1894	3	1	(4)	2	0	6
1895	2	0	(2)	3	2	7
1896	0	2	(2)	2	0	4
1897	1	2	(3)	3	0	6
1898	0	1	(1)	4	2	7
1899	2	5	(7)	6	2	15
1900	2	1	(3)	5	0	8
1901	0	0	(0)	6	0	6
1902	0	3	(3)	4	1	8
1903	2	3	(5)	3	0	8
1904	0	0	(0)	5	3	8
1905	1	1	(2)	3	0	5
1906	0	0	(0)	6	1	7
1907	0	0	(0)	5	0	5
1908	0	4	(4)	6	2	12
1909	0	1	(1)	1	1	3
1910	1	4	(5)	9	0	14
1911	3	1	(4)	5	0	9
1912	1	4	(5)	2	1	8
1913	2	5	(7)	3	0	10
1914	0	1	(1)	1	1	3
Totals	20	39	(59)	84	16	159

The figures from the FA Minute Books and those for England as a whole from the *Leicester Daily Mercury* are set forth side by side in Table 6. The figures in brackets relate to the numbers of incidents reported in the *Mercury* which do not appear in the FA Minutes.

It is clear from Table 6 that spectator misconduct and disorderliness at football matches in this period were subject to under-recording in both directions. Thus, between 1895 and 1914, 116 incidents of spectator disorderliness against which punitive action was taken by the FA are unambiguously recorded in the minutes of the national association. In the same years, fifty-five incidents in Leicestershire and eighty-two in the rest of England, a total of 137, were reported in the *Leicester Daily Mercury*. However, only three of the Leicestershire incidents and twelve from the rest of the country which the *Mercury* reported appear in the FA Minutes. Conversely, only fifteen of the incidents recorded in the FA Minutes reached the pages of the *Mercury*. In other words, the FA took action in 101 cases which the *Mercury* did not report, and the *Mercury* reported 122 cases on which the FA did not take action (or where incidents regarding which they took action were ambiguously recorded). This suggests that the actual rate of disorderliness in this period may have been higher – perhaps even considerably higher – than either of these sources suggests. Let us take the analysis one step further still.

Table 6 Annual incidence of spectator misconduct and disorderliness at Association Football matches in England, 1895–1914, as suggested by analysis of the FA Minutes and reports in the *Leicester Daily Mercury*

Year	FA Minutes	Leicestershire		Elsewhere in England		Total	Combined annual totals
1895	19	2	(2)	3	(1)	5	22
1896	27	2	(0)	2	(2)	4	29
1897	15	3	(3)	3	(3)	6	21
1898	2	1	(1)	4	(3)	5	6
1899	6	7	(7)	6	(4)	13	17
1900	5	3	(2)	5	(4)	8	11
1901	8	0		6	(6)	6	14
1902	Records	3	(3)	4	(4)	7	7
1903	missing	5	(5)	3	(3)	8	8
1904	2	0		5	(5)	5	7
1905	1	2	(2)	3	(3)	5	6
1906	8	0		6	(4)	6	12
1907	6	0		5	(3)	5	9
1908	2	4	(4)	6	(6)	10	12
1909	3	1	(1)	1	(1)	2	5
1910	4	5	(5)	9	(8)	14	17
1911	4	4	(4)	5	(5)	9	13
1912	2	5	(5)	2	(1)	7	8
1913	–	7	(7)	3	(3)	10	10
1914	2	1	(1)	1	(1)	2	4
Totals	116	55	(52)	82	(70)	137	238

The FA was dependent for its knowledge of disorderly incidents on referees' reports, and some of them evidently reported incidents which were not regarded as newsworthy by the *Leicester Daily Mercury*'s reporting staff. Alternatively, the latter may have been unaware of such incidents or may not have regarded it as their responsibility to report them.[4] Similarly, the *Mercury* evidently reported incidents which some referees did not regard as worthy of reporting to the FA, which the FA did not regard as warranting official action, or of which the referees were simply unaware. Doubt is thus cast on the adequacy of both the FA records and the *Leicester Daily Mercury* as sources for measuring the 'real' rate of spectator disorderliness in England in the years before the First World War. More particularly, both appear to under-record it. It is, of course, impossible to determine what the level of under-recording was. Based on this table, however, and taking both sources together, one can say that the total number of incidents reported as having taken place in England in the years 1895 to 1914 was 238. The figure rises to 254 if the number of cases reported by the *Mercury* for the rest of the UK (see Table 5) is added to it. It would rise even higher if the FA figures for 1902–3 were available and if our Birmingham data were included. In any case, the figure of 254 is considerably in excess of the numbers of cases – 17 and 13 – reported by Mason and Hutchinson. It is also considerably greater than the overall total of sixty-three cases reported by Vamplew. The difference becomes even greater when account is taken of the fact that our figures are for a twenty-year period only, whilst theirs are for periods ranging between thirty-five and forty-five years. In short, at least using the FA records and the *Leicester Daily Mercury* as a data base, there can be little doubt that spectator disorderliness was a problem of considerable proportions at Association football matches in this period and that none of the three historians who has studied it so far has come even close to capturing the scale on which it occurred.

In addition to calling the quantitative picture which emerges from the work of these historians into question, our data from the *Leicester Daily Mercury* also cast doubt on the contention by Hutchinson and Vamplew that a decline in the rate of football spectator disorderliness began to occur in either the 1890s or the early 1900s. The figures certainly suggest that a decline in Leicestershire may have occurred around that time. Thus, the average number of incidents reported annually in that county in the years 1894 to 1900 was 3.1, but fell to 1.4 in the years 1901 to 1907. But in the years 1908 to 1914 the annual Leicestershire average rose to 3.9, a figure more consistent with a cyclical pattern than a simple curvilinear one. The average number of incidents reported annually for the rest of England in these three seven-year periods was also cyclical but in this case, the peak – which was much lower – came in 1901–7, the years which formed the trough as far as Leicestershire was concerned. These annual averages for the rest of England were: for 1894–1900, 3.6; for 1901–7, 4.6; and for 1908–14, 3.9. Moreover, the mean overall totals (that is for Leicestershire *and* the rest of England) reported annually in these three periods remained fairly stable at 7.5 for 1894–1900; 6.7 for 1901–7; and 8.4 for 1908–14. That the trough in this case came once again in the middle period is clearly an artefact of the relatively low Leicestershire figures for those years. Of course, since the *Leicester Daily Mercury*'s knowledge of local incidents was probably more accurate than its national knowledge, the Leicestershire figures are probably more reliable than the others; namely, on the assumption that spectator disorderliness in Leicestershire followed the same trend as the rest of England, the years 1901–7 are more likely, in fact, to have seen a trough.

Rather different evidence for the view that the pattern may have been cyclical rather than simply curvilinear is provided by Figure 1, in particular by the two-year moving average depicted by line B. This suggests a more rapid and more extreme cycle, and that peaks were reached in the years 1898–1900, 1902–4, 1907–8 and 1910–11. The fact that the peak of 1898–1900 seems to have been higher than those of 1902–4 and 1907–8 is to some extent consistent with the Hutchinson–Vamplew thesis. Against this, however, line B shows a peak in 1910–11 as high as that of 1898–1900. Moreover, it suggests that the incidence of spectator misconduct and disorderliness troughed at a lower level in the 1890s than in the early 1900s, when the cycle was more nearly flat. Further analysis and research are necessary in order to establish whether this cyclical pattern reflects the 'real' incidence of disorder in this period or whether it is an artefact of the 'knowledge base' of the *Leicester Daily Mercury*'s reporting staff. It may also be a reflection of changing sensitivities on their part or perhaps indicative of a shift in public opinion regarding spectator disorderliness at football or perhaps even regarding violence and disorderliness more generally. It is also possible that it may be a function of changing editorial policies in this regard.

So far, our discussion has been about the numbers of incidents of spectator misconduct and disorderliness acted on by the FA and/or reported in the *Leicester Daily Mercury*. It says nothing about the types of misconduct and disorderliness which occurred. Nor does it touch on the relative frequency and relative seriousness of the different types, or whether relative seriousness is judged by contemporary standards or our own. Table 7 presents the results of a preliminary attempt to

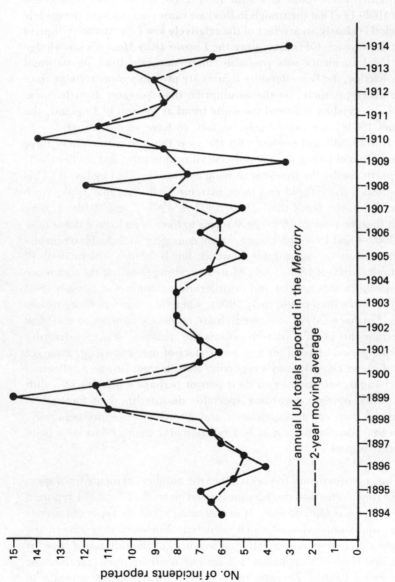

Figure 1 Spectator misconduct and disorderliness at Association Football matches in the United Kingdom reported in the *Leicester Daily Mercury*, 1894–1914.

come to grips with these issues. It breaks down the fifty-nine cases reported in the *Mercury* as having occurred in Leicestershire between 1894 and 1914 into four categories: verbal misconduct and disorder; pitch invasions, encroachments and demonstrations; physical violence and assault; and ambiguous or unelaborated (and therefore unclassifiable) references, for example to 'misconduct', 'disorderly proceedings', 'mobbing' and so on. There is a small amount of double-counting in the table because, for instance, pitch invasions are sometimes described as involving assault or attempted assault. However, in order to keep the amount of double-counting to a minimum, we have not included cases of assault or attempted assault in the 'verbal misconduct and disorder' category, even though, in most cases, the assault or attempted assault involved verbal as well as physical violence.

Table 7 Types of spectator misconduct and disorderliness reported in the *Leicester Daily Mercury* as occurring at football matches in Leicestershire, 1894–1914

Types of misconduct and disorderliness	*Years*		
	1894–1900	1901–7	1908–14
1 *Verbal misconduct and disorder* e.g., use of threatening, or foul and abusive language; barracking; drunk and disorderly behaviour	10	0	8
2 *Pitch-invasions, encroachments, interference with play, demonstrations*	3	1	15
3 *Physical violence and assault* e.g., missile throwing, assault or attempted assault in the general match-day context on players, match officials and other fans	8	4	4
4 *Ambiguous and/or unelaborated cases* e.g., references to 'misconduct', 'disorderly proceedings', 'mobbing' etc., without clarification of the behaviour involved	4	5	2
Totals	25	10	29
Numbers of incidents included twice	3	0	2

Among the more interesting things suggested by Table 7 are the apparent decline in physical violence and assault at football matches in

Leicestershire after 1900, and the apparent rise in pitch invasions and encroachments after 1907. We cannot at the moment say whether such statistical changes reflect 'real' or 'factual' transformations at the level of behaviour, whether they are an artefact of changes in reporting practice, or whether they are a consequence of changes in the two combined. What we can be sure of is that the apparent disappearance of verbal misconduct and disorder from football grounds in Leicestershire between 1901 and 1907 is an artefact of the data, more particularly of the fact that all the reported cases known to us have been included in the physical violence and disorder category. It is, of course, extremely unlikely that verbal misconduct and disorder would have continued to accompany the more physically violent forms of spectator disorderliness whilst, at the same time, disappearing more generally from football grounds in the county. The relatively high rates of verbal misconduct and disorder in the years 1894–1900, and 1908–14 add weight to this conclusion.

Whilst one cannot, at this stage, be certain regarding the representativeness of Leicestershire in the years before the First World War, whether as far as football spectator disorderliness in general was concerned or regarding its various types, the data we have introduced so far do provide a basis for working out a crude estimate of what the national figures in that period may have been. Such an estimate can be arrived at simply by multiplying the Leicestershire figures obtained from the *Mercury* by the proportion of England's population that lived in the county in those years. It will, hopefully, serve as a stimulus to further research, but, before we proceed, some of its more obvious crudities ought to be pointed out. *Inter alia*, they include the fact that it fails to take account of such probable influences on the rate of crowd disorderliness as: the differential spread and popularity of football in different parts of the country; the differential social composition of crowds in different areas; differences in the provision of facilities for spectators; and differences in the degree of experience in catering for and controlling large crowds. Nevertheless, for all its limitations, such an exercise seems to be a useful one to undertake, especially given the current dearth of reliable knowledge on this issue. In order to carry it out, we shall first return briefly to the overall quantitative dimension and then, in somewhat greater detail, work out national estimates for the different types of disorder.

At the time of the 1901 Census, the population of Leicestershire was approximately one-seventieth of that of England as a whole.

Taking that year as representative of the period 1894–1914, and assuming that the rate of misconduct and disorderliness reported in the *Leicester Daily Mercury* as occurring in Leicestershire in that period was typical of the country at large, a notional reportage figure for the whole country in those years of 59 × 70, that is 4,130 cases, or an average of 197 incidents per year, is yielded. On the basis of the same assumptions, the notional reportage figures for the three seven-year-periods 1894–1900, 1901–7 and 1908–14, are as follows: 1894–1900, 1,540 cases or an average of 220 incidents per year: 1901–7, 700 cases, or an average of 100 incidents per year; and 1908–14, 1,890 cases, or an average of 270 incidents per year. Again on the basis of these assumptions, we have estimated that the national pattern regarding the different types of disorder in this period may have been something like that reported in Table 8.

Table 8 Estimated incidence of spectator misconduct and disorderliness at football matches in England, 1894–1914

Types of disorder		Years		
		1894–1900	1901–7	1908–14
1 Verbal misconduct	over period as a whole	700	0	560
and disorder	per season	100	0	80
	per week in season*	3	0	2.4
2 Pitch invasions,	over period as a whole	210	70	1050
encroachments, etc.	per season	30	10	150
	per week in season*	0.9	0.3	4.55
3 Physical violence	over period as a whole	560	280	280
and assault	per season	80	40	40
	per week in season*	2.4	1.2	1.2
4 Ambiguous and	over period as a whole	280	350	140
unelaborated cases	per season	40	50	20
	per week in season*	1.2	1.5	0.6
Totals	over period as a whole	1750	700	2030
	per season	250	100	290
	per week in season*	7.6	3	8.8

* The calculations of weekly rates were made on the assumption that the average duration of the Football League season in this period was 33 weeks (see Green 1953).

We are aware of the arbitrary character of this exercise. It was bound to magnify the defects of our Leicestershire data and to throw up absurdities such as the apparent disappearance of 'verbal misconduct and disorder' from English football grounds in the years 1901–7.

55

Nevertheless, we regard it as a useful means of working out a provisional estimate of the national incidence of spectator disorderliness in the late nineteenth and early twentieth centuries. However, it will only serve its intended purpose if others carry out similar research using local newspapers as the principal data source. Until such research is carried out, our quantitative conclusions in this regard will retain their speculative character. In the meantime, perhaps all that can be said with a degree of certainty in this connection is that, while an estimated total of 4,130 reported cases of spectator disorderliness at football matches in England between 1894 and 1914 may seem rather high, especially when judged against the much smaller numbers reported by Mason, Hutchinson and Vamplew, the degree of distortion is probably not too excessive. At least that would seem to be a reasonable conclusion to draw from the fact that our researches on both the FA records and the *Leicester Daily Mercury* have uncovered a number of cases considerably in excess of the numbers reported by these historians. Such a conclusion is reinforced by the fact that the number of cases of spectator disorderliness known to the FA in this period which were not reported in the *Leicester Daily Mercury* was relatively high, and vice versa.

A CONTENT ANALYSIS OF SELECTED REPORTS

Our analysis up to this point gives an idea of the forms of spectator disorderliness which seem to have occurred recurrently at football matches between 1894 and the outbreak of the First World War. It also gives an idea of the relative frequency both of the different forms and of spectator disorderliness in general. However, content analysis of the reports of specific cases gives a clearer and richer picture of the kinds of behaviour actually involved and, at the same time, provides a means for provisionally assessing the relative seriousness of particular incidents. Accordingly, we shall conclude this empirical section of our essay by citing a few representative examples of such reports. They have been chosen on account of their relevance for theoretical issues raised in our critique of Taylor and Clarke. We shall start with some reports which document 'verbal misconduct and disorder'. We shall then present selected cases that document pitch invasions, attacks on referees and players, the destruction of property at football grounds, and fights between rival fan groups. Finally, we shall cite cases that deal with the occurrence of hooligan behaviour by football fans *outside* football stadia.

In January 1899, the Leicestershire FA ordered the ground of Loughborough Town FC – it was, up until that year, a member of the Football League, having joined it in 1895 – to be temporarily closed. It also forbade the team to play within a 6-mile radius of its ground. In the *Leicester Daily Mercury*, it was reported regarding the FA's decision that 'the Association are determined, as far as possible, to stop the use of foul language on the part of spectators at football matches and that referees will receive the full support of the executors' (24 January 1899). In response to this report, a supporter wrote to the *Mercury* urging the Loughborough Committee to do 'all they can to keep the game so that no self respecting man may hesitate to bring either male or female members of his family' (25 January 1899). An article published in the *Birmingham Daily Mail* in November 1899, similarly complained that 'bad language prevents a decent-minded man enjoying the game and prevents a lady attending' (19 November 1899). In a letter to the editor which appeared on the following day, a supporter wrote that he would 'have liked to take his wife and son to matches but that bad language makes it impossible' (20 January 1889). These are just a few examples selected from many more which suggest that 'bad language' at football matches was, in this period, a matter of considerable public concern. Let us turn now to the subject of pitch invasions.

In 1890, when Lofthouse scored for Blackburn in their match against Sheffield Wednesday, he was, it was reported, 'enveloped by an overenthusiastic crowd who invaded the pitch to celebrate'. The field was cleared after five minutes, owing, it was claimed, to the 'solid endeavours of the police and the military' (Dobbs 1973: 38). The Tottenham – Aston Villa cup-tie of 1906, however, was rather different: it had to be abandoned after spectators 'swarmed onto the turf at the interval . . . and a mob which was said to be violent (formed) in front of the stand' (Cotton 1926: 225). Another pitch invasion occurred at the match between St Mirren Reserves and Glasgow Rangers Reserves in the Scottish Second Eleven Cup Competition in December 1898. With Rangers leading 7–2 and only ten minutes left, the crowd broke through in what was described as 'a disgraceful outburst of rowdyism.' In the subsequent court case, an 18-year-old youth described as the ringleader was sentenced to a £3 fine or imprisonment for thirty days. According to the magistrates, 'such rowdyism is the means of reducing a manly sport to blackguardism' (*Leicester Daily Mercury*, 20 December 1898).

An account of a 'disgraceful scene' at the match between Burnley and Blackburn in February 1890, illustrates another form of event which seems to have been not uncommon at football matches in this period; namely, an attack by spectators on the referee. According to the report in the *Leicester Daily Mercury*,

the referee was mobbed at the close. . . . The official had to be protected by the Committee and so demonstrative were the spectators that the police could not clear the field. (He) had to take refuge under the grandstand, and, subsequently, in a neighbouring house. The police force was increased and eventually the referee was hurried into a cab and driven away followed by a howling, stone-throwing mob. (27 February 1890)

That it was not only referees but players, too, who were attacked, is shown by a report in the *Birmingham Gazette* in May 1885. The report also shows how 'missile-throwing' sometimes formed part of these attacks. More particularly, at the end of the Aston Villa v. Preston match in that year, it seems that

roughs congregated round the Preston team, (each of whom) . . . came in for (his) share of treatment. The Preston men, with commendable courage, turned upon the crowd surrounding them and retaliated. A free fight quickly ensued, during the course of which several aereated water bottles were hurled into the crowd and smashed, regardless of the consequences. (11 May 1885)

A much more violent and destructive sequence of events was described in an article headed, 'Football Riot at Glasgow', which appeared in the *Leicester Daily Mercury* in April 1909. The report is worth quoting from at length. The relevant sections of it read:

A serious riot took place at Hampden Football Ground, at Glasgow, on Saturday afternoon, at the close of the Scottish Cup Final. For the second week in succession, the tie between the Celtic and Rangers ended in a draw, and the crowd on Saturday demanded that the teams should play extra time, but the authorities had made no such arrangement.

On the teams returning to the pavilion, thousands of spectators broke into the playing pitch, and proceeded to tear up the goal-posts. Mounted constables arrived, and in the melee that followed, more than 50 persons were injured.

When the barricading was broken down, the rioters piled the

debris, poured whisky over it, and set the wood ablaze. The flames spread to the pay-boxes, which were only some 20 yards from a large tenement of dwellings. Great alarm prevailed, particularly when the firemen were attacked by the mob, and prevented from extinguishing the fire, for no sooner had they run out the hose than the crowd jumped on it, and, cutting it with knives and stones, rendered the efforts of the firemen useless. The woodwork of the boxes was completely destroyed, leaving only the corrugated iron roofs and lining, which were bent and twisted into fantastic shapes. The Club's heavy roller was torn from its fittings, and maliciously dragged across the turf.

Fresh detachments of police and firemen arrived, and a series of melees followed, during which injuries, more or less serious, were inflicted on some fifty or sixty persons.

Stones and bottles were freely thrown, while at least two persons were treated for stab wounds. Over a score of constables were included among the injured as well as several firemen.

Meanwhile, a great crowd, totalling fully 60,000 was swaying and rushing about to escape being trampled by police and horses. Fears were entertained for the safety of the pavilion and grandstands, but the constables kept the crowd to the opposite side of the field.

The mob repeatedly rescued the prisoners from the police, and ultimately it was deemed advisable to clear the field without taking the rioters into custody. For almost two hours the park was a scene of violence unparalleled in the history of sport in Scotland, and has created grave concern among the executives of the Scottish Football Association.

The damage to the enclosure amounts to hundreds of pounds
. . . .

An emergency meeting is to be held at Glasgow this evening to consider the whole situation. Official reports issued by the police and fire brigade yesterday show that fully 200 constables were required to cope with the mob, while nearly 70 firemen, with 6 motors and engines were on the scene. (19 April 1909)

Hutchinson's paraphrase of a report in the *Glasgow Herald* corroborates the *Leicester Daily Mercury*'s account but refers, in addition, to 'the destruction of virtually every street-lamp around Hampden', thus suggesting that the violence spread outside the ground. (Hutchinson, 1975: 14). That certainly seems to have happened in the case of the 'riot' that accompanied the match between Greenock Morton and Port Glasgow in April 1899. We are told that, when the Port Glasgow team 'began to lose goals',

> their partisans became turbulent, and several free fights took place. At the close, . . . the Port Glasgow followers broke into the enclosure, and assaulted the Morton players, and also the police on duty at the ground. In a few minutes the row assumed the proportions of a riot, and extra police were telephoned for. On the arrival of the mounted police the constables were forced to use their batons freely, but the riot continued for over two hours. Nineteen constables were injured, some of them seriously. A number of spectators were also injured. The east end of Greenock was in a state of panic for a time, and when the riot was at its height, shopkeepers closed their places of business. (*Leicester Daily Mercury*, 10 April 1899)

Spectator disorders in the Midlands and other parts of England in this period do not seem to have reached such heights of violence and destructiveness. Nevertheless, disorders do seem to have regularly occurred. Thus we hear that, at the Norwich–Chelsea match of 1913, 'the East Anglian supporters went on a rampage outside the ground, throwing missiles and damaging property' (FA Emergency Committee Minutes, February 1913). Clashes between rival supporters also seem quite frequently to have taken place. For example, it is reported that, at the Aston Villa–Notts County match in October 1900,

> a section of the spectators varied the proceedings by engaging in a free fight. . . . (M)atters were assuming serious proportions among the crowd and policemen blew their whistles noisily. Then was seen the spectacle of a football match in progress and three stalwart constables racing across the ground. The unruly folks who had leaped the barriers scuttled. But one less active than the rest was captured and he went back over the palings in a very sudden if undignified manner, the constable acting as assistant, while the crowd cheered . . . . (*Birmingham Daily Mail*, 13 October 1900)

Fighting between rival supporters also broke out at the match between Leicester Fosse and Lincoln City in April 1900. According to the *Leicester Daily Mercury*'s report, once the fighting was in progress,

> (the game) now seemed to be quite a secondary consideration with an unselect few of the spectators on the popular side – and a

Lincoln v. Leicester proceeded on two occasions in the shape of free fights. The sparring was wilder than judicious and out of place in any case, but fortunately each time a constable was at hand and promptly and firmly parted the pugilists, who showed by these actions that they were not qualified to watch a football match. (7 April 1900)

Accounts such as these, together with the figures obtained from the *Leicester Daily Mercury* and the FA Minutes, suggest that spectator misconduct and disorderliness at football matches in the late nineteenth and early twentieth centuries took place principally at football grounds themselves, sometimes spreading outside them into the immediate vicinity as in the Scottish cases of April 1899, and April 1909. Such accounts also suggest that attacks on referees and players rather than inter-fan-group fighting were the most frequent forms of physically violent disorder in that period. However, there are reasons for believing that the impression thus given of the relative frequency of the different types of disorder and their locations may be to some extent an artefact of the manner in which the data were socially produced and not a completely reliable guide to the totality of what went on. Thus, the FA relied for their knowledge of disorderly incidents upon reports by referees, and all the indications are that these officials only reported incidents which threatened either their own persons or the continuity and playing of the game. Of course, it is highly improbable that the members of FA committees were ignorant of all the disturbances reported in the press. It is rather the case that, then as now, they depended for the knowledge on which they based their actions on the reports provided by match officials.

Newspaper reports were subject to similar forms of bias. They were produced by journalists who went to football specifically to report on matches and who are likely, on that account, only to have noticed incidents inside the ground which disrupted play, occurred close to the pitch or were on a scale sufficient to make everyone present aware of them. Fights deep in the crowd and, above all, fan-group skirmishes away from the ground, are less likely to have come to their attention, and even if they did, as sports reporters, they would not necessarily have regarded it as part of their brief to report them. There are, however, at least three sources of evidence which suggest that inter-fan-group fighting and what one might call 'alcohol-related disorderly behaviour' may have been more common in this period than the predominantly available data seem to imply: namely, letters to the press, encounters witnessed by reporters who just happened to be present, and reports of court proceedings.

As a result of limited space, it is only possible in this context to give one example each from the first and second of these sources. The first just refers generally to drunkenness and disorderly behaviour, though we know that a fan died under the wheels of a train at Birmingham's New Street Station in the course of the events described. The second refers to a fairly large-scale inter-fan-group fracas which took place at a station in Cheshire.

Writing to the *Birmingham Daily Mail* in February 1902, a man who styled himself 'Citizen of Handsworth' claimed that he had witnessed in the city centre on the previous Saturday night

> crowds of young girls, about 17 years of age, and also of youths who were in such a state as to be a disgrace to a respectable citizen. Some were rolling about the pavement utterly helpless and seemed to have hardly the strength to do anything but curse, swear and endeavour to sing. I wondered what was the cause of this and found that it was due to the fact that we had thousands of visitors from Derby to see the cup-tie at Aston. . . . (A)t a low estimate, 30 per cent of the men were drunk . . . . Gentle manners and chivalry were conspicuous by their absence. Police were helpless or powerless. (11 February 1902)

Although it is one of only a few such examples that we have come across, an account of behaviour even more similar to that of present-day football hooligans appeared in the *Liverpool Echo* in April 1889. We shall conclude this empirical section of our analysis with this account:

> An exciting scene took place at Middlewich Station on Saturday evening, after a match between Nantwich and Crewe for the Cheshire final. Both parties assembled on opposite platforms waiting for trains. They commenced operations by alternately hooting and cheering, and then one man challenged an antagonist to a fight. Both leaped on the metals and fought desperately until separated by the officials. Then a great number of the Nantwich men ran across the line, storming the platform occupied by the Crewe men. Uninterested passengers bolted right and left. The special then came

in and the police guarded them off, many of them carrying away marks that will distinguish them for some time. (1 April 1889)

CONCLUSIONS

The sorts of conclusions that can be drawn from the empirical analysis presented in this chapter are limited to the use of the data we have introduced as a focus for comparison with present-day football hooliganism. That is, since we have restricted our discussion to spectator misconduct and disorderliness at and in conjunction with football matches before the First World War, we cannot draw the sorts of conclusions for the theories of Taylor and Clarke that our full-scale diachronic studies – they embrace, not only the late nineteenth and early twentieth centuries, but also the inter-war years and the years immediately following the end of the Second World War – permit. Nevertheless, there are a number of things that can be said. Our findings are also relevant to the conclusions reached by Mason, Hutchinson and Vamplew. It is with the analyses of these historians that we shall start our critical discussion.

In this chapter, we have established, *pace* Mason, that spectator disorderliness was a recurrent and relatively frequent accompaniment of Association football in the twenty-one years before the start of the First World War. It was, moreover, deeply rooted at all levels of the game, not just at that of the emergent Football League. Our conclusions in this regard are more in keeping with those of Hutchinson and Vamplew, though it seems possible that the relatively small amounts of data that their methods enabled them to unearth – we realize, of course, that each of them was working on his own –coupled with the fact that they seem to have concentrated almost solely on Football League clubs in their researches, led them to underestimate the incidence of football hooliganism in that period. Of course, precise measurement of the incidence of a phenomenon such as this is difficult if not impossible to achieve. That is principally because, as we have shown, of the manner in which most of the extant data were produced. This means that there is a 'dark figure' of spectator misconduct and disorderliness in this period consisting of unreported incidents which probably took place, partly in the depths of large and densely packed crowds, and partly, but more importantly, outside grounds. By its nature, this 'dark figure' is impossible to quantify precisely, though further research along the lines we have attempted might be revealing, if not quantitatively accurate, in this regard.

Our data also cast doubt on the hypothesis of Hutchinson and Vamplew that the incidence of football hooliganism in the late nineteenth and early twentieth centuries followed a curvilinear trend. The data are more consistent with the existence of a cyclical pattern, though, again, further research is necessary in order to establish whether the cycle reflects 'real' rises and falls in the incidence of spectator misconduct and disorderliness, or whether it is a function of changing sensitivities and perceptions. These are not, of course, mutually exclusive alternatives. Further research is also necessary to determine the structural roots ('causes') of this putative pattern, whatever its precise character turns out to be.

Perhaps more significantly from a sociological standpoint, the data we have reported here also cast doubt on the analyses of football hooliganism offered by Taylor and Clarke. Taylor, for example, is simply wrong when he claims that pitch invasions by spectators are a new development. Clarke, too, is wrong in suggesting that, in the past, swearing was accepted as an inevitable part of 'the ''man's world'' of the football subculture'. It may have been accepted by the majority of working-class males in the late nineteenth and early twentieth centuries but it clearly was not accepted by all of them. It was also regarded by the football authorities as a problem requiring remedial attention. Indeed, our data suggest that the attempt to transform football into a 'respectable', 'family' game has been going on for a very long time. Such an attempt does not, that is to say, appear to be simply an adjunct of processes of 'professionalization' and 'spectacularization' – or of 'bourgeoisification' and 'internationalization' – the start of which can be located in the 1960s and which were connected with wider social changes which began around that time. Rather, it seems to have formed part of an ongoing process associated with the development of professional football since the beginning and with the wider social developments within which the development of the professional game has taken place. Crucial in this regard, it seems, has been the continuing attempt by those who run the game to gain 'respectability' for themselves and for their 'product'. Crucial, too – although we cannot go into details here – has been the changing composition of crowds and the degree to which the (non-linear) processes of 'incorporation' and 'civilization' of the working class have affected the behavioural standards of spectators. In these as in other ways, Taylor and Clarke appear to us to see too sharp a disjuncture between the processes which occurred in the game and the wider society in the 1960s and 70s, and those which occurred in the past.

It would, of course, be wrong to suppose that the data we have reported are necessarily inconsistent with the *totality* of Taylor and Clarke's hypotheses. One cannot, for example, discount the possibility that *some* spectator disorderliness at football matches in the late nineteenth and early twentieth centuries may have been a form of resistance against the commercialization and, in that sense, 'bourgeoisification' of the game. Incidents such as the riot at Hampden Park, Glasgow, in April 1909, may fall into that category. They involved destruction of the property of clubs that were limited companies; that is, that were privately owned by shareholders and run by boards of directors. Accordingly, although the Hampden Park riot seems to have been sparked off by a 'game-specific' cause, namely, by the authorities' failure to make provision for extra time, one cannot show definitively that none of the rioters were protesting against the hegemony of middle-class groups over the emergent professional game. Thus, even though it is historically wrong in many ways, Taylor's hypothesis may retain a degree of explanatory validity.

It is important, however, to stress that there is no *direct* evidence to support such a view. Moreover, for what they are worth, the currently available data suggest that the riots and other forms of violent incidents that took place at football matches in the late nineteenth and early twentieth centuries were unorganized, relatively spontaneous and *ad hoc* affairs. That is, they cannot in any meaningful sense be described as having formed part of a 'resistance movement'. The same would seem, for the most part, to hold true for present-day football hooliganism, too. Thus, even though specific incidents, such as the 'invasion' of a terrace occupied by a rival fan group, are often planned, such planning tends to be limited to the coordination of tactics at a particular match. A central object of the planning, futhermore, seems usually to be to outwit the authorities in order to engage in an attack on the rival fans. The fact that these rivalries are acted out within a context of public concern and official condemnation appears to be one of the sources of gratification for the participants. However, it does not appear to be the case that the major target of such attacks is those who own and control the clubs. Rather, the structure of ownership and control in the game seems to be taken for granted by the fans, and football hooligan fighting seems principally to grow out of specific inter-fan-group rivalries. This suggests that, even though such activities generate conflict between the fans and a whole variety of other groups (for example, the football authorities), the agencies of social control and groups in higher reaches of the class system, greater attention has to be paid to explaining why particular forms of conflict should be generated *within* sections of the working class than is paid by Ian Taylor. In short, a more subtle and complex conceptual apparatus than the one Taylor employed, an apparatus capable of dealing with a multilayered pattern of conflict and with the interplay between the different levels, is required in order to grapple with this problem.[5]

Although our data suggest that, like Taylor, Clarke, too, gets much of the history wrong, his hypothesis appears to be more object-adequate as an explanation of the relatively uncoordinated, spontaneous and *ad hoc* character of much football hooligan behaviour. That is, even though the existence of forms of football hooliganism before the First World War suggests that it cannot be attributed in some simple sense to the 'fracturing' of working-class family and neighbourhood ties in the period following the Second World War, *one* of the principal determinants of it does appear to be the attendance at matches in large numbers of working-class adolescents and young adults accompanied solely by their age peers. However, although again limited space has prevented us from presenting the totality of our evidence on this score,[6] the data we have cited suggest that, *pace* Clarke, working-class youths and young adults have always tended to go to matches in substantial numbers unaccompanied by older relatives and neighbours. This suggests, in its turn, that Clarke has romanticized the past of the working class, attributing to it a degree of family, inter-age-group and neighbourhood solidarity it has probably never possessed. It would certainly be going too far in the opposite direction to paraphrase Dahrendorf in this connection and claim that the working class was 'born decomposed' and has remained so ever since.[7] It is, however, reasonable to suppose that, in order to move towards a more adequate explanation of football hooliganism, what is needed is a conceptual apparatus that is much more closely attuned to the changing balance between the polarities of conflict and co-operation, harmony and dissension, persistence and change as they are empirically observable in the longer term in working-class communities than is the case with the conceptual apparatus employed by Clarke.

By way of conclusion we wish to make two points. The first is that we are not suggesting that football hooliganism before the First World War was identical with its present-day counterpart. That would be an absurd claim to make if only because of the changes that have occurred both in the game and the wider society since the early years of the present century. Our central objective has been simply to provide a comparative focus for the present-day phenomenon in order to highlight what its distinctive characteristics really are. It is also our contention that, despite the occurrence of changes, elements of continuity between past and present are detectable, and that it is necessary to take account of them in attempting to develop a sociological explanation. In fact, the second major object of this chapter is to make a small contribution towards reorienting the sociological analysis of football hooliganism in a manner that will enable such complexities to be handled in a more adequate manner than has been possible hitherto. This leads on to our second and final point.

We have begun, in this essay, to present data which suggest to us that the theories of football hooliganism offered by Taylor and Clarke are inadequate in a number of ways. It is important, however, to stress that our critique is not an empiricist one. Thus, although we set great store by empirical investigation and regard it as a vital prerequisite of adequate sociological analysis, we do not believe that, in some simple sense, 'facts' exist which can be said 'to speak for themselves'. On the contrary, theories are needed to interpret 'facts' and even in order to discover them. Indeed, it is the fact that our theoretical assumptions are in many ways different from those of Taylor and Clarke that led us to embark on the research, part of which has been reported here, in the first place. These assumptions derive from a sociological perspective that has, as one of its main objectives, the unification of sociology and history.[8] It is a perspective that eschews the kind of speculative history that forms the work of Taylor and Clarke, largely because the latter appears to us to depend too heavily on heteronomous and, above all, ideological evaluations. One of the consequences of this is a distortion, not only of the past, but in many ways of the present as well.

Having said this, it is, we feel, necessary for us to record our debt to Taylor and Clarke for the stimulus provided by their work. At the same time, we feel that our approach has enabled us to move further in the direction of an object-adequate explanation. To the extent that this is true, this essay serves as a demonstration of the gains that can accrue from an approach which synthesizes the historical and sociological elements, and which, more particularly, eschews on the one hand, forms of sociological analysis that rely on speculative history and, on the other, forms of historical research that are almost or entirely atheoretical and asociological.

NOTES

1 Taylor has recently returned to the subject of football hooliganism (Hargreaves 1982; Cantelon and Gruneau 1982) but, although what he has written constitutes an advance on his earlier work in many respects, nowhere does he explicitly tell the reader which of his earlier ideas he no longer accepts. Accordingly, it is relevant to subject these ideas to testing and critique.

2 Although there are clearly two dimensions to the problem, it is not, strictly speaking, accurate to distinguish one as 'factual' and the other as 'perceptual'. That is because the 'factual' level involves its own perceptual dimension, and the 'perceptual' level factually exists in the sense of being an empirically observable dimension of the overall problem. What we are actually referring to, of course, is the *behaviour* of football fans, on the one hand, and the *perception* of their behaviour by 'outsiders', on the other.

3 In a later paper, Taylor explicitly argues that 'the examination of the relations between clubs and supporters in historical times and in the recent period tends to deteriorate into specious and anecdotal debates' (see Ian Taylor, 'Class Violence and Sport – the Case of Soccer Hooliganism in Britain,' unpublished paper, University of Sheffield, 1980).

4 Limited space precludes a detailed explication of our research methods in this context. However, we should point out that one of our aims has been to avoid exaggeration. For example, our figures relating to the *Mercury*'s reportage rate include only those incidents of disorder which clearly specify spectator involvement. We have omitted all reports which merely refer to 'disorderly conduct', etc. Two further pieces of evidence which suggest that our figures underestimate the actual rate of football spectator disorder in Leicestershire are that, firstly, the FA records include reference to two incidents of spectator misconduct in Leicestershire in this period which were not apparently reported by the *Mercury*; and, secondly, there are cases of spectator disorder in Leicestershire which were only mentioned by the *Mercury* in the context of later incidents.

5 For a useful lead in this connection, see the discussion of 'game models' in Elias 1978: 71–103.

6 In this context, the following examples must suffice:

(a) In 1903 the *Mercury* wrote of the impediment to linesmen on the Fosse ground created 'by small boys and youths who allowed excitement to carry them from their proper places' (*Leicester Daily Mercury*, 22 Aug. 1903).

(b) In 1897, the *Mercury* reported an attack on the Burton player Cunningham in a Leicester street by a 'gang of youths' following a match with Leicester Fosse, an attack which left the player in a critical condition (*Leicester Daily Mercury*, 19 Jan. 1897).

(c) As a result of two FA enquiries into crowd disorders, boys were singled out for punishment. In 1897, in addition to having their ground closed for ten days and having to post warning notices, Lincoln were also told to suspend for two months the half-price admission enjoyed by boys (FA Minutes, 28 May 1897). In 1908, in the case of Walsall, the FA went further in this regard, ordering that the ground be closed to boys for three weeks (FA Minutes, 30 Nov. 1908 – 18 Nov. 1908).

(d) In 1888, the Villa team arriving in Liverpool received a hostile reception from 'an army of young ragamuffins who met them at the station at Everton, hooting and threatening them . . . ' (*Birmingham Daily Mail*, 10 Oct. 1898).

7 This phrase is used by Dahrendorf (1959: 56) to refer to the 'new middle classes'.

8 The perspective we are referring to is the 'figurational-developmental' perspective associated principally with its main originator, Norbert Elias.

REFERENCES

Clarke, John (1978) 'Football and Working Class Fans: Tradition and Change', in Roger Ingham (ed.) *Football Hooliganism*. London: Interaction Imprint.

Cotton, J.A.H. (1926) *Wickets and Goals*. London: Chapman and Hall.

Dahrendorf, Ralf (1959) *Class and Class Conflict in Industrial Society*. Stanford, CA: Stanford University Press.

Dobbs, B. (1973) *Edwardians at Play: Sport, 1890–1914*. London: Pelham.

Elias, Norbert (1978) *What is Sociology?* London: Hutchinson.

Green, Geoffrey (1953) *A History of the Football Association*. London: Naldrett.

Hood, R. and Sparks, B. (1974) *Key Issues in Criminology*. London: Weidenfeld & Nicolson.

Hutchinson, John (1975) 'Some Aspects of Football Crowds Before 1914' in *The Working Class and Leisure*, Proceedings of the Conference for the Study of Labour History, University of Sussex, paper no. 13 (mimeo).

Mann, L. and Pearce, P. (1978) 'Social Psychology of the Sports Spectator', in D. Glencross (ed.) *Psychology and Sport*, Sydney: McGraw-Hill.

Marsh, P., Rosser, E. and Harré R. (1978) *The Rules of Disorder*. London: Routledge & Kegan Paul.

Mason, Tony (1980) *Association Football and English Society, 1863–1915*. Brighton: Harvester.

Taylor, Ian (1971) ' "Football Mad": a Speculative Sociology of

Football Hooliganism', in E. Dunning (ed.) *The Sociology of Sport: a Selection of Readings*. London: Cass.

Taylor, Ian (1982) 'Class, Violence and Sport: the Case of Soccer Hooliganism in Britain', in Hart Cantelon and Richard Gruneau (eds) *Sport, Culture and the Modern State*. Toronto: University of Toronto Press.

Taylor, Ian (1982) 'On the sports violence question', in Jennifer Hargreaves (ed.) *Sport, Culture and Ideology*, London: Routledge & Kegan Paul.

Vamplew, Wray (1989) 'Ungentlemanly Conduct: the Control of Soccer Crowd Behaviour in England, 1888–1914', in T.C. Smout (ed.) *The Search for Wealth and Stability*. London: Macmillan.

Chapter Four

FOOTBALL HOOLIGANISM IN BRITAIN: 1880–1989

Since the 1970s, the problem of football hooliganism has come to be widely considered in Europe, indeed the world at large, as solely or mainly an English 'disease'. Up until the early 1980s, there was, indeed, considerable justification for such a view. More particularly, the reputation for having the worst-behaved football fans in Europe, if not indeed the world, was gained by the English primarily as a result of the fact that, from about 1974 onwards, English fans following both their clubs and the national side were the principal instigators of a series of violent and vandalistic football-related incidents in continental countries.[1] As is well known, this series culminated in 1985 with the deaths of thirty-nine people, most of them Italians, at the Juventus–Liverpool European Cup Final in Brussels when a wall collapsed following a charge by Liverpool fans against Juventus fans who were occupying the same unsegregated terrace. As a result, English club sides – though not the national team – were banned by UEFA (the Union of European Football Associations) from European competition *sine die*. At the time of writing, the ban has still not been rescinded.

Despite the degree of justification that lay behind it, there was in one sense, at least by the time of Heysel, a measure of irony in the English reputation for having the worst-behaved fans in European football. More particularly, in the late 1970s and early 1980s the problem of football hooliganism began noticeably to spread, coming to take on more and more the dimensions of a pan-European phenomenon. West German fans, for example, began to rival the violent and vandalistic exploits of their counterparts in England, and Dutch fans even began to copy the English penchant for behaving violently abroad. (So far, however, the Dutch hooligans have not followed their national side as frequently as their English counterparts have followed theirs.)

71

In these and other countries, a minority of fans seemed to be modelling their behaviour directly on that of the hooligans from England, often forming gangs on English lines and calling them by English names. In short, soccer hooliganism appeared to be an English 'export' much in the same way as the game itself had originally been.

This general summary represents a mainly accurate description of an important aspect of football's history over the last two decades. If one adopts a slightly longer-term perspective, however, it can be seen to be misleading in at least one important respect. More particularly, in England in the 1960s there were repeated calls from the media for English sides to withdraw from European competition on account of the unruly behaviour of continental, particularly Italian, fans. The reaction to the crowd violence that erupted during Chelsea's visit to Rome in October 1965, can serve as an example. It prompted a writer in the *Daily Telegraph* to puzzle over the

> seemingly unaccountable reactions of the massed spectators to almost any sort of play, culminating in the exhibitions of violence and lawlessness that took place at Chelsea's match in Rome this week. It is difficult to imagine passions rising to such heights in this country, or to envisage the need for wire fencing to protect players from spectators.[2]

Behind this judgement, there clearly lay a stereotyped image of English 'national character' as universally characterized by sang-froid and as contrasting markedly with the higher, more open and volatile emotionality and excitability supposedly typical particularly of Southern Europeans. Another way of putting it would be to say that, at that time, the English had a dominant conception of themselves and their sports spectators as among the most 'civilized', if not the most 'civilized', in the world. Of course, it was a conception which failed, at least in contexts where the behaviour of 'foreigners' was being compared with that of 'Englishmen', to take account of class and regional differences in this regard. This may help to account for the fact that the writer in the *Daily Telegraph* seems to have forgotten or to have been unaware of the fact that problems of football crowd disorderliness were coming increasingly to be perceived as growing in Britain precisely at that time[3] and that wirefences had been installed as an anti-hooligan device in at least one English ground, that of Everton FC in Liverpool, as early as November 1963.[4]

What is the reality behind the stereotype, widely accepted not only in England but in much of the rest of the world, of the English as universally characterized by cool, unflappable reserve and by a capacity, equally shared by all social classes and regional groupings, for comporting themselves at exciting leisure events with greater moderation and a higher, more even and continuous level of self-control that their continental counterparts? And how does the fact of football hooliganism fit in with this stereotype?

In this chapter, we shall explore these issues historically and sociologically. More particularly, we shall show that the problem of football hooliganism is deeply rooted in British society in at least two senses. It is deeply rooted firstly because, contrary to popular belief, forms of it have been a frequent accompaniment of football matches in the United Kingdom ever since the 1870s and 1880s, the period when the professional game first started to emerge. Secondly, it is deeply rooted in the sense that those who nowadays engage in it most persistently are strongly committed to their hooligan behaviour. For them, football hooliganism is something to which they cling despite all the preventive measures that the state and the football authorities have tried. However, we shall also show that the incidence of soccer hooliganism in Britain declined between the two world wars and that it was precisely in that period – the 1920s and 1930s – that the myth of 'civilized' English football supporters principally arose. It was a myth that was partly based in reality in the sense that, in that period, violent and disorderly behaviour among English football crowds was declining relative to before the First World War at a time when it was continuing – and in some cases, possibly increasing – in other parts of the United Kingdom and abroad. However, the myth exaggerated the orderly character of English soccer crowd behaviour in the sense that disorderly and sometimes violent incidents continued to occur at English soccer grounds in the 1920s and 1930s, albeit less frequently than before. There was thus a potential, even in that period, for the downward trend to be reversed. As we shall show, such a process of reversal started to occur in the mid-1950s, but above all in the mid-1960s, partly in conjunction with a media-orchestrated moral panic.

In order to explore this upward trend from the mid-1950s onwards, we shall weave a two-fold comparison into our analysis. First, we shall compare the media treatment of football crowds in that period with its counterpart in the 1920s and 1930s, the period when the part-myth of the universally 'civilized' English soccer spectator arose. Second – and more briefly – we shall compare it with the part played by the

Danish media in the 1970s and 1980s in the development of the *roligan* – 'friendly hooligan' – movement.[5] But we are jumping ahead of ourselves. Let us begin to become more concrete by summarizing our findings regarding the history of football hooliganism in the United Kingdom.

THE HISTORY OF FOOTBALL HOOLIGANISM IN THE UK

The Leicester research into the history of football hooliganism in the United Kingdom is based on a systematic study (1) of the Football Association's records from 1895 to 1959, and (2) of reports in a variety of national and provincial newspapers from 1880 to the present day. Summarizing, our principal findings are as follows: before the First World War, the incidence of reported soccer crowd disorderliness in the United Kingdom was high; between the wars, the incidence of reported disorderliness declined markedly in England, though not in Scotland; up until the mid-1950s, the incidence of reported disorderliness remained low but then started rising; this rise was slow at first but became more rapid in the mid-1960s, especially from about 1965 onwards, the period just prior to the staging of the World Cup Finals, the only ones so far to have taken place in England. As we hope to show, this event was of considerable significance in this regard. Before discussing how, let us first substantiate this general picture in some detail. Since it has already been dealt with in considerable depth in Chapter 3, there is no need in this context to deal with football hooliganism in Britain before the First World War. We shall, accordingly, move straight into an analysis of crowd behaviour in the inter-war years.

CROWD BEHAVIOUR AND CROWD DISORDERLINESS IN BRITAIN BETWEEN THE WARS

A number of indications combine to suggest that the incidence of crowd disorderliness declined in England – though not in Scotland – between the wars. Table 9 compares the FA records for the periods 1895–1915 and 1921–39 in this regard.

On the face of it, the figures in Table 9 suggest that, contrary to our earlier suggestion, the incidence of disorderliness actually *increased* in the inter-war years. However, a contra-indication is provided

Table 9 Incidence of spectator misconduct and disorderliness at Football League matches recorded by the FA, 1895–1915 and 1921–39

Period	No. of seasons	No. of incidents		Totals
		Closures	*Cautions*	
1895–1915	18.5	8	17	25
1921–1939	18.0	8	64	72

Source: Dunning, Murphy and Williams 1988: 95

by the fact that ground closure was ordered in only eight out of a total of seventy-two cases reported between 1921 and 1939, whereas such a measure was applied in eight out of twenty-five cases reported between 1895 and 1915. In other words, the ratio of demanding that grounds should be closed as opposed to simply ordering that warning notices should be posted had dropped considerably, a fact which may be indicative of a decline in the perceived seriousness of the events that were being reported and dealt with.

Looked at superficially, our data from the *Mercury* also suggest that the incidence of football-related disorderliness was increasing between the wars. Table 10 compares the frequency with which the Leicester daily paper reported incidents between 1894 and 1914 with the frequency with which it reported them between 1921 and 1939:

Table 10 Incidents of spectator misconduct and disorderliness reported in the *Leicester Daily Mercury*, 1894–1914 and 1921–39

Period	Filbert Street	Elsewhere in Leicestershire*	Elsewhere in England
1894–1914	20	39	84
1921–1939	43†	22	35

* The figures in this column are indicative of the fact that disorders were by no means solely confined to matches in the Football League.

† Includes two incidents that occurred in conjunction with travel to and from Leicester City away matches.

Source: Dunning, Murphy and Williams 1988: 96

However, two things are not taken into account by the figures in Table 10 as far as the years 1921–39 are concerned: the substantial rise that occurred in that period in the popularity of the game;[6] and the precise nature of the offences that were covered in the reports. Regarding the first of these issues, it seems highly likely that the rise in the incidence of disorders in this period was, at least in part, an artefact of the growing spectator support that the rapid expansion of the game entailed. Regarding the second issue, the forty-three incidents recorded as occurring at Leicester City matches are illuminating. No fewer than twenty-six of them were instances of 'barracking', or what was described as 'unsporting' conduct on the part of the Filbert Street crowd. Eleven were instances of minor misdemeanours, including some incidents of straightforward crime such as pick-pocketing, and only six might be described as 'genuine' football hooliganism. Of these, four were incidents which led individual fans to be charged with being drunk and disorderly, and only two – one a case of assault on a railway passenger, the other a case of vandalism on a train – involved groups of any size. In other words, despite the increase in the *number* of offences recorded compared with before the First World War, the *rate* at which offences were being comitted appears to have fallen considerably. So, too, does the incidence of offences involving physical as opposed to verbal violence. Indeed, it seems possible that the increased frequency with which reports of 'barracking' and 'unsporting' conduct appeared between the wars may have been a function of the fact that higher all-round standards of behaviour had begun to be expected of football crowds and that such relatively minor behavioural infractions stood out in sharper relief as a result. If that were, indeed, the case, it would be consistent with one of the points made by Durkheim in relation to crime; namely that, as the incidence of a particular form of criminal behaviour falls, so other forms of deviant or socially unacceptable behaviour, previously regarded as less serious, will come to be regarded as just as reprehensible as the forms of crime that are declining.[7]

There are at least two further indications of the probability that the behaviour of English football crowds improved between the wars: reports comparing their behaviour with that of crowds in England in the past and with crowds in other parts of the United Kingdom and abroad; and reports that are indicative of increased attendance by unescorted females. Shortage of space precludes us from citing more than a few examples of each of these two types of reports.

Commenting in April 1928 on disturbances at a match in Northern Ireland, an editorial in the *Leicester Mercury*, headed 'Football and Truncheons', described the disturbances thus:

> at Belfast yesterday the half-time interval in a cup-tie between Celtic and Linfield was given up to a diversion which introduced the stoning of the musicians in the band, and the intervention of the police who used their truncheons to keep the more heated rivals in the crowd apart. Fortunately the excitement disappeared when

the players came out again, and the game was resumed as if nothing particular had happened. . .

In many centres in England during the next few weeks the big issues at stake in the Cup and the League will unite thousands of people in a single thought. Huddersfield's chance of a record 'double', League championships, promotions and relegations – will exact their full measure of hope and anxiety from the thousands amongst whom League football is a dominating sporting interest. And, happily, all those things will be duly settled without a single policeman having to raise his truncheon to preserve the peace.[8]

Two weeks later, the editor of the *Mercury* again turned to the subject of football crowds. This time, under the heading 'Orderly Crowds', he commented on behaviour at that year's FA Cup Final in the following terms:

There seems to have been more than usual favourable comment on the good behaviour of the great crowds assembled in London to take part in the Cup Final and its associated festivities. The comment arises, no doubt, from a legendary feeling that big sporting crowds are in some peculiar way predisposed to riotous and unseemly behaviour. . . .

Students of people in the mass will probably tell us that we are better behaved, and that we make merry nowadays without the discreditable manifestations that were at one time thought to be inseparable from these public rejoicings. Rejoicing and sobriety go hand in hand and great crowds distinguish themselves with a sense of discipline that is creditable all round. May we infer that we are in improving people?[9]

As we suggested earlier, further testimony to the fact that English football grounds came to be widely perceived between the wars as places that were not unduly dangerous is contained in reports which indicate that women began attending matches in increasing numbers in that period. Commenting on the 1927 FA Cup Final, for example, a reporter in the *Mercury* noted that 'A remarkable feature was the number of women who had accompanied their husbands and sweethearts. Many mothers carried babies in their arms and confessed they had brought them to see the cup-tie'.[10] The *Mercury's* report of a Leicester City–Clapton cup-tie in January 1922, similarly referred to

a never-ending stream of people, including a good sprinkling of women [going to the match]. Quite a number of women, in fact, faced the Cup-tie crush without a male escort. If Leicester is any criterion, then the lure of the English Cup is rapidly infecting the female mind.[11]

Such, indeed, was the popularity of football among Manchester women in the 1920s that special transport to matches was provided for them by the City Corporation.[12] The very fact that it was thought necessary to provide segregated transport may, of course, be indicative of the fact that it was regarded as desirable to protect women from the rough and, to them, offensive behaviour of male fans. If that was the case, however, one would have expected segregated provision to have been made in the context of matches as well. However, such issues are less germane for present purposes than the fact that there is a body of evidence which points to the growing attendance of women at football in the 1920s and 1930s, and that this seems to be consistent with the view that football grounds in that period came increasingly to be perceived as orderly and respectable places that were relatively safe. If that was not the case, it is difficult to believe that women, sometimes apparently carrying babies and often unescorted by males, would have been reported as attending matches in increasing numbers. Of course, women sometimes encourage aggressive behaviour in men. They are also sometimes the objects of it and sometimes they engage in aggressive behaviour themselves. However, the evidence we have collected for the 1920s and 1930s points overwhelmingly towards the probability that their attendance at football in growing numbers in that period was largely a consequence of the widening public percep-tion of grounds as orderly and safe. Indeed, since the evidence also suggests that the bulk of spectators in that period were recruited from the more 'respectable' sections of the working class and since a principal feature of 'respectable' working-class culture in England consists of norms which demand that males should comport themselves peaceably in the presence of women, it seems highly likely that their attendance in greater numbers would itself have intensified the trend towards more orderly crowd behaviour on which it was predicated. Let us turn now to crowd behaviour in England after the Second World War.

CROWD BEHAVIOUR AFTER
THE SECOND WORLD WAR

Table 11 records the incidents of spectator misconduct and disorderliness reported to the Football Association in the years 1946–59:

Table 11 Incidents of spectator misconduct and disorderliness reported to the FA, 1946–59

Year	Football League	Outside Football League	Totals
1946	2	2	4
1947	15	5	20
1948	7	11	18
1949	11	13	24
1950	15	4	19
1951	10	11	21
1952	8	7	15
1953	6	6	12
1954	6	8	14
1955	6	4	10
1956	9	11	20
1957	10	7	17
1958	21	8	29
1959	12	3	15
Totals	138	100	238

Source: Dunning, Murphy and Williams 1988: 136

As one can see from Table 11, the idea that the years immediately after the Second World War were years of peace and tranquillity as far as the behaviour of spectators at football matches in England was concerned is yet another myth. A substantial amount of spectator misconduct and disorderlinesss continued to be reported to the FA as occurring both inside and outside the Football League. By contrast, only fifty-five incidents were reported in the *Leicester Mercury* in those years, around one-fifth of the number recorded in the FA Minutes. In other words, spectator disorderliness seems then to have been substantially under-reported by the media. Such incidents as were reported, moreover, tended not to be headlined or highlighted in any other way. It is reasonable to suppose that this pattern of 'playing down' and under-reporting may have been one of the conditions contributing to the myth that English spectators in that period were invariably well behaved. Such a myth received reinforcement in at least two further ways: on the one hand, from positive comments made by foreigners about English crowds; and on the other, from reports of football-related disturbances abroad. For example, when six Italian police officers visited Filbert Street in 1955 to watch a Leicester City match, they confessed to a *Mercury* reporter that they were 'amazed how a handful of Leicester police officers manages to control large football crowds. In Italy', they said, 'the area would be "flooded" with police officers to keep order.'[13] In that period, too, the *Mercury* printed reports of football crowd disorders in countries as diverse as Sweden, Kenya, Switzerland, Portugal, Italy and Yugoslavia. Principally, however, they were reported as occurring in South America.

Perhaps in part because the experiences of the war were still to the forefront of many people's minds, the relatively high number of incidents reported to the FA between 1946 and 1950 were not singled out by the press for special treatment. In any case, the immediate post-war years were boom years for the English game, a period when attendances reached their all-time peak. By 1957, however, the loss of empire, slow relative economic growth and specific events such as the Suez débâcle of 1956 had begun seriously to undermine the national self-confidence of the British. As far specifically as football was concerned, crowd sizes had by then been in continuous decline for some six or seven years and the defeat of England by Hungary at Wembley in 1953 – the first such defeat on English soil – contributed what was experienced as another massive blow. Added to this, the after-glow of victory in the Second World War had by then begun to fade and, in such an overall context, an anxious press began to articulate and at the same time to exacerbate rising public concern about 'the problem' of working-class youth, especially the 'teddy boys'.

It was in this situation that the media began to report the misbehaviour of soccer fans more frequently than they had done immediately after the war. For example, in November 1957 the *Mercury* published the following article under the heading 'This Soccer Trend Must Cease':

On Saturday hundreds of [Everton fans] jeered West Bromwich Albion and assaulted some of the players as they went for their coach after the game. . . This season, some six teams have been booed or jeered . . . at either Goodison or Anfield. Bottles have been thrown at several players . . . and Teddy Boys have run out onto the pitch. . . Everton fans have wrecked an excursion train and had free fights with other gangs following Liverpool. . . Even in Regency Brighton . . . on Saturday, Reading manager Harry Johnson was hit on the jaw by louts and two of his players were also struck as they left the field. . . It's a trend that is increasing. They even threw fireworks at a goalkeeper at Highbury on Saturday.[14]

At first, however, there was no consistent trend as far as reports of this kind were concerned. On the one hand, press reports of spectator disorders became more frequent from 1956 onwards (especially relative to the low frequency of reporting for the years 1952–5, though not so much relative to the years 1946–51 when the frequency was roughly comparable to that for 1956–9). On the other hand, the press remained at this stage ambivalent towards disorderly fan behaviour. Typical of such ambivalence was the response from the *News of the World* to the erection of fences behind the goals at Goodison Park in November 1963. 'Hooligans?' queried the reporter, 'They're so friendly.'[15] Similar ambivalence was displayed in the *Daily Sketch*. Under the headline, 'Brave Fans – You Don't Need Cages', a *Sketch* reporter offered the following account of player and fan behaviour in the country as a whole on the first Saturday after the introduction of the Everton fences:

What? No darts? No invasions? No sendings off? No fights on the field? No protests? No menacing mobs awaiting the exits of referees? What is British football coming to? And what dull reading for the violence-hungry this weekend!. . . Everton can remove the hooligan barriers at Goodison Park, and those who plead for cages and moats and barbed wire can weep in their beer, for the British football fan is showing he can correct the stormy situation of recent weeks in the good old British manner – by common sense.[16]

As late as February 1964, a *Daily Mail* reporter was even able to express his preference for 'hooliganism rather than indifference.'[17] However, the pattern of reporting spectator behaviour at that stage seems to have marked a watershed. English fans were no longer held up to the rest of the world as models of good behaviour as they had been in the 1920s and 1930s. Nevertheless, it was still possible to point to the occurrence of serious fan violence abroad. It was in 1964, for example, that the worst football-related tragedy of modern times occurred – the deaths of an estimated 318 people at the Peru–Argentina match in Lima.[18] In fact, at that stage, it seems possible to us that, had the positive side of the ambivalence of the British press become dominant over the negative, condemnatory side, there would still have been a chance, not of eradicating hooliganism *per se*, but of halting or at least severely restricting the escalation of it specifically in football contexts which followed in the next few years. At least the currently available comparative evidence – cross-cultural comparative evidence from Denmark and historical comparative evidence from England – seems to point in that direction. Let us briefly examine the evidence which suggests that this was so.

In the late 1970s and early 1980s, the Danish press seems to have played a part in nipping an incipient problem of football hooliganism in the bud by coining the term *roligan* – 'calm' or 'friendly hooligan' – and by praising rather than condemning what one might call socially acceptable deviant behaviour on the part of football fans (such as heavy drinking, dressing-up carnival-style and so on), as long as serious violence was not involved. In this way, potentially violent fans were kept away and Danish fan groups came to be to a large extent self-policing and only minimally reliant on external interventions for the maintenance of orderly behaviour.[19] In similar fashion, despite the continuing undercurrent of crowd disorderliness in England in the 1920s, 1930s, 1940s and 1950s, the English press of those years seems not only to have reflected but also to have actively contributed to the then-dominant trend towards more orderly spectator behaviour by praising English fans relative to those from other countries and by defining football grounds as safe places where it was appropriate for 'respectable' people, women as well as men, to go. In 1965 and 1966, however, the 'national mood' in England, at least in so far as it was articulated by the press, was more conducitve to playing up the negative side of the ambivalence. The fact that the World Cup Finals were staged in England in 1966 seems to have been of decisive significance in this regard. It is to this issue that our attention will now be turned.

THE 1966 WORLD CUP

In the early 1960s, the mods and rockers took over from the teddy boys as the principal 'folk devils' of British society.[20] They were reported in the media as fighting regularly but principally at seaside resorts on public holidays and only rarely or never at football or in football-related contexts. Nevertheless, the rising public concern about them seems to have interacted with the negative side of the media ambivalence towards crowd disorderliness at football to create a climate of considerable anxiety about the forthcoming World Cup Finals. In a country where people were more confident about themselves and their position in the world than the British then were, it is conceivable that the media might have reacted calmly and with confidence to the media spotlight under which they were about to come. But the national self-confidence of the British was then at a low ebb and the reaction of at least sections of the popular press bordered on the hysterical. On 6 November 1965, for example, during a match in London between Brentford and Millwall, a dead hand grenade was thrown on to the pitch from the end where the main body of Millwall fans were congregated. Misreading the meaning of this symbolic gesture, a reporter in the *Sun* wrote on 8 November under the headline 'Soccer Marches to War':

> The Football Association have acted to stamp out this increasing mob violence within 48 hours of the blackest day in British soccer – the grenade day that showed that British supporters can rival anything the South Americans can do.
>
> The World Cup is now less than nine months away. That is all the time we have left to try and restore the once good sporting name of this country. Soccer is sick at the moment. Or better, its crowds seem to have contracted some disease that makes them break out in fury.

There was fighting at this match both inside and outside the ground, and one Millwall fan sustained a broken jaw.[21] However, the reporter chose to concentrate on the symbolic violence of the hand grenade and implicitly equated this incident with the full-scale riot that had taken place at the Peru–Argentina match in 1964. Significantly, he also chose to locate the incident in the context of the forthcoming World Cup Finals. A similar choice was made by the Editor of the *Sun* in April 1966 following violent scenes at a match involving Liverpool and Glasgow Celtic. He wrote:

> It may be only a handful of hooligans who are involved at the throwing end, but if this sort of behaviour is repeated in July, the world will conclude that all the British are hooligans. . . Either the drift to violence must be checked or soccer will be destroyed as an entertainment. What an advertisement for the British sporting

spirit if we end with football pitches enclosed in protective wire cages.[22]

There were elements of self-fulfilling prophecy in reports such as these. That is to say, they helped to set in motion a train of events over the next twenty years which led football hooliganism to be defined world-wide as 'the English disease' and which contributed to the re-design of stadia in the Football League into fortress-like constructions in which fans were segregated, caged and penned. In the shorter term, however, a series of more specific effects were produced, serving to set the longer-term trend in motion. More particularly, reports of this kind appear to have been instrumental in helping to produce a 'moral panic' over the behaviour of football fans. One of the consequences of this was that the popular press started regularly to send reporters to matches specifically to report on crowd behaviour.[23] Previously, football reporters, there to report principally on the match itself, had tended only to write about the most visibly disruptive crowd incidents. Now, however, incidents that were less obviously disruptive of the match began to be reported, too, and the increase in the frequency with which they were reported contributed to the impression that football hooliganism was increasing more, and more rapidly, than was, in fact, the case. Around the same time, too, in conjunction with growing competition for readers among the popular dailies, both match reports and reports of crowd behaviour began to become more sensa-tionalistic and to be couched more frequently in terms of a military rhetoric. As a result, soccer grounds came to be perceived increasingly as places where openly violent and not simply sporting conflict regularly takes place, and this had, as one of its consequences, the fact that their attractiveness to youths and young men for whom fighting and disrup-tive behaviour are a source of pleasurable excitement was increased. In fact, it was probably by no means accidental that, whereas the teddy boys and the mods and rockers, the 'folk devils' of the years before the 1966 World Cup Finals, had not fought regularly in football con-texts, the 'skinheads', the groups who followed them and who first became visibly active in 1967, chose the game as one of their major theatres of operation. In other words, in a context of growing national self-doubt where exaggerated fears were being generated about the anticipated world response to crowd behaviour at the forthcoming World Cup Finals, an intensifying press 'circulation war' contributed to a pattern of sensationalistic and militaristic reporting, and this appears to have had, as one of its unintended effects, the advertising of soccer as a context for fighting. As a result, young males from the 'rougher' sections of a working class that had generally been growing more 'respectable' for some thirty or forty years were drawn into attending football more regularly and in greater numbers than before. At the same time, members of the 'respectable' majority withdrew their support more and more, intensifying the already occurring trend towards lower gates[24] and contributing to the position in which we find ourselves in Britain today: namely, a situation where hooligan incidents in conjunction with football are larger in scale and a much more regular accompaniment of matches than was formerly the case and where the English hooliganism problem has been exported abroad with the consequence that the terms 'English football fan' and 'football hooligan', have come to be widely regarded on the Continent as synonymous. The mass media, of course, cannot be said to have caused this process but, via the pattern of reporting described above, they can be said, by means of a kind of self-fulfilling prophecy, to have played an important part in bringing it about.

Once these adolescent and young adult males from the 'rougher' sections of the working class had been attracted to football in larger numbers, they stayed there, largely because it is, in a number of ways, a highly appropriate context for the sorts of activities that they prize. At a football match, for example, they are able to act in ways that are condemned by officialdom and 'respectable' society in a context which provides relative immunity from arrest. They are able, that is to say, to 'take the lid off' for a while and collectively to establish a temporary reversal of the power structure of the wider society. The game, too, can generate high levels of excitement, and the focus of this excitement is a contest – a mock battle with a ball – between the male representatives of two communities. Though formally more controlled, usually less openly violent and, in a sense, more abstract and symbolic, it is in many ways homologous with the fighting of the hooligans themselves. That is to say, it, too, is a form of masculinity ritual. Also, to the extent that the away team brings with it a large number of supporters, a ready-made group of opponents is provided and, in that context, the internal rivalries of the local 'rougher' working class can be temporarily suspended in the interests of presenting a common front to the 'invading outsiders'.

But let us look at the typical motivations of the football hooligans and at the social backgrounds from which they typically come.

THE MOTIVATIONS AND SOCIAL BACKGROUNDS
OF THE FOOTBALL HOOLIGANS

In an article published in the *Guardian* in 1984, a self-confessed former football hooligan reminisced as follows about the emotions he experienced in the 1960s during his days of hooligan involvement:

> the excitement of battle, the danger, the heightened activity of body and mind as the adrenaline raced, the fear and the triumph of overcoming it. To this day, when trouble starts at a game I come alive and close to getting involved. I may not forget the dangers of physical injury and criminal proceedings but I do not ignore them.[25]

Basically similar sentiments were expressed by another self-confessed football hooligan, 'Frank', a 26-year-old lorry driver who was interviewed by Paul Harrison in conjunction with the 1974 Cardiff City–Manchester United match. 'Frank' is reported by Harrison as having said:

> I go to a match for one reason only: the aggro. It's an obsession. I can't give it up. I get so much pleasure when I'm having aggro that I nearly wet my pants. . . I go all over the country looking for it . . . every night during the week we go around town looking for trouble. Before a match we go round looking respectable . . . then if we see someone who looks like the enemy we ask him the time; if he answers in a foreign accent, we do him over; and if he's got any money on him we'll roll him as well.[26]

Here is how 'Howard', one of our Leicester informants, put it in 1981. Howard's words illustrate the sort of rationality that came increasingly to be involved in football hooliganism as police and club controls were progressively increased:

> If you can baffle the coppers, you'll win. You've just gotta think how they're gonna think. And you know, half the time, you know what they're gonna do 'cos they're gonna take the same route every week, week in, week out. If you can figure out a way to beat 'em, you're fuckin' laughin'; you'll have a good fuckin' raut (Leicester slang for a 'fight').

Finally, when interviewed for the Thames TV programme 'Hooligan', in 1985, a member of West Ham United's 'Inter City Firm' said:

We don't – we don't go – well, we *do* go with the intention of fighting, you know what I mean. . . (W)e look forward to it. . . It's great. You know, if you've got, say 500 kids coming for you, like, and you know they're going to be waiting for you, it's – it's good to know like. Like being a tennis player, you know. You get all geed up to play, like. We get geed up to fight. . .

I think I fight, like, so I can make a name for meself and that, you know. Hope people, like, respect me for what I did, like.[27]

Despite the fact that they were made over a period of more than twenty years, these statements are remarkably consistent. What they reveal, above all, are the continuing underlying motives that tend to be involved in football hooligan behaviour. More particularly, they reveal that 'core' football hooligans are engaged in a quest for status and excitement or emotional arousal; that the excitement generated by the game alone is insufficient for them in this regard; and that, for them, fighting is a central source of meaning and gratification in life. Thus 'Frank' spoke of 'aggro' as a pleasurable, almost erotically arousing obsession, while the *Guardian's* informant talked of 'battle excitement' and 'the adrenaline racing'. A quest for pleasurable excitement, of course, is a common feature of leisure activities, a counter to the emotional staleness that tends to be engendered not only by work but also by the routines of non-leisure life.[28] Also of relevance in this connection is the fact that Britain remains a predominantly patriarchial society in which males generally are expected under certain circumstances to fight. However, the dominant norms demand that they should not be the initiators in this regard and require them to confine their fighting to self-defence and to sports such as boxing. However, the core football hooligans regularly contravene these norms. For them, a quest for pleasurable 'battle excitement' engendered at football and in other contexts forms a predominant leisure interest. Sociologically, the point is to explain why. Who are the core football hooligans and what in their social circumstances and experiences explains their love of fighting and the fact that they deviate from the dominant norms of British society in this regard?

In our research, we have established that between 2 and 6 per cent of any British soccer crowd is likely to consist of professional personnel, that is to say, of members of the Registrar General's Social Class 1. A somewhat larger proportion – between 13 and 15 per cent – is likely to fall into the 'intermediate' occupational category; that is, to come from the Registrar General's Social Class 2. The overwhelming majority, however, around two-thirds or 65 per cent, are likely to be routine non-manual and skilled manual workers; that is, to come from the Registrar General's Social Class 3. By contrast, attendance by semi-skilled and unskilled manual workers – that is, by people from Social Classes 4 and 5 – tends to be considerably lower, ranging, according to our data, between 11 and 13 per cent for the semi-skilled, Social Class 4 category, and between 2 and 4 per cent for unskilled workers, members of the Registrar General's Social Class 5.

The available data on football hooligans contrast markedly with these, showing a far higher concentration towards the bottom of the social scale. In 1968, for example, J.A. Harrington collected relevant data on 497 convicted soccer hooligans and found that 206 or 41.4 per cent were employed as labourers or in unskilled manual occupations.[29] A further 112, or 22.5 per cent, were employed in a semi-skilled capacity. Some 64 per cent of Harrington's sample, in other words, belonged to the Registrar General's Social Classes 4 and 5. However, even as early as 1968, some football hooligans came from higher up the social scale. Thus, fifty, or just over 10 per cent of Harrington's sample, were skilled manual workers and a further nineteen, just under 4 per cent, of Harrington's sample belonged to the Registrar General's Social Class 3. Two were even employed in a professional or managerial capacity and thus qualify for membership of the Registrar General's Social Classes 1 or 2.

The findings of Trivizas for London in 1980 were broadly similar to those of Harrington. More particularly, on the basis of data of about 520 offences committed in 'football crowd events' in the Metropolitan Police Area during the years 1974–6, he found that 'more than two-thirds (68.1 per cent) of those charged with football-related offences were manual workers, the majority being apprentices; 12 per cent of football offences were committed by unemployed persons and 10 per cent by schoolboys. . . Only 8 football-related offences were committed by people in "intermediate occupations", 6 by students, 3 by individuals in professional occupations and 3 by members of the armed forces.'[30]

That the kind of occupational and social class distribution of football hooligans discovered by Harrington in 1968 and by Trivizas for the years 1974–6 continues, broadly speaking, to hold good is suggested by the Leicester research. Thus, of the twenty-three Leicester football hooligans we studied in 1981, five were skilled manual workers

(Social Class 3); seven were partly skilled (Social Class 4); three were unskilled (Social Class 5); and eight, at the time of the research, were unemployed. Similarly, of the 143 members of West Ham United's 'Inter City Firm' on whom we obtained data in 1985, eight, or 5.6 per cent, fell into the Registrar General's Social Class 2; thirty-six, or 25.2 per cent, fell into Social Class 3; ten, or 7 per cent, were members of Social Class 4; and twenty-five, or 17.5 per cent, fell into Social Class 5. A further fifty-four, or 37.8 per cent, were unemployed.

The currently available data thus suggest that, whilst football hooligans are recruited from all levels in the class hierarchy, the overwhelming majority come from the manual sections of Social Class 3 and from Classes 4 and 5. In fact, aggregation of our data on known hooligans provides a perfect inverese correlation between participation in football hooliganism and social class. Thus, of the total of 519 employed football hooligans active in the 1960s, 1970s or 1980s on whom we have information, two (0.38 per cent) came from Social Class 1; thirteen (2.5 per cent) from Social Class 2; twenty-nine (5.58 per cent) from Social Class 3, non-manual; ninety-eight (18.88 per cent) from Social Class 3, manual; 132 (25.43 per cent) from Social Class 4; and 245 (47.2 per cent) from Social Class 5. The data also suggest that, together with the motivational patterns of the football hooligans, this sort of distribution has remained remarkably stable since the problem of football hooliganism first began to reach its current levels and to take on its current forms in the late 1960s. Within this stable pattern, only the proportion of football hooligans who are unemployed has shown a steady tendency to rise. More particularly, the data of Harrington for the 1960s, of Trivizas for the 1970s and our own for the 1980s, all suggest that the majority of football hooligans come from towards the bottom of the social scale. A much smaller and relatively stable proportion is recruited from around the middle, and an even smaller, equally stable one from the top.

Despite such relative stability as far as the motivational and social recruitment patterns of the football hooligans are concerned, changes have occurred over the past twenty years in their patterns of organization. Such changes appear to have taken place less as a result of the internal dynamics of football hooligan groups and the broader experiences of the social strata from which they principally come and more as a consequence of an interaction between, on the one hand, what one might call the 'dialectics of control' and, on the other, the dynamics of the status rivalry among the different hooligan groups as they strive to gain media and terrace recognition as the most feared hooligans in the land. More particularly, as the controls imposed by central government, the football authorities and the police have grown more all-embracing, tighter and sophisticated, so the football hooligans in their turn have tended to become more organized and to use more sophisticated strategies and plans in an attempt to evade the controls. At the same time, football hooligan fighting has tended to become displaced from an immediate football context and to take place at times and in situations where the controls are, or are perceived to be, weak or non-existent. Similarly, as one hooligan group has developed strategies and a form of organization that has enabled them regularly both to evade the controls and to inflict defeat on their rivals, so the others have been forced to follow suit. It is to these issues that our attention will now be turned.

THE DYNAMICS OF FOOTBALL HOOLIGAN RIVALRY AND THE DIALECTICS OF CONTROL

At the time of the major 'skinhead' involvement in the late 1960s, the football hooligans tended to be organized on a relatively loose and *ad hoc* basis. Small groups of fans united primarily by kinship and neighbourhood ties or through friendships formed at work or school would forge larger alliances in a match-day context for purposes of confronting rival fans. Such alliances were organized largely in terms of the 'Bedouin syndrome' – that is, according to the following, four-fold set of principles: the friend of a friend is a friend; the enemy of an enemy is a friend; the friend of an enemy is an enemy; and the enemy of a friend is an enemy. As official controls such as the penning and segregation of opposing fan groups began to be imposed, however, what became known as the 'football ends', so called because they consisted of youths and young men who regularly watched their team from behind a particular goal, began to be created. Examples are the 'Stretford End' of Manchester United and the 'Clock End' at Arsenal. Their solidarity was enhanced by self-selection and as a response to their public vilification by officialdom and the media. They also came to see the 'end' where they stood as a territory to be defended and the 'end' where opposing fans like themselves were congregated as a territory to be attacked. The football ends also often involved the submergence of local rivalries in common opposition to the fans of the rival team. At this stage, 'taking the end' of a rival team – that is, invading 'their' territory inside the ground and inflicting a defeat on them through fighting or making them run for safety on to the pitch – was a source of great kudos in football hooligan circles. Then, as police and club controls inside grounds began to bite and as the 'end-rivalries' between the goal-terrace fans of different clubs began to be displaced outside grounds and on to and beyond the periphery of the controls, so the fans who were most deeply committed to hooligan activities in a football context formed themselves into what they called 'fighting crews' or 'fighting firms' and were forced, in order to evade the burgeoning controls, to plan and organize their activities more and more. Until the late 1970s, such organization remained largely informal, usually involving little more than meetings and discussions in pubs and clubs in the week before a match, the circulation of plans via the local 'grapevine' and perhaps the production of crudely cyclostyled leaflets detailing a time and venue for a meeting and a place for ambushing the opposing fans.

This process culminated in the emergence in the early 1980s of named 'superhooligan' gangs such as the 'Inter City Firm' (ICF) of West Ham United, the 'Service Crew' of Leeds, the 'Gooners' of Arsenal, the 'Bushwhackers' of Millwall, the 'Baby Squad' of Leicester and the 'Headhunters' of Chelsea. The ICF can serve as an example. They were one of the first 'superhooligan' gangs to emerge and they chose their name in order to signify the fact that they pioneered the tactic of eschewing travel on 'football special' trains wearing club favours, choosing, instead, the regular 'Inter City' service and what they regarded as 'smart' but 'casual' clothing with no club colours in order not to advertise themselves as football fans to the police. These successful tactics spread during the early 1980s until most major crews were practising similar techniques.

Members of the ICF tend to be in their late teens and twenties although key leaders and organizers are sometimes older. They make use of younger fans whom they call 'the Under Fives' but who are, in fact, mainly 14- and 15- year-olds, in order to reconnoitre the numbers, locations and dispositions of opposing fans and the police. The ICF use complex strategies to avoid police controls and to infiltrate home territories on their visits to away grounds. Before matches away from home, they typically roam the streets and pubs of the town they are visiting, seeking out local fans who can be identified as the opposition's equivalent to the ICF. At home matches, the ICF seek to attack and intimidate the members of visiting ends who show sufficient 'nerve' to visit West Ham United's ground at Upton Park. Sometimes frustrated by the lack of opposition or as a means of effecting a pre-emptive strike, the ICF have been known to travel to other parts of London in the hope of engaging rival London fighting crews on their own territories.

The core 'membership' of the ICF numbers about 150, though up to around 500 may travel with core members when what they regard as a major confrontation is in view. Their organization and solidarity are partly predicated on the fact that the bulk of their core members are united by bonds of close or common residence in specific communities in or near London's East End and through ties forged at school or work. Such bonds are further solidified through frequent meetings in non-football contexts – for example, at pubs and clubs. However, not all superhooligan groups have the same underlying basis of solidarity. The Headhunters, for example, come from suburbs from all around London and appear to have forged their bonds more instrumentally and specifically in a football context. They even paid subscriptions into a building society account opened by one of their lower-middle-class members, a solicitor's clerk, and used their joint savings to finance trips abroad. Some of them kept scrapbooks and photograph albums recording their violent exploits and the press reaction to their escapades.

Perhaps because they are more individualized and anomic and lack the kinds of controls that tend to be generated in a community context, groups such as the Headhunters appear to be more interested in wanton and gratuitous violence than groups such as the ICF, the majority of whom are usually satisfied simply with inflicting defeat on their rivals, fighting only when local opposition provides 'suitable' opponents, and with behaving with impunity on away trips in the territory of their rivals, thereby establishing a form of momentary control. However, the dynamics of hooligan confrontations can lead even such groups on occasion to arm themselves and they also tend to be joined by non-locals, sometimes from higher up the social scale, who are attracted by their violent reputations. These reputations have also made the ICF and similar groups a target for recruitment campaigns by neo-fascist and racist political parties. So far, however, the results of these campaigns have been patchy, meeting with a degree of success only at a small number of clubs. In fact, the ICF is racially mixed and some of its leaders are black, though, so far, it has not attracted any recruits of Asian descent.

Some of its leading members claim to be overtly hostile to racist parties like the National Front.

CONCLUSION

In this chapter, we have shown that football hooliganism in Britain is a deeply rooted social phenomenon. It stretches back to before the First World War, though in its present form it dates from the 1950s and 1960s. Since that time, it has been publicly and officially defined as a major social problem and the state apparatus has been increasingly mobilized in an attempt to eradicate it. So far, however, what these attempts have succeeded mainly in doing is increasing the solidarity of the football hooligans, displacing their activities further and further away from grounds, and increasing their organizational and tactical sophistication. At the time of writing (November 1989), the Government proposes to introduce a computerized national identity-card scheme as a means of identifying the football hooligans and facilitating their exclusion from matches. In this way, the Government and its supporters argue, it will be possible to break the link between football and hooliganism once and for all. It remains to be seen how successful this latest attempt at eradicating football hooliganism will be. The history of the problem and of attempts to control it in Britain over the last twenty years certainly do not seem to be propitious for continuing to attack such a complex social problem primarily by means of punishments and controls.

Apart from shedding light on the history and social roots of football hooliganism in Britain, our analysis in this chapter is of relevance to the complex issues of 'national character' and the stereotypes that different national groupings have of one another. At the very least, what it shows in this connection is that, to speak of 'the English' – or, for that matter, 'the Scots', 'the Welsh', 'the Irish' or any other national group – as completely homogeneous and undifferentiated is unwarranted. Britain is a complex society, and one of the principal aspects of its complexity is its complex class structure. This is a structure which, if we are right, has been conducive to the production and reproduction over time of distinctive subcultural variations on the stock of shared, national cultural themes. The pattern of 'aggressive masculinity' of the core football hooligans is one such subcultural variation, and, again if our evidence and analysis are right, it is characteristic, not solely but mainly, of the 'rougher' sections of the lower working class. It remains to be seen whether the football hooliganism of countries other than England is similarly produced mainly by social class. Perhaps in such cases, other aspects of national culture – for example, religious or regional differences – are of greater significance? That is certainly the case, at least to some extent, in Scotland and Northern Ireland where religious sectarianism interacts with social class to produce distinctive forms of soccer hooliganism. Perhaps that is the case in some continental countries, too?

NOTES AND REFERENCES

1 John Williams, Eric Dunning and Patrick Murphy, *Hooligans Abroad: the Behaviour and Control of English Fans at Continental Matches*, London: Routledge & Kegan Paul, 1984; second edition, with a new introduction, 1989.

2 *Daily Telegraph*, 9 Oct. 1965.

3 Eric Dunning, Patrick Murphy and John Williams, *The Roots of Football Hooliganism: an Historical and Sociological Study*, London: Routledge & Kegan Paul, 1988.

4 Dunning, Murphy and Williams, *The Roots of Football Hooliganism*, p. 144.

5 Birger Peitersen and Bente Holm Kristensen, *An Empirical Survey of the Danish Roligans during the European Championships 88*, Copenhagen: Danish State Institute of Physical Education, 1988. See also Chapter 7 in this volume, 'Soccer hooliganism as a European phenomenon'.

6 Dunning, Murphy and Williams, *The Roots of Football Hooliganism*, p. 91.

7 Emile Durkheim, *The Rules of Sociological Method*, Glencoe, NY: Free Press, 1964, esp. Chapter 3, 'Rules for Distinguishing between the Normal and the Pathological', pp. 68ff.

8 *Leicester Mercury*, 10 April 1928.

9 *Leicester Mercury*, 23 April 1928.

10 *Leicester Mercury*, 23 April 1927.

11 *Leicester Mercury*, 7 Jan. 1922.

12 *The Times*, 5 Feb. 1926.

13 *Leicester Mercury*, 2 Feb. 1955.

14 *Leicester Mercury*, 4 Nov. 1957.

15 *News of the World*, 24 Nov. 1963.

16 *Daily Sketch*, 25 Nov. 1963.

17 *Daily Mail*, 11 Feb. 1964.

18 Williams, Dunning and Murphy, *Hooligans Abroad*, p. xxi.

19 Peitersen and Kristensen, *An Empirical Survey of the Danish Roligans*. In supporting the argument of Peitersen and Kristensen on this score, it is not our intention to single out the media as the *sole* factor of explanatory significance in accounting for the combination of heavy drinking and relatively non-violent behaviour that appear to

be characteristic of the majority of Danish roligans. For one thing, as Peitersen and Kristensen themselves point out (p. 71), the roligans tend to come from higher up the social scale than the majority of English hooligans. Above all, for a fuller explanation it would be necessary to look at such things as: norms and patterns of masculinity in Danish and English culture; the balance of power between the sexes in the two countries; the characteristic patterning within them of gender roles; their (i.e. the Danish and English cultures') norms and values associated with the consumption of alcohol; the comparative rates among them of violence and violent crime; and class, ethnic, religious and regional differences within the two countries in *all* of these regards. Only in the context of a broader study focused on a range of influences such as these would it be possible to specify more adequately and precisely the part played by the media relative to other social processes and factors in the generation/prevention of football hooliganism.

20 Stanley Cohen, *Folk Devils and Moral Panics*, London: Paladin, 1973.
21 The *Sun*, 27 Sep. 1966.
22 The *Sun*, 21 April 1966.
23 Stanley Cohen, 'Campaigning Against Vandalism', in C. Ward (ed.) *Vandalism*, London: Architectural Press, 1973, p. 232.
24 For two or three seasons following England's World Cup victory in 1966, attendances at Football League matches rose. From about 1970, however, the downward trend became dominant once again and continued until 1987. Since then, an upward trend, though only a relatively slight one, has been recorded.
25 E. Taylor, 'I Was a Soccer Hooligan, Class of 64', *Guardian*, 28 March 1984.
26 Paul Harrison, 'Soccer's Tribal Wars', *New Society*, 29, 1974, pp. 602–4.
27 Interviewee on the Thames TV programme 'Hooligan', Aug. 1985.
28 Norbert Elias and Eric Dunning, *Quest for Excitement: Sport and Leisure in the Civilizing Process*, Oxford: Blackwell, 1986.
29 J.A. Harrington, *Soccer Hooliganism*, Bristol: John Wright, 1968.
30 Eugene Trivizas, 'Offences and Offenders in Football Crowd Disorders', *British Journal of Criminology*, 20 (3) (July 1980): 281–3.

Chapter Five

SOCCER CROWD DISORDER AND THE PRESS:
Processes of amplification and de-amplification in historical perspective

To our knowledge, the majority of media studies carried out to date have been present-centred, concerned to shed light on contemporary correlations and effects.[1] Fewer have been concerned with processes over time and fewer still with the long-term social processes that are at work in this regard.[2] An implication of this has been a tendency to seek timeless correlations, generalizations about the media that take too little account of spatio-temporal variations. This chapter is a contribution towards remedying that deficiency. More particularly, it is a study of the newspaper reporting of football crowd behaviour in Britain over a period of approximately 100 years, and of the relationships between the changing patterns of such reporting and the changing patterns of behaviour of football crowds themselves.

The essay is based on data from a wider study of the roots and development of British – particularly English – football ('soccer') hooliganism (Dunning *et al.* 1988). Newspapers formed one of the principal sources of data for this study.[3] However, since they are not simply passive reflectors of events, but play both an intentional and unintentional part in their construction, one of the central sociological tasks that faced us in this regard was to determine the ways in which changing modes of press coverage played a part in the development of football crowd behaviour *per se*. It was also necessary to probe the reliability of newspaper data. To what extent was the frequency with which incidents were reported indicative of their frequency in fact? Has the nature and character of the coverage exaggerated or minimized the seriousness of disorders? In this chapter, we address the latter question in greater depth and detail than we have done in our work to date. That is, we focus on the context, content and tone of press reports, the extent to which journalistic comment intruded into accounts, the degree to which issues were regarded as sufficiently important to be discussed at editorial level, and the standards that were applied in that connection. In sum, through an analysis of such issues we shall attempt to assess the differential contribution made by press treatment to the development of football crowd behaviour in Britain over the last 100 years.

Although our research led us to draw extensively on a variety of national, London and provincial newspapers, our most comprehensive survey involved use of the *Leicester (Daily) Mercury*. Such differential reliance – as will be seen, it is certainly not exclusive – is reflected in this article. As a Leicester newspaper, the *Mercury* necessarily displays a local bias with respect both to the sorts and numbers of issues covered and the kinds of judgements offered.[4] However, it also dealt with national issues reasonably comprehensively and in detail throughout the period covered by our research. In any case, as will be seen, the broad picture we obtained from the *Mercury* is by and large confirmed by the other papers and sources that we used. In short, differential reliance on a single local newspaper does not, in our view, seriously detract from the general relevance of the thesis we develop.

In order to facilitate the task of analysis and exposition, we have divided the period to be covered into four 'eras': (1) the years before 1914, more especially the two decades before the outbreak of the First World War; (2) the inter-war years; (3) the decade and a half following the end of the Second World War; and (4) the period from the mid- to late-1950s to the present day. We shall argue that each of these eras was characterized by differing patterns of interaction between press reporting and football crowd behaviour. Our general findings regarding the eras are as follows: that the reported incidence of crowd disorderliness in Britain was high before the First World War; that it fell in England – though not necessarily in Scotland – between the wars, though nowhere near to zero point; that the reported incidence remained low between 1945 and the mid-1950s but then started rising, slowly at first but more rapidly from the mid-1960s. This general picture forms an essential backcloth for understanding some of the points to be made later on.

PRESS REPORTAGE AND CROWD DISORDERLINESS BEFORE THE FIRST WORLD WAR

In the years before the First World War, the channels of communication

97

available to the press, perhaps particularly to provincial newspapers, were by present standards rather limited and unsophisticated though interest in sport in the national and provincial press, especially in football, grew considerably towards the end of the nineteenth century (Mason 1986). Despite the growing importance of, for example, press agencies and the telephone for news gathering purposes in this period, newspapers generally continued to operate with standards that were undifferentiated compared with those that govern what counts as 'newsworthiness' today. That is, reporters and news-collecting organizations seem to have been less discriminating than their present-day counterparts regarding the items which they sent to editors' desks, and the latter seem to have been less discerning regarding the items that they used. In the *Mercury*, this approach is perhaps best exemplified by a residual daily column called 'Epitomy of the News'. Typically, it consisted of between thirty and forty stories, each of three or four lines, which captured the 'bare essentials' of the items covered. Incidents that would count as 'serious' and be given much more prominent treatment in the press today, local as well as national, were frequently treated in this manner. On 30 June 1900, for example, this column related that 'There has been an epidemic of assaults on the police in Birmingham, and at present nine constables who have been victims of violence are lying disabled'. Today, such a story would surely attract more attention in the *Mercury* and similar local papers. Moreover, it hardly taxes one's powers of imagination to envisage how the present-day tabloid press in Britain would treat a story of this kind.

A more general indication of this relatively undiscriminating approach is provided by the column after column of tiny print throughout the paper which is only occasionally broken up by larger lettering. Even this, for the most part, was different from the headlines of today, for the aim seems to have been to inform rather than to catch the eye and shock, titillate or sensationalize. It was a uniformity unbroken by photographs and relieved only by the odd cartoon. This general format found one of its expressions in the paper's treatment of football crowd disorders.

Accounts of such disorders reached the pages of the *Mercury* in five main ways. First, they were the result of observations by match reporters or journalists who penned a general column devoted to 'the football scene'. Second, stories were relayed to the *Mercury* by contacts in other regions. Third, they emerged out of reports on the proceedings of the Football Association's disciplinary committees, usually a committee under the immediate jurisdiction of the Leicestershire FA. Fourth, they took the form of reports of court proceedings. Fifth, they came in the form of letters to the editor by citizens who were 'concerned'.

The manner in which football crowd disorders were reported in this period is best illustrated by presenting some representative examples from across this range.

1 Reports on Local Matches

Leicester Fosse[5] v. Lincoln City (*Leicester Daily Mercury*[6], 8 April 1904):

> Pleasant weather prevailed and there was at the outset a 4,000 gate included amongst which was a train-load from Lincoln. . . The match now seemed to be quite a secondary consideration with an unselect few of the spectators on the popular side and a Lincoln v. Leicester proceeded on two occasions in the shape of free fights. The sparring was wilder than judicious and out of place in any case, but fortunately each time a constable was at hand and promptly and firmly parted the pugilists who showed by these actions that they were not qualified to watch a football match.

Loughborough v. Gainsborough (*Leicester Daily Mercury*, 3 April 1899):

> Loughborough had much the best of matters and the Gainsborough goal survived several attacks in a remarkable manner, the end coming with the score:
>
> Loughborough, none
> Gainsborough, none
>
> The referee's decisions had caused considerable dissatisfaction, especially that disallowing a goal to Loughborough in the first half, and at the close of the game he met with a very unfavourable reception, a section of the crowd hustling him and it was stated that he was struck.

The first press boxes began appearing at major football grounds from the beginning of the 1890s. Prior to that, football journalists often found themselves 'at a table just in front of the spectators, with no cover, exposed both to the vagaries of the crowd and the weather' (Mason 1986). It is difficult to tell the reporters' locations from the accounts provided here. Nevertheless it is clear from the Leicester – Lincoln match report that the writer took exception to the unruly conduct he described. Despite this, his comments were measured and restrained. As regards the account of the Loughborough–Gainsborough game, it is difficult to detect any note of condemnation. Indeed, there might even be said to be a hint of empathy for the aggrieved Loughborough supporters and of understanding for why they acted as they did.

Incidents of crowd trouble at matches in Leicestershire – usually at matches at the lower levels of the game – also appeared in general columns, whether football 'round-ups' or feature articles. Here are two examples of this genre.

On 26 November 1904, the *Mercury* contained a section characteristically headed 'Association Football Notes'. It was less characteristically subtitled, 'Bad Language on Football Fields', and it cited the comments of the Chairman of South Wigston Albion FC, a local club. He was reported to have

> referred to the prevalence of bad language on football grounds and it has to be admitted that this is something of a blot upon the pastime, although the contention sometimes put forward that it is impossible to witness a football match without hearing a lot of language of the wrong sort is absurdly wide of the mark, as all football patrons know. Football is no worse in this respect than anything else which of necessity brings together a crowd largely composed of the man in the street.

The following item appeared in a column providing a round-up of local match reports in the *Mercury* of 3 February 1899:

> In a Loughborough and District League match at Shepshed last Saturday, between the Albion and Loughborough Corinthians, regrettable scenes were witnessed. At the close Loughborough players were stoned and struck, and altogether roughly used. The matter has been reported to the Association by the Corinthians whose experiences in the district on account of their superiority have been far from satisfactory.

'Blot upon the pastime', 'regrettable scenes', 'far from satisfactory': words such as these may have carried heavier tones of condemnation eighty or ninety years ago than would be the case today but, even making due allowance for a convention of writing in a restrained style, this hardly seems to be the language of great concern.

Some incidents which occurred in other regions also filtered through to the *Mercury*. For present purposes, two examples must suffice as illustration. Both serve to confirm the paper's penchant for what seems to have been, at least by present-day standards, a low-key form of presentation.

2 *Reports from Other Regions*

A match in Birmingham (unheadlined report, *Leicester Daily Mercury*, 7 February 1903):

> During the hearing of misconduct cases at the meeting of the Birmingham Youths and Old Boys Association, an organisation controlling close upon 5,000 juniors, on Friday night, a referee when asked why he did not stop a match in which disgraceful conduct had occurred said he was afraid. There was a gang of 500 roughs present. A member of the Association said the attitude of the crowd was so threatening that a supporter of the visiting team fetched two pistols to protect the players.

Sunderland v. Small Heath (unheadlined report, *Leicester Daily Mercury*, 5 April 1902):

> At the close of the Sunderland/Small Heath game, a crowd numbering several hundred, principally youths, waited outside the dressing-room for the referee, Mr Sutcliffe. So threatening was their attitude that the police eventually had to attire the referee in a policeman's suit, and smuggle him out at the side gate. Being too small for the suit, he was at once recognised, but the cabby galloped away and defeated the attempt of the section of the crowd to stop the cab. The decisions of the referee had been very unpopular. He was not hurt.

In the first story, the casual and unelaborated reference to fire-arms is worthy of note. In the second, despite the fact that he evidently became caught up in the excitement of the fracas, the writer nevertheless continued to use what is, by present-day standards, a restrained and largely descriptive style.

FOOTBALL ON TRIAL

3 Reports on Court Cases

Leicester Daily Mercury, 31 March 1897:

Stone-throwing at a League
Match
The Culprit Sent to Prison

At Burnley, today, a collier, named Smout, was sentenced to one month's imprisonment for assaulting Hillary Griffiths, a footballer in the Wolverhampton Wanderers team, on Saturday week last during the football match, Burnley v. Wolverhampton. The defendant threw a stone at complainant, striking him on the head. Griffiths had to be carried off the field and has not since been able to work or play.

Leicester Daily Mercury, 2 February 1896:

Sequel to a Football Match
Attack on Police

At the Gloucestershire Assizes on Tuesday, three young men were charged with the wilful murder of a police-sergeant, and the attempted murder of a police-constable, during a disturbance when returning from a football match. One prisoner was found guilty of manslaughter and the other two pleaded guilty to assault. They were given good characters and the judge sentenced George Morgan to 12 months'. James Morgan to six months' and George Hill to one month's imprisonment.

Local newspapers, even today, tend to concentrate on local issues for their front-page, headlined stories. Around the turn of the century, constraints of time could also, obviously, have been a problem in this regard.[7] Nevertheless, the reportage of these two cases, particularly the second one, is, relative to present standards, worthy of note both from the standpoint of the space allocated and the total absence of comment. This silence and the rather muted expressions of distaste which characterize the other stories cited are representative of the general treatment given by the *Mercury* in this period to football crowd disorders. That the newspaper did not reflect or affect the attitudes and opinions of all its readers, however, is evident from the letters column.

4 Letters to the Editor

Leicester Daily Mercury, 22 January 1903:

Sir, Will you through your paper allow me to thank the Rev. J.W.A. Mackenzie for coming forward and denouncing the language used on the Fosse Football ground? I have been surprised that someone has not taken it up before. It is not of remarks made to the players only that I complain, but the use of chanting language and cheers all over the ground. I can understand a man getting excited and expressing his opinion on good or bad players but it should be without the use of such language. I like a good shout or a clap of the hands as well as anyone. Surely those who use this bad habit should have a little feeling for their neighbours.

Before we cite the next letter, it is interesting to juxtapose it with the *Mercury*'s (17 December 1900) account of the events to which it referred. In December 1900, the Arsenal visited Leicester and they were accompanied by some 1,500 travelling fans. The paper depicted their activities in the following appreciative terms:

with musical instruments of varied nature they kept things very lively, while their knowledge of choruses of music-hall songs was predictably unlimited. However, they are a good-natured lot, and by other people besides the Fosse directors, their visit was appreciated.

This vote of thanks was not endorsed by a correspondent to the letters column of the subsequent issue. Signing himself 'Social Order', he wrote of the London visitors:

We noticed early in the day a lot of these sportsmen, already dead to the football world. But at night the conduct of these people was most reprehensible, and our local hooligans must have learned a further lesson in the art. But there is enough drunkenness, filthy language and disorderly conduct without strangers swelling the number.

Such letters to the editor are clearly invested with a vocabulary of disapproval, not a little class prejudice and, in a city noted at the time for strong views on drink, 'pro-Temperance' feeling. Similarly, the punishments meted out by the FA to clubs whose fans were found guilty of engaging in disorderly conduct[8] and the fact that some cases reached the courts is indicative of a determination to curb the 'unruly element'. And yet the *Mercury* seems to have felt under no compunction to underscore such negative judgements. Apart from its generally prosaic treatment of the incidents described, it is this virtual absence of journalistic comment that is most striking. On this front at least, it is almost as if the paper was content to act as a simple conduit for the concerns of others.[9]

While a bland heading such as 'Football Association Notes', or, indeed, no heading at all was the standard response of the *Mercury* in this period to incidents of football crowd disorder, there were one or two notable exceptions. Here are two examples, the first from the *Leicester Daily Mercury*, on 19 April 1909:

Football Riot at Glasgow
Over forty persons injured
Bonfires on the field

A serious riot took place at Hampden football ground at Glasgow, on Saturday afternoon, at the close of the Scottish Cup Final. For the second week in succession the tie between the Celtic and Rangers ended in a draw and the crowd on Saturday demanded that the teams should play extra time, but the authorities had made no such arrangements.

On the teams returning to the pavilion, thousands of spectators broke into the playing pitch and proceeded to tear up the goal-posts. Mounted constables arrived, and in the melee that followed, more than 50 persons were injured.

When the barricading was broken down, the rioters piled the debris, poured whisky over it, and set the wood ablaze. The flames spread to the pay-boxes, which were only some 20 yards from a large tenement of dwellings. Great alarm prevailed, particularly when the firemen were attacked by the mob and prevented from extinguishing the fire, for no sooner had they run out the hose than the crowd jumped on it and, cutting it with knives and stones, rendered the efforts of the firemen useless. The woodwork of the boxes was completely destroyed, leaving only the corrugated iron roofs and linings which were bent and twisted into fantastic shapes. The club's heavy roller was torn from its fittings and maliciously dragged across the turf.

Fresh detachments of police and firemen arrived and a series of melees followed, during which injuries, more or less serious, were inflicted on some fifty or sixty persons.

Stones and bottles were freely thrown, while at least two persons were treated for stab wounds. Over a score of constables were included among the injured, as well as several firemen.

Meanwhile, a great crowd, totalling fully 60,000, was swaying and rushing about to escape being trampled by police and horses. Fears were entertained for the safety of the pavilion and grandstands, but the constables kept the crowd to the opposite side of the field.

The mob repeatedly rescued the prisoners from the police, and ultimately it was deemed advisable to clear the field without taking the rioters into custody. For almost two hours the park was a scene of violence, unparalleled in the history of sports in Scotland, and has created grave concern among the executives of the Scottish Football Association.

Luton v. Spurs, (*Leicester Daily Mercury*, 4 February 1898):

> Exciting Scene at a Football Match
> A Loughborough Referee Mobbed
> Players Assaulted

. . . neither side were above a bit of bluffing if some advantage might in this way be gained. A London contemporary, commenting on the game on this point, says: 'The referee was not taking any of these little diplomatic moves and showed himself unusually indifferent to the powers of penalisation invested in a person of his capacity. This unappreciativeness of the visiting brutality as seen by the local eye roused the home spectators to a frenzy of indignation somewhat inconsistent in its warmth. Mark Anthony at Her Majesty's addressed a very fine frenzied mob in his oration over the haughty Julius, but if Anthony had had to face "the honourable gentlemen" who composed the crowd at Northampton Park on Thursday, I am afraid the famous oration would have had to go by the board. During the last two minutes of the game the Spurs made a despairing effort to get ahead, and just before the call of time the ball was put through. Ecstasy immediately reigned supreme, but only for a fleeting moment! It turned out that a too zealous Hotspur had fisted the leather sphere past the watchful Williams, and the referee with a heroism which I humbly admire had the courage, in the face of an illogical passionate crowd, to disallow. This settled it. When the players came off the field some ill-disposed ruffians, encouraged to a more practical emulation of the well-dressed yelling yahoos on the grandstand, rushed across and struck some of the Luton men. A few blows were freely exchanged, one of the visitors being particularly smart with his ''bunch of fives''. Although this attracted a deal of attention, the referee did not escape, Mr Rudkin receiving a very hostile reception as he left the ground.'

Despite the higher profile given to these two stories, each in its own way reinforces our general impression. The first exemplifies the tradition of detailed reporting uninterrupted by the injection of journalistic comment. The second, with its references to an 'exciting scene' and use of such phrases as 'ill-disposed ruffians' and 'yelling yahoos', captures the ambivalence of the paper towards the sorts of events described.

Allowing for changes in language use, the *Mercury*'s treatment of football crowd disorders in the years before the First World War thus appears to have involved standards which could be judged as complacent compared with those that are dominant today. Concern was expressed but usually only in unsensational terms and the readership was, for the most part, left to draw its own conclusions. This absence of any sustained expression of concern probably in part reflects the different role and market situation of the press in Britain at the turn of the century. However, it might also be indicative of higher thresholds of tolerance for disorder than those which are nowadays characteristic of the majority of people. Support for such a judgement is provided by the *Mercury*'s treatment of the case of George Cunningham. It is a case which merits discussion at some length.

In January 1897, Leicester Fosse entertained local rivals, Burton Wanderers. After the match, Cunningham, a Wanderers player, was attacked in a Leicester street. The *Mercury* (18 January 1897) caught up with these events belatedly and reported them in the following terms:

The Visit of the Burton Wanderers
Reported Attack on Cunningham

The following has been received from a correspondent at Burton-on-Trent. A disgraceful piece of rowdyism was perpetrated at Leicester on Saturday night after the match with Leicester Fosse.

One of the Burton Wanderers' players, George Cunningham, was returning to the station to catch the special at 11 o'clock when he was set upon by seven ruffians who beat him with straps and kicked him. He was found bleeding and insensible and conveyed to the station, and now lies in Burton Infirmary in a very critical condition.

Inquiries made in Leicester by our representatives have not resulted in obtaining any confirmation of the alleged assault. The police have no information of any such occurrence and railway officials state that nothing of an untoward nature was observable when the special train to Burton left just after 11 o'clock on Saturday night.

The next day, under the innocuous heading, 'The Fosse v. Wanderers Match – the Attack on Cunningham', the *Mercury* (19 January 1897) began to piece the story together:

A Burton evening contemporary states: 'The meetings of Leicester Fosse and the Wanderers have always been of a keenly interesting character and little quarter has been either given or taken, but whatever feeling has arisen has generally subsided with the blowing of the referee's whistle. Such was not the case, however, on Saturday, when Cunningham . . . came in for such rough treatment that he is now an inmate of the Burton Infirmary' . . .

[He] left the ground in company with some Derby friends, and nothing more was seen of him until just before 11 o'clock when he was brought to the railway station by two Leicester men. His clothing was covered with blood and dirt, his companion saying they had found him lying in the gutter in Church Gate. On getting into the salon, the unfortunate man was seen to be seriously injured, having nasty wounds on the temples, head, ear and jaw, while his top lip was also badly cut as if by a kick. Judging by his appearance he had lost a large quantity of blood, and he became unconscious. . . . When the train arrived and after a brief examination [a doctor] ordered Cunningham's removal to the Infirmary, whither he was taken on a railway ambulance. . . .

With reference to this matter, a correspondent writes: 'About 10.45 p.m. on Saturday last I was walking down Church Gate when I heard a lot of rowdy youths running behind me. Turning round I saw about 12 running after the man Cunningham and when about half-way down they caught him up, and at once attacked him unmercifully by punching his head whilst one or two were using their feet about his body. He cried out for help, and I and several others ran up and a policeman appearing also on the scene the youths immediately made off. That the policeman did not hold one of them was the surprise of all who witnessed the affair. The Burton report was much overdrawn for Cunningham was certainly not unconscious or he would not have walked away, which he did. He was, however, bleeding from a nasty cut on the temple. I have the idea that the police know the gang.

The *Mercury*'s treatment of this incident is an example of a style of reporting which seems to have been obsessed with detail. The disgust felt by the Burton correspondent was dutifully reported but one has to search hard for any further words of sympathy for the victim or condemnation of his assailants. Indeed, at certain points the paper almost seems to convey doubts that the incident ever took place and even allows a Leicester correspondent to express the unsubstantiated view that the initial account of the attack on Cunningham 'was much overdrawn'.

Finally, the coverage of the 'Cunningham incident' provides an insight into the rudimentary nature of local communications networks in this period. For example, when the police were approached by the *Mercury* to confirm that the incident had taken place, they were found to have no knowledge of it. Later, however, as we have seen, an eyewitness made reference to the presence of a policeman. It may be that the officer in question did not wish to report his failure to apprehend any of the culprits – an outcome which is said to have surprised the onlookers. It may also have been police practice before the First World War not to record incidents in which there were no arrests and the victim(s) 'left the scene' without bringing charges. Such dimensions are difficult to penetrate at this distance. Nevertheless the whole affair does seem by the standards of today to have been characterized by an air of unconcern, even casualness, that was inconsistent with the injuries inflicted.

Just by way of a postscript regarding the level of sensitivity of the age as reflected at least by the press, the following items appeared in an unheaded column in the *Mercury* of 15 November 1898. The middle item is also indicative of a level of violence, at least in association football, that was higher than we are accustomed to today:

Fosse Reserves go to Brighton on Saturday to oppose the United. The match is a friendly and the return will be played at Leicester on Shrove Tuesday, 14 February. The game on Saturday should be interesting as three old Fosse players – McLeod, McWhirter and McArthur – are in the Brighton team.

Herbert Carter has died at Carlisle from injuries received while playing football last week, when he was accidentally kicked in the abdomen. Two other football players also died on Saturday from injuries received in the course of play, viz. Ellam of Sheffield, and Parks of Woodsley. These, together with the case of Partington, who died on Wednesday last, make a total of four deaths during the past week.

W.L. Bunting, the English international rugby three-quarter who turned out once or twice for the Midland Counties in the championship games last season, is said to have definitely retired from football.

This matter-of-fact and unsensational mode of reporting fatal injuries to soccer *players* is consistent with the view that newspaper practice before the First World War involved neither the excessive over – nor under – reporting of football violence on or *off* the field. It is, of course, impossible to measure its exact extent but the data presented so far, together with our more extensive analysis of football crowd behaviour before the First World War (Dunning *et al.* 1984, 1988), leaves us in little doubt that match-day disorder was common in this period. Moreover, judging by the *Mercury*'s treatment of the phenomenon as a whole, the general impression conveyed is perhaps best described as one of 'controlled concern'. This is perhaps especially significant if one agrees with the judgement of Shattock and Wolfe (1982) that during the Victorian period the press, in all its manifestations, became a medium from which more and more people derived their sense of the outside world. It was these sorts of conditions and experiences which came to constitute one of the measuring rods against which commentators in the inter-war years formed their assessments of then-contemporary football crowds. It is to the inter-war years that our attention now turns.

PRESS REPORTAGE AND CROWD BEHAVIOUR IN THE INTER-WAR YEARS

During the inter-war years, the style of presentation of the provincial press changed significantly. Advertising grew in importance as a source of revenue, headlines and print in general both became larger and, as a consequence, stories began to be picked out. In a word, there was more white and less black, and photographs began to appear in increasing numbers. These innovations squeezed the amount of space available for the reporting of news. Under the twin constraints of lessened space and the emerging, competition-induced desire for a more attractive presentation, editors seem to have become more sensitive to the issue of 'newsworthiness' and the need for selectivity. In the *Mercury*, although the number of pages increased, there occurred a considerable reduction in the number of news items covered compared with the pre-1914 era. Under these conditions, editors generally were both able and constrained to indicate their priorities and concerns by being more selective about stories and giving them differential emphasis to a greater extent than had previously been the case. This can be illustrated by the way in which the *Mercury* handled what was held at the time to be one of the most serious public order problems in Britain – the so-called 'racecourse riots' of the 1920s. Here is an example of the sort of treatment given to this issue (*Leicester Mercury*, 29 September 1924);

Short Shrift for Race Gang Terrorism
Police to Begin Immediate Suppression Campaign
Flying Squad to be Armed with Revolvers

A violent outbreak of fresh race gang outrages directed against bookmakers and their assistants, and the fatal affray in a Tottenham Court Road club, have determined Scotland Yard to embark upon a drastic campaign of suppression.

Under control of Sergeant McBrien, a special 'arm' of the famous 'Flying Squad' has been organised to deal with the violent pests who are the dangerous camp-followers of the turf. Police protection is now being accorded to certain bookmakers, who are thus able to resist blackmail threats.

Bogus social 'clubs' used as a 'clearing house' for racing pests; bookmakers terrorised into heavy payments for protection against hostile gangs; racing hangers-on who track down lucky turf winners and rob them with impunity; 'Flying-Squad' CID men to be armed. These are some of the sensational features in the race gang evil and the counter-measures devised by Scotland Yard.

The size of the headline and tone of this report stand in marked contrast to the paper's mode of presenting stories involving violence before 1914. In this regard as far as we can tell, the *Mercury* was reflecting changes which occurred to newspapers generally in this period, national as well as local. It is with such changes in mind and with the knowledge that papers were now more predisposed to respond to 'causes for concern' that we must understand their approach to football hooliganism.

Throughout the inter-war years, football crowd disturbances continued to occur, albeit at a declining rate in England, and some were reported in the press. In this context, three examples drawn from different newspapers must suffice in order to illustrate the resilience of the phenomenon:

(1) the following incident was reported in the *Daily Express* in November 1924 under the headline 'Mob Breaks Loose at Brighton':

> There was a disgraceful scene on the Brighton ground on Saturday . . . the referee being chased and a policeman stunned by a blow from a corner flag . . .
>
> Immediately after . . . the match, hundreds of the 11,000 spectators jumped the barriers and rushed across the ground. The police barred the way to the players' and the officials' quarters, but it was only after an exciting melee that the hotheads calmed down and dispersed.
>
> A policeman was stunned by a blow from a corner flag hurled by a hooligan, and was carried behind the West Stand in a dazed condition.
>
> The 'sportsmen' who joined in the baiting should be utterly ashamed of themselves.
>
> (*Daily Express*, 1 November 1922)

While this presentation is embellished with the language of condemnation, the criticism was directed at a transgression of the ethics of 'sportsmanship' and a failure to exercise self-control. In common with the style of reporting news at the local level at the time, it was not, as tends to be the case in press reports today, couched in terms of a dehumanizing rhetoric that denounces such behaviour as 'animalistic', 'lunatic' and 'barbaric'.

(2) A graphic account of an incident which occurred at the Birmingham ground in 1920 is provided by the testimony of an oxyacetylene welder who had taken the West Midlands club to court:

The affair happened on 'Spion Kop'. . . Immediately after the interval, 'bottles were flying around like hailstones'. Witness tried to get away, but he was struck on the head, and received an injury which necessitated seven stitches. He had seen other disturbances on 'Spion Kop', and on one occasion a week or so before he was injured, he saw men using bottles as clubs instead of using their fists. The bottles were half-pint stout bottles.

(Birmingham Post, 14 October 1920)

At least two points emerge from this report. First, the incident only came to light because the injured fan took legal action; second, his testimony suggests that this was not an isolated affair. That such disturbances could often go unreported by the local press may have something to tell us about the capacity of match reporters to keep informed about what was going on deep in a crowd. It may also have something to say about journalistic perceptions of 'newsworthiness', the reaction of victims to attack, or both.

(3) The following report describes the return of Leicester City fans on a 'football special' from a match in Birmingham in 1934:

Everything had gone smoothly from the time of the departure at New Street and it was feared that something extraordinary had happened to cause the train to pull up in such a manner only 300 or 400 yards from its destination. After a thorough search of all the coaches, it was found that the communication cord had been pulled. It is understood that the railway representatives questioned a number of people regarding the matter.

From other sources, it was ascertained that the hooligan element sometimes found on the trips had caused not a little damage to the rolling stock, some of it almost new. Windows were smashed, seats cut and torn and the leather window straps slashed with knives.

(Leicester Mercury, 19 March 1934)

Any notions that might have been harboured at the time regarding the 'one-off' character of this incident are casually dismissed by reference to 'other sources'. In short, as with the Birmingham incident discussed above, the implication was that a good deal of unreported football hooliganism was going on between the wars.

Despite the continued occurrence – and occasional reporting – of football crowd disorders and fan-related incidents in the interwar years, newspaper journalists and editors seemed in little doubt about the general trend, at least as far as England was concerned. For example, commenting on the crowd that attended the 1928 Cup Final between Huddersfield Town and Blackburn Rovers, *The Times* football correspondent wrote:

> The spectators may well have marvelled at the order and restraint with which such a vast crowd followed the thrills accompanying the defeat of a great side like Huddersfield Town. No less remarkable . . . was the quiet behaviour of the crowd before and after the match. . . [S]omehow the old roar of the North in triumph or despair was lacking.
>
> (*The Times*, 23 April 1928)

There is undoubtedly an element of condescension and class and regional prejudice in the surprise expressed here that members of the Northern working class could comport themselves with order and restraint. It is clear, nevertheless, that, in the judgement of the author, Cup Final crowds had often behaved less well in the past.

A further indication that crowd behaviour was widely perceived to be improving is provided by the *Mercury's* editorial comment on the same match. It appeared under the headline 'Orderly Crowds':

> There seems to have been more than usual favourable comment on the good behaviour of the great crowds assembled in London to take part in the Cup Final and its associated festivities. The comment arises, no doubt, from a legendary feeling that big sporting crowds are in some peculiar way predisposed to riotous and unseemly behaviour. . .
>
> Students of people in the mass will probably tell us that we are better behaved, and that we make merry nowadays without the discreditable manifestations that were at one time thought to be inseparable from these public rejoicings. Rejoicing and sobriety go hand in hand, and great crowds distinguish themselves with a sense of discipline that is creditable all round. May we infer that we are an improving people?
>
> (*Leicester Mercury*, 23 April 1928)

Testimony to the fact that this kind of judgement was not restricted to Cup Final crowds but had come to be extended to English football spectators generally is provided by a *Mercury* editorial which appeared some two weeks earlier. It was headed, 'Football and Truncheons', and was referring to disturbances at a match in Northern Ireland:

[A]t Belfast yesterday the half-time interval in a cup-tie between Celtic and Linfield was given up to a diversion which introduced the stoning of the musicians in the band, and the intervention of the police who used their truncheons to keep the more heated rivals in the crowd apart. Fortunately the excitement disappeared when the players came out again and the game was resumed as if nothing particular had happened. . .

In many centres in England during the next few weeks the big issues at stake in the Cup and League will unite thousands of people in a single thought. Huddersfield's chance of a record 'double', League championships, promotions and relegations – will exact their full measure of hope and anxiety from the thousands amongst whom League football is a dominating sporting interest. And, happily, all these things will be duly settled without a single policeman having to raise his truncheon to preserve the peace.

(*Leicester Mercury*, 10 April 1928)

In order to reconcile the continued occurrence of disorder with complimentary comments such as these, one has to recognize that these sorts of favourable judgements were being made relative to the more frequent and serious disorders of the pre-1914 period and alongside the more violent disturbances which were continuing to occur in such contexts as football in Scotland and Northern Ireland and horse-racing in England. It is possible, though, as far specifically as the latter is concerned, that the scale and seriousness of the 'racecourse riots' of the 1920s may have represented a decline, for a witness in a court case in 1921 was reported to have said that, 'racing is a garden party compared with before the war' (*Leicester Mercury*, 12 September 1922).

There is additional evidence to support the view that football crowds in England became more orderly in the 1920s and 1930s (see Dunning *et al.* 1988). Our present concern, however, is with the ways in and the extent to which, if any, the press portrayal of this tendency contributed to such a processs. The probability is that newspapers were on balance trend reflectors. That is to say, the currently available evidence suggests that the growing orderliness of football crowds had its roots largely in wider and more complex social processes (Dunning *et al* 1988). Nevertheless, the mode of reporting seems to have facilitated the progression of this trend. More particularly, their own unselfconscious neglect or unresponsiveness to many of the disturbances that continued to occur in and around football grounds in the inter-war years led newspapers to form an exaggerated view of the extent to which English football crowds deserved to be included in the description of the English more generally as 'an improving people'. In so far as such an improvement actually occurred, there seems to have been an element of self-fulfilling prophecy in the reaction of the press.

PRESS REPORTAGE AND CROWD BEHAVIOUR IN THE YEARS IMMEDIATELY AFTER THE SECOND WORLD WAR

The decade or so following the Second World War is crucial for understanding the development of English football hooliganism as a national cause for concern. It is a period that tends to be recalled overwhelmingly as one in which peace and tranquillity reigned in soccer grounds. As such, it has come to form the principal, much-lamented benchmark against which the present state of the game is judged. Then-contemporary newspaper characterization of football crowds in these years was more or less consistent with this picture and no doubt helped to shape these memories. Crowds were presented for the most part as being enthusiastic but orderly. From time to time a disorder was reported, but the infrequency with which this occurred encouraged the belief that these were discrete and isolated incidents. There were two dimensions of football crowd behaviour – 'gate-crashing' and 'barracking' – that caused some temporary consternation, but neither seems to have affected the collective memory. Thus it was against this halcyon image that the at first slowly growing problem of football hooliganism came to be placed.

But is this image of football crowds in that period an accurate reflection of reality? In order to address this question, it is necessary to go beyond the press and draw upon our second principal data source – the records of the Football Association. These demonstrate that the football terraces of England immediately after the Second World War were not quite as orderly as collective memory would have it. The following examples of disorders are all drawn from this source. At the Millwall–Barnsley match of 1947, a linesman reported that, during the game, he had been struck on the chest by a pellet fired from an airgun. Trouble occurred once again at Millwall in their match with Exeter in 1949. This time, the referee and a linesman reported that, when they were some 50 yards from the Millwall ground after the match, they were subjected to abuse and hostility by a crowd of between 150 and 200 people. The referee received a blow on the back and teacups were thrown at both match officials. A final example comes from the Queen's Park Rangers ground in 1951 when missiles were thrown at the Sheffield Wednesday goalkeeper. In fact, the Football Association had long been concerned about the issue of missile-throwing and, in 1947, feelings had been sufficiently high as to lead the FA to circulate the following edict to all member clubs:

> The Football Association is disturbed at the growing practice of throwing missiles at officials and players on football grounds. All clubs are asked therefore to inform the spectators through the medium of the programmes or speaker apparatus of the serious consequences which may result from such disorderly conduct and to emphasise that such is likely to bring both clubs and the game generally into disrepute.

During the years 1946–59, a total of 238 incidents of spectator disorder were recorded in the FA Minutes. Of these, 138 occurred at Football League grounds. Given that, it is difficult to avoid the conclusion that newspaper coverage in that period underplayed the extent of then-contemporary disorder. Even though attendance levels in the immediate post-war years reached an all-time high, the level of officially recorded hooliganism was remarkably low. We should, however, recognize that the FA record was derived from referees' reports which tended to be confined to incidents related directly to the match itself. Therefore, such data are bound to underestimate the actual level of disorder. This is not to argue that anything even remotely approximating the levels of the late 1960s and after was reached in the 1940s and 1950s. It is, however, to suggest that, in order to understand how the later heights were reached, it is necessary to approach the problem developmentally. More particularly, it is necessary to try and establish why, from the second half of the 1950s onwards, increasingly anxious voices began to be raised in the press at the spectre of disorder at football and elsewhere. It is a process with labyrinthine roots. Hall *et al.* (1978) have attributed what they see as the growing propensity of British society to generate moral panics in and after the 1950s to the decline of the British Empire and the feelings of insecurity which gripped the 'establishment', particularly after Suez. We think that there is something in this view but, as Hall *et al.* themselves concede, it is difficult to substantiate such connections with precision. Here, it must be sufficient to limit ourselves to aspects of the broader domestic context.

In the mid-1950s, a period when both wages and officially recorded levels of juvenile crime were rising, Britain was gripped by a moral panic over youth and violence. It focused especially on the working-class youth subcultural fashion of the 'teddy boys'. One indication of the extent of this concern is that, in a twenty-seven-month period towards the end of the 1950s, the *Mercury* carried no less than thirty-one editorials on youth, youth violence and the need for the courts to adopt a harsher sentencing policy. Increasing media anxiety proved to be infectious, the concern of the press feeding, and in turn feeding upon, the concern of the public. The tabloid press in particular – it was just emerging in its present form and its representative organs were locked into fierce competition both with each other and with the also newly emerging television – developed an increasingly voracious appetite for stories of youthful misdemeanour. One area of social life subjected to the more penetrating scrutiny which resulted was association football. The disorderly incidents which had traditionally characterized the game but which were probably on the increase began to be reported more frequently in national as well as local newspapers and presented in more dramatic relief. Therein lay the seeds of a classic amplification spiral. In order to examine this process, we shall call on a greater range of newspapers than we have in our analysis so far.

PRESS REPORTAGE AND CROWD BEHAVIOUR FROM THE MID-1950s: THE TAKE-OFF TO HEYSEL

The processes in the course of which football hooliganism achieved the status of a national and then an international cause for concern were both long-drawn-out and complex. In order to unravel the complexity, it is useful to start in 1956 for, in that year on 5 March, *The Times* reported that the train-wrecking antics of Liverpool and Everton fans had reached a historical peak, thus implying a build-up over the preceding years. In November 1957, the *Mercury* addressed the problem under the headline 'This Soccer Trend Must Cease':

This season, some six teams have been booed and jeered for long periods at either Goodison or Anfield. Bottles have been thrown at several players . . . and Teddy Boys have run out onto the pitch and played 'practice' matches in the goal mouth before the match at Preston when Everton were playing away. Everton fans have wrecked an excursion train and had free fights with other gangs following Liverpool. It makes you wonder . . . especially when you hear that similar things can happen elsewhere. Even in Regency Brighton. For there, on Saturday, Reading manager Harry Johnson was hit on the jaw by louts and two of his players were also struck as they left the field at the end of the game. It's a trend that is increasing. They even threw fireworks at a goalkeeper at Highbury on Saturday.

(Leicester Mercury, 4 November 1957)

Despite expressing concern, the paper was still wary about becoming unduly alarmist and, in September 1959 under the heading 'Don't Fence Our Players In', it published an article that was evidently designed to calm growing fears. A portion of it reads:

Will the time ever come when our Football League matches have to be played in, say, 'cages' or wire netting to protect the players and officials from the fans? Such an idea seems unthinkable, although some Continental and South American countries already have been forced to go to these lengths to protect the footballers from the volatile crowds when things have gone wrong on the field.

Admittedly there has been a minor outbreak of acts of hooliganism this season on the part of individuals here and there, but for the most part English soccer crowds are good-natured and well behaved, comparing favourably with any in the world.

(Leicester Mercury, 12 September 1959)

The ambivalence of the *Mercury* seems to have been characteristic of the press response in general at this time. The disorderly exploits, particularly of Merseyside (and Glasgow) fans, were given a treatment that was colourful and concerned, yet the press were still prepared on occasions to dismiss the official response as unneccessarily draconian. 'Hooligans?' queried a puzzled *News of the World* on 24 November 1963, 'they're so friendly!' In that month Everton FC became the first English club to erect fences behind its goals and the response of the *Daily Sketch* to this action was by no means atypical. Under the headline 'Brave Fans, You Don't Need Cages' the *Sketch*'s account of fan behaviour continued with heavy irony:

What! No darts? No invasions? No sendings off? No fights on the field? No protests? No menacing mobs awaiting the exits of referees? What is British football coming to? And what dull reading for the violence-hungry this weekend! . . . Everton can remove the hooligan barriers at Goodison Park and those who plead for cages and moats and barbed wire can weep in their beer, for the British football fan is showing he can correct the stormy situation of recent weeks in the good old British manner – by common sense.

(*Daily Sketch*, 25 November 1963)[10]

In the following year, at a time when match attendances were sharply declining (see Dunning *et al.* 1988: 132–3), the *Daily Mail* (11 February 1964) even benignly expressed its *preference* for 'hooliganism rather than indifference'. Henceforth, though, reacting to the increasingly violent and destructive activities of a minority of fans, the press (and television) began more and more to portray the fans to which it attached the 'hooligan' label as among the major 'folk devils' of present-day Britain.[11]

The prospect of England staging the World Cup Finals in 1966 intensified this effect. In the two or three years before the tournament, newspapers began to express dire warnings of the consequences that would follow from spectator misbehaviour during the Finals. The *News of the World*, for example, lent its support to the erection of fences at Everton by reminding its readers that 'Goodison is one of the principal venues for the World Cup in 1966. Complete discipline and control must be established' (*New of the World*, 24 November 1963). In the months which followed, several incidents of spectator misbehaviour were accompanied by similar warnings or prescriptions. 'Eighteen months from now', wrote the *Daily Mail* towards the end of 1964, 'the widespread and curious world of Association Football will look at the game in the land where it was born. They will shudder to see how tired, worn, even wicked it is' (*Daily Mail*, 16 December 1964).

At this stage, however, the press were still able to point to crowd troubles abroad as a means of keeping the domestic 'crisis' in perspective. On 9 October 1965, *The Times* even went so far as to recommend the withdrawal of British clubs from European competition until the continentals had 'put their house in order'. Two days later, however, following fighting between opposing fans at Old Trafford (Manchester United's ground) and between police and youths at Huddersfield, the press had apparently become convinced that English supporters had been 'infected' by what was now a universal 'disease'. Since these events followed so closely on its earlier 'anti-continental' arguments,

The Times displayed suitable humility in its comments.

Let us not be chauvinistic about it. Disorder does not only occur at the football grounds of Italy, Argentina, Brazil or elsewhere. It now seems to be a universal disease . . . but now more widespread and given greater publicity than before.

(*The Times*, 11 October 1965)[12]

In fact, according to the *Sun* on 8 November 1965, Manchester United fans were, by that time, staging their own 'Roman Riots'. That same month, during a 'local derby' between London rivals, Brentford and Millwall, a 'dead' hand grenade was thrown on to the pitch from the Millwall end. Of course, prior to investigating its contents the police could not have known that the hand grenade was inert. Nevertheless, even after that had been established, some sections of the popular press chose to misread the meaning of this symbolic gesture. 'Soccer Marches to War', screamed the *Sun* on 8 November. Its story continued:

The Football Association have acted to stamp out this increasing mob violence within 48 hours of the blackest day in British soccer – the grenade day that showed that British supporters can rival anything the South Americans can do.

The World Cup is now less than nine months away. That is all the time we have left to try and restore the once good sporting name of this country. Soccer is sick at the moment. Or better, its crowds seem to have contracted some disease that causes them to break out in fury.

Appeals like this and from the *Daily Sketch* aimed at ending 'the creeping menace which is blackening the name of soccer' (*Daily Sketch*, 10 December 1965) reached a crescendo in the months before the Finals. On 21 April 1966, it was the turn of the *Sun* again. Following violent scenes during the visit of Celtic to Liverpool, its editor commented:

It may be only a handful of hooligans who are involved at the throwing end, but if this sort of behaviour is repeated in July, the world will conclude that all the British are hooligans. . . . Either the drift to violence must be checked or soccer will be destroyed as an entertainment. What an advertisement for the British sporting spirit if we end with football pitches enclosed in protective wire cages.

Young fans from abroad did not attend the 1966 Finals in large numbers. This was probably one reason why the widely feared spectator misbehaviour failed to materialize. However, the domestic game had by this time begun to be characterized by large contingents of away fans travelling regularly to matches and, in that context, the media and official fears were rather more firmly based. Nevertheless, there was still a tendency to exaggerate the frequency and seriousness of the disorders that were occurring. Several aspects of media production combined to produce these distorting effects. For example, it was around the time of the 1966 World Cup that the popular press started sending reporters to matches to report on crowd behaviour and not simply on the game itself (Cohen 1973). Previously, football reporters had tended to report only the most visible incidents. Now, less visible incidents, incidents that were less obviously disruptive, began to be reported, too, and the increase in the frequency with which they were reported contributed to the impression that football hooliganism was increasing more rapidly than was, in fact, the case.

Around the same time, too, reflecting the intensifying moral panic about youth violence – part of which consisted of opposition from the predominantly conservative press to the de-criminalizing legislation that was being debated in parliament in the second half of the 1960s[13] – and perhaps because it helped to sell papers in an industry that was growing more competitive, the popular press started to report incidents sensationally, often using a military rhetoric. We have already noted the *Sun*'s 'Soccer Marches to War!' Here are a few more examples: 'War on Soccer Hooligans' (*Daily Mirror*, 16 August 1967); 'Courts Go to War on Soccer Louts' (*Daily Mirror*, 22 August 1967); 'Soccer Thugs on the War-path' (*Sunday Mirror*, 27 August 1967). At the start of the 1967–8 season, after describing how potters' clay had been added to the list of missiles recently thrown by fans at the Stoke city ground, the *Sun* even asked its readers rhetorically: 'What next? Napalm? (*Sun*, 11 November 1967). By 1969, *The Times* and the *Guardian* had begun to use a similar rhetoric, and were informing their readers of the Home Secretary's determination to 'make war' on soccer hooligans.[14]

There were signs, too, that the media coverage of football hooliganism was contributing *directly* to its escalation. For example, trouble in and around London grounds gathered momentum towards the end of 1967 and, as this happened, so the role of the press in moulding and helping to trigger incidents became more pronounced. A Chelsea fan convicted of carrying a razor said in court in his defence that he had 'read in a local newspaper that the West Ham lot were going to cause trouble' (*The Times*, 31 October 1967). This sort of predictive reporting was now becoming commonplace. So, too, were threats passed on the football 'grapevine' between groups of rival fans. What might be termed the 'real' and the 'perceptual' dimensions of the phenomenon became more and more inextricably intertwined. By defining matchdays and football grounds as times and places in which fighting could be engaged in and aggressive forms of masculinity displayed, the media, especially the national tabloid press, played a part of some moment in stimulating and shaping the development of football hooliganism. In particular, the more or less sustained portrayal of football as a venue for group confrontations seems to have attracted to the game growing numbers of youthful members of the 'rougher' sections of the working class, males from communities where values of 'aggressive masculinity' predominated (Dunning *et al.* 1988).[15]

So it was that, in the later 1960s, in part as a result of press treatment, football hooliganism began to take on its distinctively present form, that is, to involve regular confrontations between named rival groups. The media played a part in shaping the phenomenon in another way as well. When they were not engaged in predicting or reporting disorders, they were leading the call for remedial action. However, the policy measures introduced to combat football hooliganism over the last two decades, partly as a result of pressure from the press, have tended to be narrowly focused and aimed at specific phases of the match-day. As such, even when they have had ameliorative effects, they have tended to displace the disorder on to the streets outside football grounds, sometimes at considerable distances from them, rather than to eradicate it. There has also been a tendency for this sort of response to generate higher levels of solidarity and greater organizational awareness within the hooligan groups (Sports Council/SSRC 1978). The press has helped further to consolidate them by publicizing their exploits, hence giving them the public notoriety which they prize(d).

From the mid-1970s, the growing cohesiveness and sophistication of the groups which attached themselves to certain English clubs began to find a new outlet in trips to continental Europe. In that context, English hooligan 'crews', by now well-versed in a range of disruptive practices, began to test unwary continental club officials and relatively inexperienced police forces. This aspect of the continuing process of displacement culminated in May 1985 in the tragic events at Heysel where thirty-nine fans died, most of them Italians. The disaster itself had its immediate antecedents in a combination of the presence of belligerent groups of rival fans, complacent, profit-orientated officials, and a crumbling stadium. Its main relevance for present purposes, however, is that it intensified the activities of what the press characteristically chose to call Prime Minister Thatcher's 'War Cabinet' to combat football hooliganism and resulted in English clubs (but not the national side) being excluded from European competition. Heysel undoubtedly constituted a watershed in the developing structure of the English game. It would, however, be easy to mistake the media and public *furor* which followed the disaster for effective action 'on the hooligan front'. In the season following Heysel, the fact that arrest figures were down was widely acclaimed by the press, but numerous serious incidents that occurred away from grounds were not reported. Moreover, the arrest figures for the 1986-7 season showed a significant increase relative to 1985-6, and already in the 1987-8 season (the time of writing), a number of serious outbreaks have occurred. So the notion, ironically in part fostered by the media, that, in the wake of Heysel, England's problem of football hooliganism has been brought under control could well turn out to be a false dawn.

CONCLUSION

The press are not neutral observers of the social scene. They are active elements in the development of social processes and the defining of social problems. Their contribution is characterized by varying degrees of conscious intent. However, that they can play both amplifying and de-amplifying roles is suggested by their manner of reporting football crowd disorders after the 1950s as compared with their treatment of football crowds in the inter-war years and in the decade or so immediately following the Second World War.

Whilst perhaps accepting what we have said about their de-amplifying role in the past, a defender of the press might want to argue that the interpretation we have offered regarding their amplifying role since the 1950s is slanted against them. Our analysis, it might be suggested, involves a speculative leap from press treatment to the decline or growth of football crowd disorder. However, it has been our aim to avoid any such simplistic and mechanistic account of the effects of press coverage on the long-term balance between socio-cultural change and persistence that we have been concerned with. It might also be argued that our material is susceptible to an alternative interpretation, namely that the press throughout the period we have covered were simply commenting on events and played no part at all in influencing attitudes, opinions and behaviour. The principal weakness of such an argument is that it is predicated on a false dichotomy, that between the press as 'initiators' and the press as 'reflectors'. However, our analysis not cast in terms of such polarities. We are not suggesting that the press *caused* present-day football hooliganism. Its roots are deep and very complex. Rather, we have argued that newspapers – in particular, the tabloid press – have made a contribution of some significance to the rise of present-day hooliganism and to giving it its distinctively contemporary form.

One way of shedding further light on to this issue is to recall the press response to the publication in 1984 of 'Football Spectator Violence', a report by a working group in the government's Department of the Environment (1984). Among the recommendations in this report was the suggestion that the police might find it useful in planning their counter-hooligan measures to compile a 'league table' of t he country's most notorious football hooligan groups. Wrongly assuming that the implication of this proposal was that the putative table should be published, a number of newspapers responded with ridicule and condemnation, blaming the government for threatening to incite hooligan competition by presenting rival fan groups with an official 'league table' charting their relative progress.

Such press reactions provide unambiguous recognition of the belief that the printed word can combine with events to exacerbate a phenomenon. More specifically, these papers were in effect arguing that publicity can and does influence the phenomenon of football hooliganism, in this case by contributing to an intensification of the status competition between rival hooligan groups. Insights of this kind probably have some validity. However, they only seem to register with Britain's popular press when they coincide with the greater god of 'newsworthiness' as they define it. For confirmation of this scale of priorities one needs only to reflect on the number of times that newspapers themselves have published 'league tables of hooligan notoriety'. For example, in May 1974, the *Daily Mirror* carried the following story under the headline 'Soccer's Season of Shame':

Today the *Mirror* reveals the end-of-term 'arrest' record of First Division clubs' supporters covering every League match played by 22 teams. The unique report compiled with the help of 17 police forces reflects the behaviour of both 'home' and 'away' fans at each ground. The record speaks for itself; Manchester United were bottom of the League of Shame by more than 100 arrests.

(*Daily Mirror*, 6 May 1974)

Interestingly, the *Mirror* chose to place the *best*-behaved fans at the top of its table. However, when in September 1974, the *Daily Mail* followed suit, it preferred to give pride of place to notoriety with its headline 'Chelsea top thugs league'. Just by way of variation, in a centre-page spread on 29 July 1975, the *Evening Standard* produced its 'London league of violence' in alphabetical order. Regardless of variations of this kind, the fact remains that these and other newspapers have made great play of such 'alternative' league tables over the years. It may be the case, of course, that the vehemence of the press reaction to 'Football Spectator Violence' was partly engendered by their realization that their own past treatment of football hooliganism had helped to nurture the phenomenon. To our knowledge, however, no newspaper has admitted as much. In fact, many of them continue to devote editorial space to denying any role for their stories in exacerbating or shaping the hooligan problem.[16]

It has to be acknowledged in the interests of balance that, from time to time – largely on television and in 'quality' newspapers – the issue of football hooliganism has been the subject of more circumspect and analytical media treatment.[17] But these pools of insight have been engulfed by the mass circulation dailies with their screaming headlines, calls for immediate action and advocacy of punitive solutions. Thus, having done much to stimulate the rise of present-day football hooliganism and having, by their crass treatment of the phenomenon, contributed to the generation of a smoke screen of misunderstanding, the tabloids stand back in apparently unselfconscious innocence and berate politicians and football officials for their failure to eradicate the problem. The editorial policies responsible for such treatment seem to be a consequence of political opportunism, the increasingly fierce battle for circulation, a scant regard for any explanation that ventures beyond the simplistic, the narrow or the monocausal, and a lack of either the time or the taste for reflection, save the regulation doses of nostalgia.

Let us reiterate by way of conclusion that it has not been our intention to replace one simplistic explanation by another. As we have shown elsewhere, a range of processes have combined to produce football hooliganism in its present-day forms (Dunning *et al.* 1988). Nevertheless, it is also our view that the media, especially the popular press, played a part of some importance in directing hooligan behaviour into the football context. Its roots, however, go far deeper and wider than the game itself. The media mentality that restricts the problem solely or largely to the narrow confines of football, perhaps out of fear that a broader perspective might have unpalatable implications, is at base self-deceiving. Those who cling to such ideas might with equal profitability spend their time sweeping up leaves in a gale.

NOTES

1 This is certainly true of studies of the media portrayal of football hooliganism and its effects. See, for example, Stuart Hall (1978) and Gary Whannel (1979).

2 There are, of course, a number of important historical studies of both the national and the provincial press. These include those by Lee (1976); Harris and Lee (eds) (1986); and Shattock and Wolfe (1982).

3 In addition, we relied on the records of the Football Association and our own direct and participant observation.

4 Such a bias also depends, for example, on local traditions and on the ownership and control of local newspapers.

5 'Leicester Fosse' was the original name of what is now Leicester City FC.

6 Since the end of the First World War, Leicester's local paper has been called simply the *Leicester Mercury*. Despite changing its name, it remains a daily paper.

7 In his study of the provincial evening press, Jackson (1971: 82) concludes that 'except when major non-local news stories are to hand, (e.g. a macabre crime, a serious industrial disorder, significant "consumer" news, etc.) about half the evening papers sampled tended to select the leading local story for their main headline'.

8 These punishments consisted principally of the posting of warning notices and the closure of grounds.

9 This coincides with the findings of Hall *et al.* (1978) who speak of the greater tendency for newspapers today to adopt 'political' positions and to speak *on behalf* of rather than through their public.

10 The *Daily Sketch* was one of the fatal casualties in the circulation war between the tabloids which took place in this period.

11 As Pearson (1984) and others have shown, concern about crime and the behaviour of young people is by no means confined to the post-war period. However, it is arguable that the 1950s brought the first authentic, media-orchestrated 'moral panic' about young

people on a national scale.

12 By the mid-1970s, of course, it was the British, particularly the English, who were accused of exporting hooligan behaviour to the Continent.

13 For an account of the controversy surrounding the emergence of the Children and Young Persons Act, 1969, see Bottoms (1974).

14 For an extended analysis of the 'militarization' of language used by the press in the 1970s to describe outbreaks of hooliganism, see Hall (1978).

15 In our view, it is probably not accidental that, whilst the principal folk devils of the 1950s and early 1960s, the 'teddy boys' and the 'mods and rockers', fought principally in dance halls and at seaside resorts on public holidays, their immediate sucessors in the years beginning in 1967, namely the 'skinheads', were the first to use soccer as a major sphere of operations.

16 In most instances of this kind, newspapers argue that the game and its spokespersons accuse the press of *causing* the problem as a means of deflecting criticism from themselves. There may, indeed, be some truth in this view. More recently, however, some commentators have argued that the media are *under-reporting* hooligan incidents. See, for example, Peschardt (1987).

17 Examples include BBC Television's 'Panorama' feature on Millwall fans, first broadcast in 1977, and Thames Television's documentary, 'Hooligan' directed by Ian Stuttard, which was first broadcast on 20 Aug. 1985.

REFERENCES

Bottoms, A.E. (1974) 'On the Decriminalisation of English Juvenile Courts', in R. Hood (ed.) *Crime, Criminology and Public Policy*. London: Heinemann.

Cohen, S. (1971) *Folk Devils and Moral Panics*. London: Paladin.

Cohen, S. (1973) 'Campaigning against Vandalism', C.Ward (ed.) *Vandalism*. London: Architectural Press.

Department of the Environment (1984) 'Football Spectator Violence'. London: HMSO.

Dunning, E.G., Murphy, P., Williams, J. and Maguire, J. (1984) 'Football Hooliganism in Britain before the First World War', *International Review for the Sociology of Sport*, 19 (3/4): 215-40.

Dunning, E.G., Murphy, P., and Williams J. (1988) *The Roots of Football Hooliganism*. London: Routledge.

Hall, S. (1978) 'The Treatment of Football Hooliganism in the Press', pp. 15-36 in R. Ingham *et al.* (eds) *Football Hooliganism*. London: Inter-Action Imprint.

Hall, S. *et al.* (1978) *Policing the Crisis: Mugging, the State, and Law and Order*. London: Macmillan.

Harris, M. and Lee, A.J. (eds) (1986) *The Press in English Society from the*

Seventeenth to the Nineteenth Centuries. London: Acton Society Trust.

Jackson, I. (1971) *The Provincial Press and the Community*. Manchester: Manchester University Press.

Lee, A.J. (1976)*The Origins of the Popular Press, 1855–1914*. London: Croom Helm.

Mason, A. (1986) 'Sporting news, 1860–1914', in M. Harris and A.J. Lee (eds) *The Press in English Society from the Seventeenth to the Nineteenth Centuries*. London: Acton Society Trust.

Pearson, G. (1984) *Hooligan: a History of Respectable Fears*. London: Macmillan.

Peschardt, M. (1987) 'Football Hooliganism: Is There an Official Cover-up?', *The Listener*, 15 Oct: 4–5.

Shattock, J. and Wolfe, M. (eds) (1982) *The Victorian Periodic Press: Samplings and Soundings*. Leicester: Leicester University Press.

Sports Council/SSRC (1978) *Public Disorder and Sporting Events*. London.

Whannel, G. (1979) 'Football Crowd Behaviour and the Press', *Youth, Culture and Society*. 1: 327–42.

Chapter Six

LIFE WITH THE KINGSLEY LADS:
Community, masculinity and football

The study of the 'Kingsley lads' reported in this chapter is based largely on a programme of intensive participant observation and interview research that was carried out in 1980 and 1981. It focuses on their activities in a whole variety of settings – in the Kingsley neighbourhood itself, at school, on their weekend trips 'down-town' but, of course, primarily at football. We shall start with a brief discussion of the Kingsley estate itself. As will be seen, the west part of the estate is predominantly 'rough' today and many of its initial residents were recruited from what was the 'roughest' of Leicester's pre-war inner-city slums. In short, the West Kingsley estate is a community that is characterized by many of the features that are typical of 'ordered segmentation' and, despite the various changes that have occurred, it has evolved largely from an earlier variant of such a social configuration.

The Kingsley estate stands on the south-west fringes of Leicester. It was constructed as part of Leicester Corporation's rehousing programme of the 1920s and 1930s. The estate as a whole consists of two geographically separated sections – East Kingsley and, on the other side of Kingsley Park, West Kingsley, the focus of the present chapter. With just under 1,800 households, the West Kingsley estate is one of the largest areas of council housing in the city. At the time of the 1971 Census, its total population stood at 6,579. However, the eastern side of the Kingsley development was built and occupied first, more particularly between 1924 and 1926. Potential tenants for the new houses in East Kingsley are reported as having passed through a 'fairly rigid selection process' with only 'well-paid skilled artisans accepted as tenants'.[1] The West Kingsley estate was built in the late 1930s to rehouse the poorer slum-clearance tenants from the notorious

Quay Street slums in the city centre. In the earlier parts of the century, the Quay Street area was the home of Leicester's version of the 'dangerous underclass' whose lifestyles and public standards led them to be despised and feared by ruling groups and social revolutionaries alike – the 'social scum' of Marx and Engels.[2] The tension and conflict generated between the residents of East and West Kingsley was, from the outset, considerable.

In terms of its residents' occupational status, the West Kingsley estate is rooted firmly at the bottom of the socio-economic scale. Data from the 1971 Census have 82 per cent of the persons from West Kingsley who were in employment at that time working in manual occupations. A more detailed occupational breakdown, comparing West Kingsley with the 'inner area' and the city of Leicester as a whole, is provided in Table 12.

Table 12 Socio-economic group structure for West Kingsley, the Inner Area and the City of Leicester as a whole (percentages)

SEG	Description of group	Leicester	Inner Area	West Kingsley
1, 2	Employers and managers	8.6	4.5	0.3
3, 4	Professional workers	3.1	1.1	—
5, 6	Non-manual workers	16.9	17.9	9.4
7	Personal service workers	2.1	3.9	7.4
8	Foremen and supervisors	3.8	2.2	0.7
9	Skilled manual workers	30.5	28.6	31.5
10	Semi-skilled manual workers	15.7	19.4	22.1
11	Unskilled manual workers	7.1	8.3	19.1
12–17	Others (inc. 'own account')	12.0	13.9	9.5

Source: 1971 Census

As one can see, in 1971, the proportion of Kingsley residents working in unskilled jobs was more than twice the proportion in the inner city and not far short of three times the proportion in the city overall. The proportion of semi-skilled workers in West Kingsley was also higher. Moreover, by the early 1980s, the period when our research on the estate was done, the level of unemployment on the estate stood at over 30 per cent. It is important, however, to note that, despite the overall skewing towards the lower socio-economic levels, West Kingsley in 1971 had a slightly higher proportion of skilled workers in its ranks than either the city as a whole or its inner-city regions. Some non-manual workers, together with a sprinkling of people in the foreman, supervisor, employer and manager categories, also lived there. In other words, it is, in socio-economic terms, a 'mixed' estate. It is also one which is 'rough' overall but in which there are significant pockets of 'respectability'.

As we have said, many of West Kingsley's residents were recruited from the Quay Street area which had been demolished under the slum-clearance programme of the late 1920s and 1930s. Partly for the sake of convenience but also partly in recognition of the strong neighbourhood and kinship ties which had been characteristic of the city-centre slum, movement to the new estate was conducted so as to replicate many existing community ties. In some cases, whole streets were transplanted into the new setting *en bloc*.[3] Such strategies contributed to the maintenance on West Kingsley of the shifting divisions between 'rougher' and 'more respectable' families which had characterized the Quay Street area. Self-selection as well as labelling and housing-department 'dumping' policies have accentuated these divisions. There are also extensive kinship networks which continue to knit sections of West Kingsley together by blood and marriage. Virtually all 'the lads' had more cousins, uncles and aunts living on or close to the estate than they cared to or were able to remember. In 1981, an inner area research report noted that, of all the council estates in Leicester, 'the closest network of family contacts was found in Kingsley where 94 per cent had family or relatives in (the city), two-thirds of whom lived in Kingsley'.[4] This kind of close-knit neighbourhood and family ties are features reported in a number of studies of lower-working-class communities.[5] As we suggested in *The Roots of Football Hooliganism*, they are one of the constitutive features of ordered segmentation.

By many of the people who live there and by many who live close by, the West Kingsley estate is known as 'Dodge City'. The origins of this label are not difficult to trace. It refers to a violent town in the American West, notorious for its lawlessness. It is a connection that the Kingsley lads, some of whom sport 'Dodge' tattoos, find attractive. Since West Kingsley is noted locally for its toughness, it is also a label which has a degree of validity. But the 'Dodge' label is used by outsiders – as well as, with a sense of irony, by the lads themselves – to describe the estate in another sense. More particularly, because of the persistently high levels of poverty and crime in the area, West Kingsley residents are alleged to *dodge* the milkman, the rentman, the police and so on. In fact, in the late 1960s British Debt Services named the estate, alongside one in Liverpool, as the 'biggest debtors' haven in Britain'.[6]

The smaller area of council housing to the east of Kingsley Park is known among the 'young Kingsley', and by members of the youthful gangs that are produced in East Kingsley itself, as 'Texas'. The area of largely private housing to the south of 'Dodge' is known locally as 'Queensway'. Along with the more distant council estates of Eastern Park and Old Gardens – the traditional estate rivals of West Kingsley gangs – these local corporate identities, which are cross-cut to some extent by school and racial affiliations, constitute the most obvious aspects of the gang *cum* territorial rivalries that are endemic to West Kingsley and the surrounding area. The latter provide a source of enduring fascination for young males – and some females – who are socialized into the traditions of the West Kingsley estate.

It might not be easy for an outsider to understand the strength of local attachment to West Kingsley, especially among the lads. Those whose families have left often yearn to return and, in many cases, actually do. Although many families on the estate are seeking transfer because of its forbidding reputation, poor facilities and troublesome tenants, the lads won't be told that Kingy isn't 'the best fuckin' estate in town'. Yet it contrasts markedly with the neat and differentiated orderliness of the East estate. With its overgrown fronts, crumbling walls and delapidated houses, West Kingsley has an appearance of decay. The houses which face on to Kingsley Park are probably the most sought-after by the least badly-off families on the estate and they present a relatively healthy façade. Inside the estate, however, the occasional pocket of 'respectability' vies in a manifestly uneven contest with the well-documented characteristics of poorer council estates: rubbish and debris sprinkled liberally across pavements and roads; parts of cars or vans abandoned on the estate and dismantled by groups of eager young kids who roam the streets until late at night; packs of snarling dogs which threaten the unwary pedestrian, cyclist or motorist; gates and fences removed or demolished, in earlier days for firewood; overgrown, rubbish-strewn gardens; several vacant and boarded-up houses; iron-grilled and graffiti-daubed shops whose doorways are eagerly colonized at night by the 'young Kingy' and their girl-friends; couples, married young and trailing poorly clothed and dirty kids; prematurely old men and women, standing on doorsteps or hanging over fences, watching the noisy, daily street pageant pass by; the omnipresent, drifting police car and the cat-calls or frozen stares which follow it. Especially in the summer months and at night, life in Kingy is *about* the streets. But let us begin to focus on the group we have called 'the lads' who, during the time of the research, were all in their late teens and early twenties. 'The lads' are: Brad, Dibbo, Howie, Macca, Smig, Merf, Ritchie, Tammy, Allo, Sammy, Jacko, Simmo, Jimmy, Nicky, Mark, Johno and Smarto. The 'Young Kingsley', who will also be mentioned in this chapter and who included Stench, Tommy, Ronny, Stello and Stevie, were all in their early to mid-teens. The 'townies', including Fletch, Lindsey, Paulie, Derek, Liam and Dicky, were older 'hard cases' who did the bulk of their drinking 'down town'. Not all of the townies were from West Kingsley but the group was linked to the lads via their down-town exploits and through neighbourhood and kinship ties. The townies, by this time, were only infrequently involved in the football action. Their ages ranged from the mid-twenties through to the early forties. We shall start with a consideration of some aspects of the family life of the lads and the young Kingsley and the conflicts which are recurrently generated in that connection.

Family life and specific family duties were important parts of life for the lads. They found it difficult to imagine different situations. Bureaucratic settings were particularly alien to them. They found it difficult to operate in such a context, and extensive family contacts meant better prospects of finding work via relatives who had already 'got a foot in'. Families, too, were perceived as providing support ('back-up') in troubled times. Family reputations required defending in turn. Thus, insults aimed at females in the family but particularly at the undisputed head of the household – the mother – were treated in the most serious fashion. Adult sons and, then, other male members of the family if required, were duty bound to avenge or extract apologies for slurs of this kind which were perceived in the social circles of the lads as affronts to their identities as males. Male proprietorial rights over females – especially over their sexuality – were viewed in similar fashion. A considerable number of street disturbances in Dodge were ultimately traceable to minor incidents or disputes – often involving sexual indiscretions, insults or fights between kids – which had inexorably escalated into full-blown family rows which, on occasions, lived on as simmering vendettas:

JW: (*Researcher*) What about fights on the estate between families?

DIBBO: Yeah, there are fuckin' loads, ain't there?

JW: Well, how do they start?

BRAD: People knockin' other people's missus off. That's the main thing that start things round here.

DIBBO: Someone shagging someone else's missus.

BRAD: It always happens around here, don't it Dibb?

DIBBO: Well, y'know, you're playing football in the street or something and you break someone's window. Starts over little kids for a start.

BRAD: Yeah, and then the big 'uns come out.

DIBBO: If a little 'un hits another little 'un, the one who lost goes in roaring, then his mam comes out shoutin' at the other one. Then *his* mam comes out shoutin' at her, so you've got the fuckin' women arguing. Then, probably, the old blokes come out and then its fuckin' started between the whole families, like. All the fuckin' lads get into it then.

MERF: Sometimes you've got to stick up for your fuckin' family, haven't you? If someone hit me little kid, you'd be fuckin' fighting then. There's always fights between families. Most of the fights are between families. Mostly, the kids start it. Y'know, the kids get into rows and it just goes on from there.

Merfo's family had, in fact, moved out of Sparrow Road, then the most notorious street in West Kingsley, because of continuing and painful aggravation at the hands of a particularly troublesome Kingsley family which had since left the estate. During the course of this series of incidents, Merf, Paulie and Mr Teal, their father, had all been given 'good hidings' by the menfolk of the rival family who, according to Merf, had the apparently insurmountable advantage of expertise at kung fu. Smig's relationship with the Macs was similarly fractious because he had managed to get one of the Mac girls pregnant. Extramarital pregnancies were by no means unusual on the estate. In this case, Smig declined the prospects of marriage and the affair threatened a major family feud. 'If you live in Kingy', said Smig, 'you don't take on fellahs. You take on families. You might be able to have Macca but you'd have a fuckin' army after yer.' Smig was undoubtedly correct. He and others among the lads were especially wary of McInley, a Mac in-law only recently come from Scotland and, according to common consent in the area, 'a fuckin' nutter'. The stereotypical image of the Scots in West Kingsley was one of alcohol-soaked violence, an image which McInley seemed keen to live up to. Scots, according to local lore, 'don't mess about', and 'blades' (knives) and even guns were reputed to be routine weapons in the armouries of 'crazy Jocks'. During the period of fieldwork on the estate, McInley's wife – Macca's sister – was involved in 'a row' with the female Stewarts, another large family of Scottish descent who lived on Sparrow. The initial incident ended with Mary – McInley's wife and no mean fighter herself – getting 'smacked' by a couple of the Stewart girls. The numerical imbalance of this affair brought the long-standing antagonism between the Stewarts and Macs to a head, and convinced McInley, dragging Macca in tow, that male intervention was necessary in order to salvage the family's 'good name'. The Stewarts, however, well aware of the likely next stage, lay in wait. As McInley broke in through the Stewarts' front door, he was greeted with a blow from an axe or machete which resulted in a visit to the infirmary and thirty-nine stitches to a wound in McInley's head. Police involvement in the affair was, at the Macs' insistence, predictably limited. Like many other families on the estate, they did not turn easily to 'the law' to solve domestic 'dust-ups', even of such a serious kind. Instead, arming himself with a carving knife, McInley and the other Mac males returned to Sparrow Road only to find that, in Macca's words, the Stewarts 'had shit themselves and fucked off', rumour had it, back to Scotland.

Family quarrels did not usually result in such serious injuries. However, quarrels occurred regularly on the estate and often led to fist fights between the male members of the families involved rather than to negotiated settlements. Young and adult males in the area experienced a shared cultural milieu that was expressive, fundamentally, of four sets of common experiences: the common experience of manual work and/or unemployment; the common experience of deprivation and shared leisure interests (the pub, the club, gambling and sport); the common experience and interpretation of gender relations as in most respects heavily patriarchal; and the common experience of the traditions of West Kingsley, especially those connected most directly with the masculine characteristics that were prized on the estate. Let us begin to consider these masculine characteristics in greater detail.

It would be wrong to say that the lads simply 'received' the masculine traditions of the estate from older 'significant others'. As we suggested in *The Roots of Football Hooliganism*, the *structure* of 'problem' housing estates like West Kingsley tends to approximate to ordered segmentation, and the resultant *life experiences* of their members, shaped in part by the shifting circumstances which each new generation faces, lead to the production and reproduction within them of slowly changing but still strongly parochial and masculine street styles. Nevertheless, both the lads and the 'young Kingsley', the middle teenage males on the estate, were acutely aware of the reputation and traditions of the area and were pledged to carry on its 'good name' in the manner in which they perceived the males of previous generations had done:

JW: Why is it important for Kingsley lads to be harder than anyone else?

BRAD: I don't fuckin' know, really. It's 'Jack the lad', isn't it? It's your name – Kingsley – reputation. You've got to keep it up to its standards, ain't yer? 'Cos them that's older than us now, when they were our age, they were the fuckin' same as us, weren't they?

JW: You think you're carrying on the name?

BRAD: Yeah, well we are, ain't we? We're still fuckin' doing it now.

DIBBO: You see, it's got a good reputation, Kingsley. Most people say: 'Don't go up fuckin' Kingsley. You'll get your fuckin' head kicked in. It's what you've heard, isn't it?

Knowing that they come from one of the toughest parts of the city is of great importance to the lads and their juniors. It gives them dignity and respect, especially in the areas that they and their elders have 'colonized' down town – a few pubs and clubs, and of course, the home-end terraces at Filbert Street – where status depends fundamentally upon connections and estate credentials. Stories of prospective opponents 'fucking off' on hearing that their rivals come from Kingsley are continuously retold. Unwanted 'trouble' can usually be avoided, according to the lads, simply by telling the source of irritation where you come from. They even claim to have national status. The hardest inmates of borstals and youth custody centres, they say, have *always* heard of Kingsley. In the informal, heavily masculine circles which young males from the estate seek out and move within, the Kingsley tag and the 'back-up' provided by the estate ('no Kingsley lads leave mates in trouble') are essential struts for a satisfying, masculine street identity. Let us enquire into some of the ways in which the lads are socialized into these masculine traditions.

Looking at young kids on the streets of West Kingsley, it is easy to visualize the Kingy lads beginning their own aggressive careers on the streets of the estate. The tendency for young children in lower-working-class areas to colonize the streets at an early age is well documented.[7] It is also one of the main constitutive features of ordered segmentation. Like Howard Parker's 'tiddlers', the current crop of Kingsley street kids are not afraid to tell anybody to 'fuck off'.[8] Cars visiting the area are forced to slow down by 8- or 9-year-olds, already emerging as the leaders of local gangs, who strut contemptuously across the road, fixing the driver with an aggressive stare. Their games of 'war' and 'dare' involve dangerous escapades – the lighting of fires and throwing bricks and lumps of wood – and invariably end in fights or accusations of cowardice. They cheek the local teenagers mercilessly, the young boys goading girls twice their age into fights (and getting them). Before they are 10, they are conning the young Kingy and the lads for 'ciggies', and are already on the look out for coppers who threaten to spoil their assaults on the houses of 'old bags' who have given them a mouthful for their late night noises.

In Kingy, as in most similar areas, the bulk of child-rearing is in the hands of the mother – except, of course, when the kids 'go too far' or when 'mam' finds out a little more than is usually available about the antics of her younger children. In such cases, dad is still called in with the strap or the slipper. Almost all the lads remember hidings from 'the old fellah', though, characteristically, some blame their lack of sufficient punishment when young for their current penchant for 'thieving' and 'getting into trouble'. Already as kids, the important distinction between public and private domains, more particularly between the male preserves of the street and the pub and the world of feminine domestication, is imprinted firmly in their minds. Many recollections of 'my old man' strongly reflect the 'man's world' of which they themselves were soon to become part.

SMIG: Our dad was always in the fuckin' Woolpack [the pub on the estate]. You couldn't get him away from the fuckin' place. Every dinner, every night, he'd be fuckin' up there boozin'. And he'd always be gettin' into fuckin' fights an' all. He got sent down for eighteen

137

months once for something he didn't even fuckin' do. One night we were sittin' in our house and there's this knock on the door and it was one of me dad's mates and he said, 'Come up to the Woolpack 'cos some of your mates are in a fight there.' So our dad goes up there, and he got fuckin' nicked before he could do owt.

You want to see me mam, though, I remember her, when we were kids, taking us all up to the fuckin' pub and saying to our dad, 'Here, you fuckin' look after 'em,' 'cos he was always in the pub, y'see. I've seen her take him his dinner up there and all. He took me up to the Woolie one day when I was about 10. I could see 'em playing cards through the window. Anyway, this big fucker must've been losing because he just stood up and tipped the whole fuckin' table up like it were a Wild West film or summat. The manager told him to fuck off out of it. When our dad left, we were walking along the road and this fuckin' big fellah was waiting around the corner, and kicked our dad in the stomach. He went down, like, and so he kicked him again and then fucked off. Our dad just got up; he never said nothing or anything. He just got up and walked home. I was fuckin' roaring [crying], I was, seeing me dad get kicked like that. I've never forgotten it.

The lads were adamant that their own interest in fighting – in 'standing up for themselves' – was a product of their formative experiences on the estate. They broadly supported Allo's bland assertion that 'When you're brought up in Kingy, there's nothing there. You're brought up with violence in Kingy.' In this world of street hierarchies, playground intimidation and character contests, kids – especially males – were ill-prepared for the rigours of life on the estate without some parental guidance on the 'realities' of the world outside. As Ritchie put it: 'It was no good coming home roaring in our house when someone had picked on you. My old fellah would tell you not to be so fuckin' soft and to smack him back next time.' According to Howie, his 'mam' had taught him to fight at home, at the cost of the occasional black eye. Time and again, the importance of 'not being taken for a cunt'; of not 'lettin' yourself down'; of 'being able to battle', were stressed as imperatives for lads who 'wanted to be somebody' on the streets of the estate. Such requirements did not mean, of course, that the lads were fighting all the time. There were 'crazy bastards' with an almost pathological attraction to 'trouble' and who, as a consequence, were almost permamently 'inside'. In the lads' eyes, these sorts of characters – in the McInley mode, for example – were dangerous to knock around with because of their almost indiscriminate attitude to violence and fights. As Jimmy put it: 'Fuckin' hell! If you went around with McInley for long, you'd either end up battered or locked up. He's mad, that boy.' More important to the lads than McInley's almost compulsive search for aggro regardless of the odds or the prospects of 'getting nicked' was the quality of loyalty and performance among members of the group when 'trouble', as it frequently did, came calling.

The lads' earliest memories of school are shot through with recollections of their dislike for desk work. They also fondly recall their escapades in search of relief from the emasculating monotony of activities better suited to 'swots' and 'divs', and from what they perceive as the arbitrary, 'do this, do fuckin' that' discpline of formal education. The ethos as well as their experience of school clashed starkly with their emerging views on the priorities of life. The 'benefits' of education were already clear to them through their encounters with 'posh cunts' and 'snobs' who in fact, of course, 'know fuck all'. The formality of schooling, with its stifling preoccupation with discipline and rules and its dogged insistence on exploring the abstract and the intellect at the expense of the concrete and the physical which are central to the lads' experiences and values outside the classroom, progressively place school – and other formal institutions – at a sharp tangent to the overall experience of being a working-class, male teenager on an estate like Kingsley. The lads' opposition to the character and ideology of formal schooling constitutes a rejection of the threatening alliance between what they regard as the 'feminizing' tendencies of book-work (with its associated aims of exploring the consciousness; of unearthing the 'truth' about 'feelings' the lads like to deny they possess), and what they perceive as the oppressive and unimaginative hand of formal authority which 'won't let you do nothing'. In circumstances like this, the peer group is important because it is that which allows individuals to sustain the alternative maps of social reality which are offered and reinforced in the playground and on the estate. In the lads' eyes young males imprisoned in the inactive, castrating world of pen-pushing and intellectual

deliberation are to be both ridiculed and pitied. In the masculine hierarchies down-town, in the street, at football and in the shop-floor
culture of manual work, different and, for the lads, superior forms
of knowledge are at a premium.[9] There are no 'laughs', no 'good
nobbles' within the formal curriculum of school. School is for 'boring
bastards'. Education is for 'them' – and 'they' can keep it.

JW:	Most of the lads went to Radford [School], didn't they? How did you get on?
SMIG:	I never liked school. A lot of us didn't hardly go when we were kids. Always bunking off. Used to get the odd probationer coming round, y'know, or the School Board man, y'know, once a week or something like that.
JW:	But why didn't you like going?
SMIG:	I just couldn't sit down and listen. I just used to fuckin' hate it. If the teacher turned his back, y'know, something was going to happen to him. Somebody was going to chuck something at him. Then, when you got older, if the teachers started hitting you, you'd start fuckin' hitting 'em back. You weren't gonna have it.
HOWIE:	None of us liked it at school. It was no good. I was always fighting at school. They had these rules like no fuckin' running in the corridors. I took no fuckin' notice, and ended up with the cane. That put me off. I didn't go to school. I thought, I'm not going to get the cane just for fuckin' running. When I did go, I never fuckin' bothered. I just didn't bother about the lessons. There's nowt to know. They don't learn you properly. They didn't learn me to read and write, did they? Fuckin' useless.
JW:	How did you get on, Macca?
MACCA:	Well, I used to be a nuisance to tell you the truth, pal. Used to get caught smokin' all the time. We always got taken down to Fuller's room [Headmaster]. He was a foul bastard. No, he was all right but he used to get on us nerves. We used to fuck off every Friday afternoon and every Monday morning, we didn't have to be told. We just went down for the stick, down to Fuller's room.

JW: Did you like school?

MACCA: To tell the truth, I hated it. I didn't like the teachers.
          I couldn't get on with them. I didn't like their attitudes,
          like. Do fuckin' this, do that.

SAMMY: Naw, it were terrible; really fuckin' boring, the
          schoolwork, like. You used to have a fuckin' laugh in
          class, though, 'cos you could fuck around with the
          teachers. I can read and write, though, better than
          those ignorant bastards can. Trouble was, I was
          expelled from Radford when I was 14 and no other
          fuckin' school would have me. I got expelled for
          smashing up this teacher's car after he fuckin' threw
          me out. I kicked the fuckin' lights in and everything,
          like a mad cunt.

DIBBO: That was like me, kicking me out of King John's for
          smacking this girl who was grassing me up. It wasn't
          even me!

JW   Didn't you think learning to read and write were
          important at all?

DIBBO: Not me. I fuckin' hated it. Sitting around all fuckin'
          day listening to those stupid fuckin' teachers rabbitin'
          on. We used to fuck off up to the top of the stage for
          a fuckin' smoke. Nobody used to bother us there, did
          they Merf?

MERF: 'Course they fuckin' didn't. It was a waste of fuckin'
          time, school. Of all me mates who went to school with
          me, I can't think of one of 'em who can read and write
          properly now.

JW: What about any kind of qualifications, then?

MERF: Well, all those were for the clever cunts, weren't they?
          All the fuckin' dills. What we wanted was to get out
          and get a fuckin' job. Learn your job like. No need
          for fuckin' reading and writing for that.

Apart from their intense dislike of the academic curriculum and
the formal authority structure of the school, the lads' strongest
memories of education centred, on the one hand, on their routine concern with subverting the very processes which threatened to enchain
them by 'livening up' lessons, and, on the other, on their compulsive
fascination with the aggressive and hierarchical social relations of the

141

playground. Here, the roles of the classroom were dramatically reversed. The 'dills' and the 'swots', who were sickeningly successful in class, were generally targeted outside for bouts of intimidation and extortion by those who were destined – and themselves determined – to live by their hands rather than by the sorts of brainwork encouraged in school. The playground, where the strong and the 'smart' reigned, was a satisfying oasis in the midst of a desert of rules and standards which had little or no meaning in the lads' narrow vocabulary of values and experiences. Here, save for the occasional challenge from the 'lower orders' and 'interference' from teachers who were too conscientious, the 'cock of the school' (the school's best acknowledged fighter) and the young 'cocks' of each year ruled their roosts. In short, the playgrounds of schools that serve areas like West Kingsley are not quite the idylls painted by Marsh *et al.* in which consensus emerges out of processes of negotiation and compromise among equal parties.[10] Physical strength and fighting ability are central. That is, a fundamental characteristic of such playground worlds consists of the aggressive ordering and re-ordering of fighting hierarchies – the lads were not only able to name the school cock but also the second cock, the third cock, the fourth cock and so on. Also characteristic are the (in that context) mundane tales of intimidation and theft from the playground 'also-rans'. The latter might produce the goods in class but, partly as a result of that fact, they were fatefully unattached to the more powerful playground cliques and gangs. Jacko's forte while at Radford, for example, was to tread on the sandwiches of one unfortunate 'dill': 'No fucker I knew had sarnies, so I used to stand on 'em and make him eat them.' Other victims experienced the humiliation of toilet duckings and the forcible redistribution of valued objects such as sweets:

> MERF: Fighting at school was going on all the time. It was important, otherwise you'd get fuckin' bullied and that. You got sweets off other kids. You know, if someone came up to you and said, 'Give us a rock [sweet], you just had to tell 'em to fuck off. Most of the kids couldn't do that, like, against someone who could fight, who had a reputation for it. 'Cos if they did, they'd get fuckin' punched then. So that's how you got your sweets.

Attendance at a particular school formed the basis of a number of local rivalries, some of which cut across West Kingsley–East Kingsley allegiances. Traditionally, the school affiliations of West Kingsley's young teenagers produced assaults on King John's, a secondary school serving the nearby Northern Parks estate. During the fieldwork period, in fact, Radford and 'the Johnnies' were involved in a series of lunchtime exchanges at the heart of which were the young Kingsley who reportedly routed the Johnnies' cocks of *all* years. Eventually, acting on the advice of the staff of both schools, the police intervened to stop the midday excursions of up to fifty of the Radford 'hardest' on the short trip to Johnnies. Predictably, according to Kingsley sources, the Johnnies, once again, had 'shit it'.

School-based loyalties were of less importance than the gang groupings established on the streets of the estate, however. Streets provided a natural focus for gang affiliations and these affiliations were also operative in the football context. For the purposes of gang attachments, the estate is divided roughly between the Woolpack and the Sparrow Road sections, with Landy Avenue which runs through the centre of the district generating its own gang loyalties. Sometimes, depending on the presence or otherwise of two or more rival 'hard cases', the longer streets are split in half as far as their gang affiliations are concerned. And within these broader territorial and street alliances smaller cliques or groupings - 'best mates' and 'family' - complete the complex picture of 'alliances within alliances' which characterizes the loyalties of male teenagers in the area.

At the time of the research, the general view among the lads was that the really 'major rows' - those that involved some degree of collective mobilization across the generations against an external target - the 'mass fights', as Sammy called them, were no longer in the offing. This gloomy conclusion was offset, however, by the widely held view that it was the increasingly formidable reputation of the estate which had, in recent years, deterred outside groups from 'having a go'. 'Let's face it', as Jacko approvingly remarked during a Friday evening downtown session, 'you'd have to be fuckin' mad to try to do Kingsley. Fuckin' crazy!' The last 'mad' assault of this kind was collectively agreed to have occurred in 1975 when, according to local lore, 'the niggers had come to Kingsley'. The precursor of this particular episode was a fight involving young males from Kingsley, who were returning 'steaming' from a Friday night in town, and a group of Asian youths. The Asian youths, outnumbered and caught sufficiently close to the estate to be presumed to be 'up to no good', were given a 'good hammering' for this territorial violation, but they vowed to return to the estate in numbers on the following Sunday morning. Sure enough, on the morning in question up to 100 Asian males armed with sticks and other weapons (in re-telling, the lads' estimates soared into the high hundreds, even the thousands) arrived on Kingsley Park in the hope of obtaining revenge for the Friday night assault. The presence of adult Asians in their ranks and their arrival on the very doorstep of the estate were sufficient to stir not only the younger Kingsley males into collective mobilisation but also to arouse some local family heads into turning out 'to see off the niggers'. Before the police could mobilize in numbers sufficient to intervene, a number of men from both sides received injuries from bricks and clubs. Unimpressed by the police response and simultaneously angered by what they saw as this unwarranted interference in a fight of which, in their perception, *all* native whites should have approved, more than 100 Kingsley residents, some of whom had decided tactics over a few lunch-time pints, gathered again in the afternoon to attack the new police station. This largely unwelcomed addition to the estate was still under construction, and Dibbo, Jacko, Brad and Howie were among those convicted for causing damage to it. In Dibbo's words: 'They were putting the thing up and we were knocking the bastard down.'[11]

These incidents were sufficiently out of the ordinary to arouse debate among males in the area some five or six years after they had occurred. Less remarkable were the regular gang confrontations involving large groups of young Kingsley males and representatives from rival estates, especially from nearby and traditionally reviled Old Gardens. As young teenagers, the lads had organized regular expeditions to the neighbouring estate or to the slightly more distant Northern Park. For manoeuvres of this kind, the local street, territorial and kinship affiliations within West Kingsley tended to be subordinated for the sake of *estate* solidarity. This required a gathering of the various Kingsley forces, usually in the Woolpack car park, before setting off in search of action against groups of Old Gardens teenagers with similar views of masculine prowess and identity. Particularly attractive testing grounds for this collective assertion of estate credentials were the sites of the travelling fairs which were regular visitors to the areas around the Kingsley and Old Gardens estates. A fair guaranteed the attendance of Old Gardens in considerable numbers, especially if, as was usually the case, it was sited in territory close to that estate. Today's young Kingsley continue this practice of group attendance at the local fair, though their confrontations with Old Gardens teenagers were derided by the older lads as being 'all running and no fighting'. There were rumblings, too, when, in the summer of 1981, the young Kingsley, around fifty strong and on their way to a planned showdown on Northern Park, were successfully ambushed by a combined gang of Old Gardens and Northern Park youths. Smig's younger brother, Tommy, gloomily admitted that, on this occasion, the young Kingsley had been 'well bricked' and had scattered in disarray.

It was inconceivable that an assault of this kind could have happened *within* West Kingsley. The home turf was viewed as being virtually impregnable. In West Kingsley, one ran the risk of falling foul of local cliques or gangs from unfamiliar parts of the estate. There was also the chance of being drawn into family disputes. Outside West Kingsley, however, things were rather less clear-cut. The world beyond the confines of the estate and the city-centre pubs which were 'solid Kingsley' was a potentially dangerous and exciting terrain with almost limitless possibilities. According to the lads, coming from Kingsley provided considerable safeguards when trouble loomed elsewhere – 'no one picks on Kingsley'; 'Kingsley lads stick together'. But the Kingsley tag also provided increased risks of attack in the hostile territories which they perceived to be lurking beyond the comfortingly familiar streets on the estate. If Kingsley lads together were 'unbeatable', alone or in small groups they were reputed to be targets for any groups of 'cowboys' on the look out for 'strays'. Areas beyond the estate were seldom viewed in terms of the potential they offered for leisure exploration, except, of course, when the lads moved 'team-handed'. Alone or in small groups, new locations were 'dodgy', 'shit holes' and frequently just plain 'boring'. Even in their late teens and early twenties, the Kingsley lads were firmly tied for leisure purposes to the estate, to a severely limited number of city-centre pubs, and to football. Apart from a mere handful of city-centre streets, locations outside the estate were simply not known.

The lads' strong attachments to Kingsley, their reliance on the area for identity and status, and their severely limited social and geographical horizons combined to produce a profoundly conservative view of social space and a correspondingly stereotyped view of residential areas in other parts of the city. Hightown, for example, was simply 'where the niggers live' or, alternatively, 'little India'. Sefton Lane was 'full of pros' (prostitutes) and so on.[12] Lads who had moved off the estate for short periods claimed to be unable to make friends in other areas because of the peculiarities of the locals or because of the latters' perceived hostility towards Kingsley lads. Merfo, for example, moved briefly to Sefton Lane and 'never went out' because the locals were 'all queer cunts' and 'on the look out' for ex-Kingsleyites. Relations of this kind were reciprocal, of course. The Woolpack was particularly hazardous for non-locals who made the mistake of establishing fleeting eye contact with one of the male members of the 'Ando' or Handicott families whose next move was usually to enquire threateningly 'what you wanted'. Another favourite ploy levelled against outsiders involved accusations about 'eyeing up' Kingsley women. The end result in almost all cases was the same: a swift exit for the 'offender'. In the lads' terms, such episodes were not explicable as examples of simple intolerance. Instead, they were presented as rational pre-emptive strikes that were essential to protect the 'good name' of the estate. A *lack* of response in situations of this kind could too easily be interpreted as a sign of weakness: an invitation to an intolerable future. In Sammy's words, 'before long you'd have any fucker thinking they could come down here'. Visits to the area by groups of young working-class males were *naturally* presumed to be offensive. After all, the formidable reputation of the estate was well enough known and the lads' own motivations in exploring potentially dangerous ground were scarcely disguised. Moreover, their experiences of nights down-town and at football proved that 'trouble' was not something that you had to look too hard for. 'Trouble' was a fact of life.

Their weekend exploits down-town and at football were, without doubt, the highlights of the week for the Kingsley lads. Other experiences paled immeasurably by comparison. Fridays and Saturdays were occasions for drinking *par excellence*, times when you 'don't give a fuck' and you don't care who knows it. Down-town and at football for a West Kingsley lad provided both status and a degree of collective security and strength. By general agreement among the lads, however, football was the best site at which to celebrate one's Kingsley credentials. In theory at least, it also gave you a better chance of 'getting back' at the 'bastard coppers'. Accordingly, let us look at the football exploits of the Kingsley lads in order to show how the norms, values and modes of behaviour acquired in the course of their socialization on the estate are carried over into and adapted in a football context.

Most of the Kingsley lads who were regular attenders 'down City' enjoyed football. Many of them played or had played in local leagues. However, the regularity with which Kingsley sides – or their supporters – transgressed the norm of competing 'hard but fairly' brought teams from the estate a constant stream of reprimands, fines and expulsions. (Macca, for example, liked to warm up for Sunday afternoon play by getting 'tanked up' in the Woolpack.) Eventually, it was difficult for teams with 'Kingsley' in their name to gain acceptance in local leagues, though this problem was easily overcome via the use of imaginative and suitably anonymous titles for the 'new' teams which regularly sprang up from the disgraced older versions.

Despite the undoubted interest that many of them had in the game, however, the Kingsley lads were not typically the stuff of Daniel and McGuire's hard-core football supporters from 'the Paint House' who were 'very knowledgeable about their team, its history, past and present players, and content and result of particular games'.[13] Nor were the Kingsley lads generally like Harrington's sample of convicted offenders who 'surprised' that author for similar reasons.[14] Knowledge of the game and about Leicester City's tactics and players varied widely in the group from Ritchie's sometimes considered opinions to Smig and Jacko's almost total incomprehension even of the rules of the game. Ritchie and Jimmy probably cared most about Leicester's performance and favoured assessments beyond the usually bitter collective post-match analysis that, in defeat, all the City players had 'played like cunts'. For the Kingsley lads, however, 'good times' on the terraces were related less to good performances on the field than they were to the size and vociferousness of Leicester City's home end and travelling contingents. Above all, they were related to their own manoeuvres before, during and after matches. For the Kingsley, conversations about football usually meant discussions not about players, managers or matches, but about rival ends, fights and the 'liberties' taken by the police. Football was defined in terms of their own showing against rival crews and ends. Defeat on the field could be stomached, forgotten almost immediately. But disgrace in the 'real' business of terrace rivalries was much more difficult to swallow. Noteworthy matches, at home or away, were invariably etched in the collective memory as occasions when prominent characters in the group or in the Leicester end as a whole had been arrested. Alternatively, they were remembered as 'a right fuckin' nobble', 'a fuckin' good laugh', 'a brilliant raut', or, as Pat expressed it, for the opportunities they provided for an afternoon's 'boozing and wrecking'. Even in Ritchie's dreams about City reaching a major Cup Final, pride of place was reserved for the vision of Leicester's followers overpowering the collective might of the combined London crews.

It is inevitable, of course, that the lads' stress on the importance of 'fucking about' at matches brings them into conflict not only with rival crews but also with the police and more orderly fans with different views on what constitutes acceptable match-day behaviour. For the Kingy lads and others like them, 'the match' is a collective physical enterprise that embraces far more than the ninety minutes of their team's endeavours on the field. 'Spectatorship', for them, is a frequently intermittent, chaotic and halting affair. Nor is it restricted simply to relatively passive observation of the match itself. It involves, for example, clearing 'home' territories of opposing fans by fighting or by threat; shouting, chanting, singing, gesticulating, spitting and throwing missiles at opposing spectators, players and the police; settling local disputes; monitoring, goading and obstructing stewards and the police; engineering crowd falls; wrestling with one another; hanging around toilets and refreshment stalls in order to plan post-match strategies and assess the prospects for 'thieving'. A 'good nobble', in short, means that things must be *made* to happen. 'Posh bastards' who are 'acting the cunt' need to be 'woken up'. It is important to get 'steaming' and to show away fans that they can't walk through town 'cocky like, as if they fuckin' owned the place'. The shaky parts of 'shitty little grounds' (anywhere away from Leicester) are damaged or demolished to 'remind' the locals of the Leicester visit. None of these things, of course, is held by the football authorities, 'respectable' members of the public or the police to be characteristic of 'true' supporters. The lads beg to differ. As they see it, they are defending the reputation of the city, and more particularly of the estate, for producing 'good lads' or, in Jimmy's approving terms, 'typical fuckin' Kingy lads'. A few more supporters like the Kingsley, according to the lads, and Leicester City would really amount to something.

According to one of Robins and Cohen's interviewees talking about Arsenal's North Bank in the 1970s: 'Some of the kids there, they came 'cos they'd heard about the North Bank aggro and all this. They're demented. They don't know nothing about the game.'[15]

The Sports Council/SSRC report of 1978 similarly revealed that:

It has been put to us from a variety of sources that some individuals appear to show little or no interest in the game, may only rarely, if ever, have played football themselves, and come to watch the match mainly because of the opportunities it affords for hooliganism. Such individuals would not wear 'favours' or conform to the stereotypes of the 'soccer hooligan', nor would they have any fixed location inside the ground for their connection with football is incidental. They are, in fact, the terrace drifters seeking maximum cover for their activities from the crowd and probing areas of the ground which are conducive to disorderly behaviour.[16]

Smig, Jacko and other 'non-footballing' Kingsley lads who attended matches on a regular basis were not 'demented', though they claimed to know of individuals in the City end – 'nutters' who would fight uncontrollably and against any odds – who might fit that description. Nor were the Kingsley lads the unattached 'terrace drifters' described in the Sports Council/SSRC report of 1978. Far from it: they were an established and recognized focal point of the Leicester end. Part of the end's masculine character was defined – by members of the end themselves – through the Kingsley and the other gangs' defence of the home turf and of the city's reputation for not being a 'soft touch'. The Kingsley lads attended football as part of a collective enterprise which held out the prospects for 'good times' as defined in the lads' parochial and heavily masculine cultural milieu. Not least important in this context was the likelihood of Kingsley involvement in match-related trouble. As Brad explained, 'going down City' was not simply a matter of individual choice. 'When you're on Kingy, in a gang like, and someone says, "Let's go down the fuckin' match", then you *all* go.'

The lads' entry into the senior world of match-day drinking and 'rauting' had been mediated in a variety of ways: through reputations already honed on the estate; by simply 'hanging around' the end's 'establishment' and performing with 'bottle' and 'style' when challenged; or through the ever-important kinship links. Jimmy's older brother, for example, was a 'townie' with 'Mad Mob' credentials.[17] When Jimmy was 15, he had 'filled in a place' on a number of football trips from the Vines (a Leicester city-centre pub) on the understanding that he didn't 'shit himself' to the embarrassment of his brother. His brother need not have feared. Fired by the excitement of hired-van football travel – 'thirty lads, pissed up, in the back of a transit' – Jimmy had since gained a reputation as one of the estate's most reliable hard cases. Dibbo began his career when a young teenager, simply by following Liam, Lindsey and his brother, Derek, into 'yobs' corner' (the term used by the police to describe the section of terracing at Filbert Street used to house young away fans in the early 1970s). Fighting and ejection from the away end was followed by the intoxicating experience of 'the parade'; that is, of being 'paraded', under police escort and in full view of the rest of the crowd, back into the home pen. Such experiences involved not only the complex cocktail of fear and excitement that is generated by a venture into enemy territory but also, in the end and on the estate, a considerable leap in status terms.

Football is an arena in which it is possible to establish a reputation not only among one's peers but among the end's 'lower orders', too – among the young 'apprentices' from Kingsley and the other estates who have not yet 'graduated' to 'the action', for example, and among the 'hangers-on' who come for the singing and chanting but not the fighting. The game provides the possibility of 'being someone', of being recognized, not only by 'coppers' who are tempted to 'nick you' because they know you are 'looking for trouble' but also by other young Leicester males whose identities are, to varying degrees, tied up with the fortunes of the local end. Howie, fresh out of Borstal for a football offence, remembered his reintroduction to 'going down City' as a time of realization that, through his footballing endeavours, he had become something of a celebrity on the local networks. Here is how he put it:

I remember it. I'd just got out of Borstal. It was a lovely day, y'know what I mean. Beautiful day. Leicester was playing Man. City. I didn't have much money. I only had about a fiver, if that, but some of the lads bought me beer, y'know, since I'd just come out. And I thought, 'Hold on, there's a catch here somewhere. I'd seen these kids. I didn't know 'em, like, but they must've known I'd just got out and they all came to see me in this pub. Loads of Leicester, like. Loads of 'em. I just sat there, minding my own business and someone came up and said, 'All right, Howard?' I said, 'I don't know you, mate,' and he said, 'I know you down the football, what you've done.' You know, they were saying, 'We want to drink with you like, 'cos we know you don't run'. They were buying me beer and everything. . . .

I've had do's with just me and Simmo stood there, fighting. We've been fighting and the fuckin' Leicester [fans] have been watching us! Afterwards, they'd be coming up to you saying, 'You all right?', as if they know you. They fuckin' respect you, like, know what I mean? That's what it is. It's about fellahs fuckin' respecting you.

Respect – getting a 'good name' for 'battling' at football – can be read from a variety of small gestures in the football context: the excessively watchful attentions of the police; the avenue which seems magically to open out for the Kingsley as they move through the Leicester ranks; the obsessive concern among other young Leicester males from the home end to be seen to be on at least nodding acquaintance with prominent Kingsley lads; the caution shown by other estate crews who involve themselves uneasily in informal alliances with the Kingsley for the visits of major ends; and the stiffening of bar staff and clientele as the Kingsley make their menacing entrance into pubs off the usual Kingsley circuit.

On match-days at home, the young Kingsley monitored the downtown scene, relaying information to the older Kingsley lads about the movements of large groups of visiting fans.[18] During these lengthy periods of 'hanging around', of eyeing up visitors from other 'manors' as well as the youthful Asian and Afro-Caribbean gangs which cruise the city centre on a Saturday afternoon, the young Kingsley would energetically ape their elders in recounting tales of past terrace success. Although they lacked the physical capacity and suitable targets for becoming involved at the serious, fighting end, members of the young Kingsley cliques nevertheless recalled incidents at City and elsewhere *as if* they had been central characters. Many of these accounts stemmed directly from being at or near fights and attacks. While 'ordinary' fans pretended not to notice or hastened away from the scene in fear, Stench and Ronnie, for example, two of the young Kingsley who were close to 'graduation', would resolutely follow on the heels of 'hard cases' like Pat and Howie as the latter purposefully pursued visiting stragglers into side streets and car parks. Here, a young Kingsley boot might be aimed, from within the ranks of the older Kingsley crew, at a grounded or running foe, and dutifully reported as a major *personal* fighting success. It was a stage in their own terrace careers that the older Kingsley lads remembered clearly. According to Brad:

> It starts when you're getting 12, 13, 14, and then your mates say, y'know, 'I'm going football,' and they all fuckin' want to go, don't they, so you all fuckin' go, don't you? . . . 'Cos when you're 13 and 14, y'know, you're just watching the trouble. You're saying, 'I've hit a couple,' but you haven't, not really, 'cos you know, you can't then. You're not hard enough. You're still a kid. You know what I mean? So you come back then and brag about it, but you

haven't done fuck all then. Then you start getting in the pubs when you're a bit older.[19]

The young Kingsley begin their terrace careers at home matches by enthusiastically joining with their seniors in the ritualistic 'piss-taking' of the police and visiting fans, and by scouring the local pens for non-local accents. (Kids asking the time from unfamiliar faces arouse less suspicion than older enquirers.) The young Kingsley are also quickly schooled in the reputation of the estate 'down City'. Graffiti on the back wall of the Kop announce the pre-eminence of Kingsley in local football fighting circles. So do the endless Kingsley chants and surges into other groups of supporters. The occasional rows at football with lads from other local estates or with crews of Leicester supporters from outside the city – from Loughborough, for example, or Hinckley – also testify to the distinctiveness of the Kingsley *within* the Leicester end. Information of this kind is quickly assimilated into the pre-match discussions and rituals of the young Kingsley. Ronnie, for example, instructed his young apprentices never to reveal to policemen at the turnstiles that they came from Kingsley: 'What! Fuckin' Kingsley! Troublemaker! Out!' This advice was delivered not only with bitterness towards the police on account of what the lads alleged to be their prejudiced view of Kingsley males but also with a degree of pride. The young Kingsley were well aware of the estate's recent footballing traditions and aimed to continue them.

Entry into the ground was one source of opportunities for 'action' – for a 'good nobble' as expressed through the cheek and 'street-wise' inventiveness of the younger Kingsley. A 'daft old fucker' on the turnstile, for example, provided possibilities for 'shoving in behind' and getting two persons into the ground on one turn of the turnstile. Away grounds were classified in terms of the prospects offered for free or reduced-price entry. Older allies would mysteriously 'lose' their money at the turnstiles while younger fans crawled free of charge into the ground between their open legs. Smaller grounds on Cup or Second Division visits were carefully scrutinized for doors or fences which might be scaled or which might give way if subjected to the right sort of treatment. A cup-tie at Oldham, for example, provided free entry for young and older Kingsley alike after a hole had been ripped in an insubstantial corrugated iron fence. (That evening's affairs were climaxed by an assault on the police with slabs of concrete torn from the crumbling terraces and by running fights and damage to vehicles in the car park after the match.) Away grounds, especially those outside the top bracket, were considered fair game by the Kingsley. 'Successes' of this kind away from home were felt to provide further confirmation of Leicester's capacity, but especially that of the estate, to produce 'fuckin' good lads' against whose street deviousness the people in official and authority positions – turnstile attendants, stewards, the police – were perceived as having no effective answer.

Whether at home or away, once inside the ground the young Kingsley pin themselves against the segregation fences, boldly point out 'wankers' among the rival contingents, and make half-serious arrangements to see opposing fans, many of them twice their size and their seniors by years, outside. They make dismissive fun of the 'little kids' who respectfully take their places at the front of Spion Kop. These are, in fact, youngsters of similar age to themselves but they lack estate traditions and street and terrace attachments to match their own. Any hint of 'trouble' in or around the ground and the young Kingsley are there, eager to be at least on the fringes of some 'real action'. Attitudes to the police, already well-established through Kingsley lore and reinforced through conflictual contacts on the estate, are honed at football where stories about and experiences of 'heavy' policing abound. The young Kingsley need little encouragement to join in the 'gobbing' sessions that are invited when 'the law' intrudes on to the terraces in order to break up fights or drag off suspects and offenders.

'Revenge' or 'repayment' for attacks by rival fans was extracted by the Kingsley on a general rather than a specific basis. Thus, an assault by Arsenal fans could be avenged by serving up similar treatment to *any* likely-looking Arsenal supporter. Similarly, the lads' images of particular towns and cities as 'dangerous', or of the local police as especially violent and offensive, were frequently generalized out of a single concrete experience. For example, Ritchie had *all* Derby policemen as 'bastards' because of the rough treatment he had received from a *macho* sergeant on the way to a match at the Baseball Ground. Macca bristled at the mere mention of Bristol and persons from the West Country city because of a slashing he received during a football visit which had left him with scars over both eyes. According to the lads, Bristol was simply a city of 'mad fuckin' dockers'. Their collective views of other cities were similarly framed. Like the 'Paint House boys', major Northern cities – Liverpool, Manchester and Newcastle – were viewed almost solely in terms of the likelihood of attack by locals.[20] The North-east, for example, was 'cowboy country' in which the safety of large numbers was the only effective form of defence. The lads found it difficult to conceive of circumstances in which groups of Midlands males could go out drinking 'up North' without being 'forced' into 'trouble'. The picture painted by the lads of relations between Leicester and London was even more fractious. The major London clubs, they argued, had singled out the City end for special attention on a *quid pro quo* basis: 'We wreck their pubs. They come up here and wreck ours.'

The justification given by the lads for attacks on fans visiting Leicester rested largely on a projection on to them of their own motives for visiting rival manors. In short, when a large away contingent was in town, it was *bound* to contain 'cunts looking for trouble' and, in such circumstances, it was vital to get your own strike in first. In effect, and while they readily admitted their enjoyment of fighting – Howie, especially, used to tremble with anticipatory excitement when a fight was looming – the lads saw themselves as being locked into a national network of violent rivalries from which there was little prospect of escape. This was part of Jacko's thesis: 'Wherever you go at football, there'll always be someone looking for aggro'. On match-days, then, large groups of visiting young fans walking unsupervised around Leicester were, by definition, 'looking for trouble'.

To the casual observer, the Kingsley lads and their rivals are probably scarcely distinguishable. The lads do, in fact, identify their match-day targets as 'fellahs like us'.[21] (The bobble-hat and scarf brigade were rarely attacked directly, though lads wearing scarves were sometimes considered fair game.) At the same time, however, any identifiable group of intruders in Leicester on a match-day were perceived by the Kingsley as like the members of an invading tribe. The lads claimed they were able to 'smell' these Saturday aliens, though it would, of course, be more accurate to say that their sensitivities were finely tuned to picking up tell-tale signs of strangers in town. Cautious deliberations outside pubs, for example; quizzical glances at road signs; or minute differences in street styles – these were all clear signs that 'they' were in town and required attention.

Fighting on match-days was also bound up with the notion of culturally defined territories. Marsh *et al.* are in some ways correct to describe home territories as 'action facilitating'.[22] But the Oxford group's conceptualization of such territories is restricted to the banks of terracing inside grounds that are populated by the mainly young fans who constitute the home end. By contrast, the Kingy lads – and

this is typical of such groups in the country at large – take exception
to visiting supporters, not only inside the ground during matches, but
virtually anywhere in the town and its environs before and afterwards.
In particular, large groups of away fans who 'walk around town, all
fuckin' cocky like, as if Leicester's fuck all', require to be challenged.
Otherwise, as Brad put it, 'any fuckin' cunt'll do the same, and that's
when your Leicester gets a bad name'. But, of course, as this extension of an estate tradition to the town as a whole clearly shows, it is
not the territory *per se* which is significant in such cases but the lads'
identification with it. In other words, it is their *collective pride* which
is threatened by the rival group and such threats can be experienced
mutually even on 'neutral' territory, as, for example, when two rival
groups encounter each other by chance at a motorway service station.

In attempting to explain their fighting, the lads fell back time and
time again on the claim that visiting 'lads' who travel around Leicester
en masse, or who pack into its pubs, were simply 'asking for trouble'.
Any questioning of the validity of this claim merely invited gestures
of incredulity as befits someone who clearly does not know the score.
Away fans, however, were supposed to understand and were expected
to face the consequences of making what the lads regarded as
unpardonable mistakes or as taking outrageous liberties. When the
bitterly opposed local rivals, Nottingham Forest, arrived to play
Leicester in 1981, for example, even the combined efforts of the
Leicester police and a 'door guard' could not prevent two Forest fans
from taking up residence in the Vines bar. Pat's response when the
two Nottingham lads failed to take his advice that they should both
'fuck off', was to 'glass' one of them across the head with a pint mug.
The Forest fan retired to the infirmary for treatment. For Pat and most
of the Kingsley lads, the episode was put down either to the visitors'
gall or to their recklessness for drinking in the Vines without sufficient 'back-up' to cope with the inevitable 'trouble'. 'They must be
fuckin' divvies,' reasoned Jimmy. 'They must know that the Vines
is a hard pub but they still come in, only a couple of 'em. Fuckin'
crazy!'

The members of some ends visiting Leicester were easier to spot
than others, of course. The visits of clubs like Chelsea, West Ham,
Manchester United and Spurs, for example, had the city centre
swarming with visitors from early in the morning. Clubs like these
fell squarely into the first rank of a rule-of-thumb guide to visiting
factions against whom the Kingsley and their allies would expect to

be fighting something of a rearguard action. In the early 1980s, much to the disgust of the Kingsley and the 'townie' crews who turned out to support them on such occasions, the combined Leicester home end would often disintegrate when faced by visitors such as these. The Kingsley were staunchly defensive of their own fighting prowess but scathingly realistic about the performance of the home end when faced with visiting contingents which had, in Pat's words, 'a bit of class'. These were occasions of frustration and no little serious danger even for the reputable fighters amongst the Kingsley. Desperate to defend their conceptions of local masculine pride and their own local standing as 'formidable hard cases', it was often Kingsley lads like Howie, Pat, Stevie, Nicky, Simmo and Macca, together with the Vines townies, who were left outside the ground shouting at locals to stand as the Leicester end, sometimes up to 400 strong, seemed to melt away in the face of more cohesive and experienced 'mobs'. These were the times to remember Howie's warning that: 'If you go with the bad 'uns, then you'll get kicked to fuck.' 'Bad 'uns', of course, were City fans who followed the Kingsley lads but who were 'on their toes' as soon as the 'rauting' began. Ritchie, for example, was one of a number of City 'hard cases' hospitalized after the visit of Chelsea in 1981. A combined Kingsley-Vines crew, including Liam and a notorious bouncer from a city-centre club, Roy White, were involved in running fights in the city centre and *en route* to the ground. Chelsea fans seemed to have taken over the whole of the west side of the city centre and it was impossible to reach Filbert Street without 'crossing' Chelsea's numerous 'mobs'. The Kingsley lads were torn between emotions of disgust that 'fuckin' Cockneys' were roaming the city, tracking Leicester crews on their own manor, and elation at the prospects of the stirring events that undoubtedly lay ahead. There was something especially exciting about a football situation that was 'getting out of hand'. The lads talked about an 'atmosphere', a 'feeling', when it was clear that the hours to come would involve more than simply the play fights and the 'fucking about' in the seats and stands which often provided the only entertainment at home matches during the club's stay in the Second Division when clubs like Shrewsbury, Charlton and Preston brought with them only handfuls of supporters. These were the 'really boring' games which sometimes had the Kingsley attendance severely depleted and which had those who did attend picking 'domestic rows'. In these situations, crowd falls which disturbed the Kingsley would be used as justification for an attack on members of the home end. Nicky and Pat, for example, led a charge up the terraces on an otherwise uneventful afternoon when Shrewsbury were the visitors. A spot in the crowd at which 'some cunts were fuckin' about' was none too carefully selected and, at their point of arrival, Nicky promptly butted a clearly bemused Leicester fan in the face. As a hole in the crowd opened up to allow whatever fight might develop to take place, Nicky, leading Pat, Ritchie, Jimmy, Macca, Liam and Mark, with an exhilarated Stench in the rear, asked if anybody 'wanted it'. A voice further back on the Kop informed the Kingsley that these were 'all fuckin' Leicester' (hence there was no need to fight), and the Kingsley lads slowly returned to their spot further down to discuss the incident and the extent to which their targets had been 'shitting themselves'. The head-butted fan, in his early twenties, now had a large swelling under his right eye and was seeking treatment from the St John Ambulance Brigade.

Attacks of this kind on fellow Leicester fans or the match-day run-in with a gang from a rival estate which occasionally occurred were generally absent for the visits of clubs like Chelsea. On such occasions, inter-estate and other intra-Leicester rivalries tended to be muted in the face of the massive and threatening outside challenge. As Sammy put it: 'You watch when Chelsea or any of them teams come down. There'll be no rauting in the City end. Every fucker will be after the Cockneys.' Internal divisions would have been suicidal against a set of visiting gangs like those which follow Chelsea. Despite their avowed determination not to be 'run' on home territory, the sheer size of the visiting Chelsea mobs meant that evasive action was sometimes unavoidable, even for the Kingsley and Shortstop crews. Such indignities were not suffered lightly, however, and, having been run, it was important to strike back with whatever means at hand. This usually meant 'bricking' rival crews from a suitably safe distance. An open site behind the south end of the ground provided ample ammunition and, at the time of the research, it was usually not adequately policed. 'Bricking' was dangerous, of course – in many ways more so than hand-to-hand fighting. Milk bottles as well as stones and bricks were used in these aerial bombardments. Sammy had five stitches for a head wound received in a post-match 'bricking' with Nottingham Forest fans in 1981. Brad and Mark took him to the nearby Royal Infirmary for treatment and reported later that they had ended up rauting with a group of Forest fans who were also at the hospital awaiting treatment for 'football-related' injuries.

For the visits of major ends like West Ham and Chelsea, there is more shouting, staring, gesticulating and running than actual fighting. Here, the police are thicker on the ground, the prospects of arrest proportionately greater. The lads, picking up other members of the Leicester end – acquaintances from down-town and elsewhere – stalk the area searching out rival factions and looking for the chance to throw in boots and fists before escaping out of the way of the law. Here, before and after the match, is where most arrests will be made. The police are looking for the chance to get prominent members of the Leicester end off the streets and, when they are 'pissed up', it is not always easy for some of the Kingsley to resist the temptation of threatening or attacking 'provocative' visitors, even under the noses of the police. Simmo, for example, was arrested outside the ground prior to a match with Arsenal for loudly inviting a group of black 'Gooners' to fight whilst a group of police officers who were supervising the entry of Arsenal fans into the ground looked on. Brad and Howie who had been trying to calm Simmo down, had little sympathy. Simmo had acted 'like a silly cunt' and, for that, deserved to get nicked.

Despite the lads' claims that they were drawn into trouble at football by forces beyond their control – mainly, of course, by visiting fans who were 'looking for it' – they grudgingly accepted arrest for fighting and 'bricking' opposing fans as the price they had to pay for defending the home turf and giving City (and themselves) a 'good name'. Everyone, they argued, 'deserves to get done' for fighting sometimes. The lads knew, for example, that whilst 'ordinary' fans might not have been their match-day targets, fights and 'bricking' sessions did frequently impinge upon and frighten people who did not want to be involved. It was for this reason, according to the lads, that football match 'rauting' was *understandably* frowned upon by the authorities. Otherwise, they reasoned, two sets of lads who *want* to fight ought to be allowed to get on with it *without* intervention by the law. In the lads' eyes, however, the police are too quick by half to get involved at football when fans are 'doing nothing'. At home matches, the lads, sometimes fresh from fighting *outside* the ground, were regularly arrested or ejected simply for what they regarded as 'fucking about':

PAT: The coppers, though, they're right bastards. The young ones are the worst.

JW: Why's that?

PAT: I don't know. They just fuckin' nick you for anything now. You've only got to put your arm up . . . in the ground, y'know, and you're threatening behaviour. Fuckin' court on Monday morning. They say, y'know, you've been shouting 'You cunt' and all that and there's fuckin' three of them as witnesses. You've got no fuckin' chance.

HOWIE: That's it. You can't say owt against them, can you? . . .

PAT: It's not so bad though, is it, at away games? The coppers don't bother you so much. I've only been nicked once at away games. We get nicked all the time here. You've only got to walk down the fuckin' street here. Mind you, I deserved to get fuckin' nicked at the away games, like. Fuckin' fighting all over the place. . . . (*laughing*)

Generally, however, inside the ground when City were playing clubs with major ends like Chelsea, the police had rather more to concern them than simply chucking out locals for shouting abuse. On the occasion of Chelsea's visit in 1980, Pat, Howie and Nicky had joined with some of the Vines 'townies' in the Main Stand Enclosure (see Figure 2, p. 160). Here, they were soon in combat with a group of Chelsea infiltrators. The fighting in that section of the ground was sufficiently intense for other fans to spill on to the field, and the match was halted for several minutes while the police returned the Chelsea fans involved – about fifty in all – to the visitors' pens. Meanwhile, in SK3, the rest of the Kingsley, assisted by other estate and pub crews, were involved in repelling the advances of Chelsea infiltrators up the stairwell at the back of the pen. Macca received a bad cut behind the ear for his trouble – probably from a ring worn by an opponent. Once again, the police intervened to clear out the visiting faction. Throughout the match, however, missiles continued to be exchanged between Kopites and the Chelsea crews who, by this time, had begun to specialize in monotonous, moaning chants which sometimes went on for minutes and were completed by Nazi salutes. Despite the black following of the club, Chelsea was harbouring a sizeable racist element within its travelling contingents.

The Kingsley and the Leicester end were 'ready' for the visits of

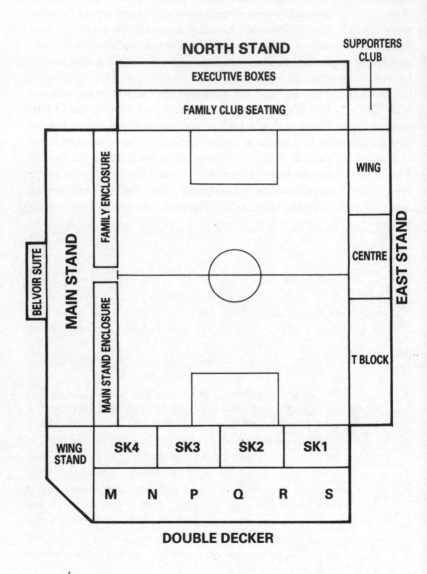

Figure 2 Leicester City Stadium

clubs like Chelsea whose supporters, Mark gloomily admitted, 'shit on City'. The visits by other major ends also promised 'action', though the Kingsley lads recognized stylistic differences between them. Chelsea, for example, brought many small crews, drawn from a wide area. According to the lads, they were 'flash and dangerous'. Chelsea were wreckers and they attracted 'nutters' and, as Merf put it, 'cunts looking to make a name for themselves by getting tooled up'. Chelsea were entertaining, too, of course, because, as far as the lads were concerned, *anything* could happen with Chelsea the visitors. Spurs were a 'mixed' end; 'plenty of niggers'. Blacks needed watching, according to the lads, because of their penchant for 'carrying' (knives). Arsenal fans – 'the Gooners' – were also 'mixed' and, at the time, favoured sheepskin coats. The Arsenal end had 'gone', though. They rarely brought more than 1,000 fans for visits to Leicester in the early 1980s. Liverpool fans – 'Scallies' – would 'have' the Arsenal sheepskins, given half a chance. They were 'tea leaves' (thieves) and also reputed to carry 'blades'. Newcastle fans were liable to be big, beer-bellied and wearing scarves – but good fighters. West Ham, unlike Chelsea, only had one main crew, the Inter City Firm (ICF). At the time (1980–2), core sections of the ICF favoured an uncompromising skinhead haircut and a 'uniform' of jeans and green, zippered combat jacket. The ICF were disciplined and tough. They 'carried' – axes, even – but usually only for purposes of display. They had not, as yet, achieved national recognition via television and the press. But the ICF were already well known around the terrace circuits as a formidable force. They were, in Simmo's words, 'good value'.

The lads eagerly awaited the visits of the major crews. Rumours about the visitors' plans to 'fuck over' Leicester were seized on as a sign that the local end needed to 'plot up' before the event. Such rumours emanated from almost untraceable sources: a mate of a mate who had been in London; 'some kid' who 'knows' the London crews; a mysterious visitor from out of town. Occasionally, however, the source was less enigmatic. A miserable visiting contingent from Charlton passed on a message to the Leicester home end during an otherwise uneventful match at the beginning of the 1981–2 season. The message was that the ICF were planning to turn the city over during their visit in a few weeks' time.

Over the next couple of weeks, the visit of West Ham was rarely out of down-town and estate discussions about events 'down City'. Older townies and the bouncers among the Kingsley were instructed to recruit for the 'forthcoming attraction'. Rumours circulated that the ICF plan was 'to wreck the town' before the match and, largely on this basis, when the day arrived non-footballing townies with local reputations manned likely city-centre targets from opening time. In the event, the ICF, over 100 strong, struck at the Turks Head, a pub on the Kingsley Friday-night circuit situated behind the Leicester market. Glasses and chairs were thrown and windows smashed. Waddo, a townie who had been inside the pub at the time, described the scenes later as resembling a 'wild West fight'. Frustrated at missing out at the Turks Head showdown, the Kingsley were not disappointed by the rest of the afternoon's events. Inside the ground, for example, the two rival contingents on Spion Kop threw missiles at each other almost without respite. Ball bearings, pieces of glass, stones and coins rained into the Leicester pens. Most of the ICF, however, had paid to go into the Double Decker, immediately above the Kop, and it was only on their way out of the ground that they were met by the Kingsley and other Leicester hard cases. The police, by now posted on the streets outside to maintain segregation after the match, seemed completely outflanked as surge and counter-surge up and down the stairwell at the back of the Kop produced hand-to-hand fights under the Double Decker. A single policeman who was manning the stairwell and attempting to keep the rival factions apart with a swirling truncheon, was overwhelmed by the sheer number of visiting fans coming down the stairs. Their ferocity and momentum forced the Leicester contingents outside, sending 'ordinary' fans fleeing away in all directions. The scenes outside the ground were as charged and uncontrolled as they had been against Chelsea. After the Chelsea match, Ritchie had 'dived in' on the black pad – the area behind the Kop – and was swamped by visiting fans. He was kicked about the head so badly that doctors told him he was lucky not to lose an eye. Against West Ham, he got another 'shiner'. Jimmy had badly grazed knuckles, and blood was coming from somewhere on the top of Nicky's head. Macca and Howie were agitated and excited, both visibly shaking. Jacko confessed later to have been 'shitting himself' but unable to leave. Nicky, Simmo and Howie urged the gathering City forces back up into the stand, but the real fighters were heavily outnumbered by young Leicester fans keen to be seen around this exciting incident but less sure about tangling with the ICF. For the Kingsley's part, it was agreed that there were 'too many coppers' on the scene for comfort and that it was best to 'fuck off' and set up ambushes at the back of the ground.

The Kingsley lads enjoyed their football. They enjoyed the camaraderie it brought; the excitement; the shared sense of danger and masculine commitment; the pleasure and honour of standing up for something they felt to be worthwhile – 'having a good name', whether it was of the city, the estate or particular individuals. All the Kingsley lads mentioned in this chapter had convictions, many for football-related offences. Some, like Howie, Macca, Simmo and Pat, had been convicted many times. Some had been in Borstal or to prison as a result. All had been fined. Fines were not easy to pay. Even in weekly instalments, fines were a drain on the resources of lads many of whom were already involved in illegal enterprises for raising money and whose commitment to such enterprises was increased as a result. In other words, far from acting as a deterrent, fines for football-related offences often led to further cime. The 'problem' for the lads was that, in the immediate moment of the football 'day out', the prospects of getting caught and convicted were catapulted into some distant, barely considered future. Lads gave up 'the football' for a wide variety of reasons: financial; marital; a 'stretch inside'; 'growing out' of the football gang. Other Kingsley males moved in to take their place, however, despite changes in the character of the Leicester end. By the mid-1980s, a new terrace force, 'the Baby Squad', was attracting considerable public attention, drawing in young 'hard cases' from estates around the city, including Kingsley. Fashion and planning began to become the new by-words in the emerging terrace order. The old estate solidarities at football were becoming less exclusive. More significant, perhaps, young Leicester blacks began for the first time to involve themselves in football aggro around this time. Despite these developments and much to the lads' pride, voices would still urge 'hard men' on the pitch to deliver their opponents 'a Kingsley kiss' (a head butt). Smig summarized a key aspect of the Kingsley 'philosophy' as follows:

It doesn't make any difference to me how things work out. There ain't nothing you can do about it, is there? I've had some fuckin' good laughs, I have, with all me mates, like. I'm not like you, say. I live more from one day to the next. Nothing fuckin' worries me. I mean, there's no point, is there? If you've got

50p, then you'll spend it. If you've got £50 then you'll spend that an' all. I don't give a fuck, I don't. Y'see, it's different for me, too, 'cos I don't have to worry about me house or me grub or anything like that like you do. I can come back here to me mam and she'll have the tea on the table, won't she? You can't do that. You have to think about those kinds of things. I s'pose, y'know, that I'd like a nice house, me own house p'raps, and a decent job – bricky or summat, but I'm not fucked about anything. I s'pose it's like going to court or something like that. I mean, I like a few pints, I do. Now once I've had a few of those, I don't care what the fuck I do, y'know what I mean? I could go out now and get nicked and it wouldn't fuckin' bother me. All I'd be thinking about is, well, a night in Charles Street, your grub an' that, you'll be all right. I mean, you'd feel a bit worse in the morning when you think, 'Fuckin' hell, I've been nicked again!' And then, when court comes up, you might be shittin' yourself in case you go down. Like Dibbo now is saying, y'know, 'I don't fuckin' care' and all this but when Crown [court] comes along he'll be the fuckin' same. That's how you think about it, isn't it? There's nowt you can do to change it.

NOTES

1   Alan S. York, 'Voluntary Associations and their Leaders on a "Difficult Housing Estate" ', University of Leicester, unpublished MA thesis, 1972, p. 639.
2   A similar point is made by J. White in *The Worst Street in North London: Campbell Bunk, Islington, Between the Wars*. London: Routledge & Kegan Paul, 1986, pp. 31–2.
3   York, 'Voluntary Associations and their Leaders', p. 37.
4   'Inner Area Research Project Social Survey First Report', Centre for Mass Communications Research, University of Leicester, 1981, p. 52.
5   See, for example, Howard Parker, *View from the Boys: a Sociology of Down-Town Adolescents*. Newton Abbot and London: David & Charles, 1974; Owen Gill, *Luke Street: Housing Policy, Conflict and the Creation of a Delinquent Area*. London: Macmillan, 1977; James Patrick, *A Glasgow Gang Observed*. London: Eyre-Methuen, 1973; J.B. Mays, *Growing Up in the City*. Liverpool University Press, 1964.
6   Quoted by York, 'Voluntary Associations and their Leaders', p. 80.
7   See, for example, Parker, *View from the Boys*; Gill, *Luke Street*; Mays,

Growing Up in the City; M. Kerr, *The People of Ship Street*. London: Routledge & Kegan Paul. 1958; and T. Morris, *The Criminal Area*, London: Routledge & Kegan Paul, 1957.

8 Parker, *View from the Boys*, pp. 47–55.

9 This issue is one which is dealt with at some length by Paul Willis, *Profane Culture*, London: Routledge & Kegan Paul, 1978, chs. 3 and 4.

10 Peter Marsh, Elizabeth Rosser and Rom Harré, *The Rules of Disorder*, London: Routledge & Kegan Paul, 1978, p.3.

11 One reason why a new police station in the area seems to have been a priority for the authorities was the high level of crime on the estate. Writing in a *Leicester Inner Area Report* on Kingsley prepared by the City Council in 1978 (p. 12), the Leicester Police referred both to the 'magnitude of the crime problem on the estate' and to the fact that figures on crime in the area were 'indicative of the persistence of offenders, those prosecuted normally being classed as recidivists'.

12 Parker makes a similar observation about the perceptions of the 'Roundhouse Lads', *View from the Boys*, p. 31.

13 S. Daniel and P. Maguire, *The Paint House: Words from an East End Gang*. Harmondsworth: Penguin, 1972, p. 91.

14 J.A. Harrington, *Soccer Hooliganism*. Bristol: John Wright, 1968, p. 10.

15 David Robins and Philip Cohen, *Knuckle Sandwich: Growing Up in the Working Class City*. Harmondsworth: Penguin, 1978, p. 144.

16 *Public Disorder and Sporting Events*, Sports Council/SSRC Report. London, 1978, p. 18.

17 The 'Mad Mob' are a group of older 'townies' (late twenties to late forties) whose activities in the Leicester City centre have almost a mythical status. They are well known to the police and regular city-centre drinkers for their occasionally violent and destructive escapades. At least some of the members of the 'Mad Mob' are Kingsley-based. Typically, they do not become involved in the football action unless, of course, outsiders come across them by accident.

18 A more organised version of these activities is provided by the ICF's 'Under Fives'. See Thames TV's 'Hooligan', Aug. 1985.

19 Marsh *et al.*, *The Rules of Disorder*, concentrate their attentions on the 'Rowdies' who are aged between 12 and 17 years and who constitute, according to Marsh and his colleagues, the most active and vocal participants in terrace life. Perhaps this is one of the reasons why the Oxford group discovered so little violence at Oxford United?

20 Daniel and Maguire (eds), *The Paint House*, pp. 92–3.

21 So, too, do groups like the ICF. (See Thames TV's 'Hooligan'.) Of course, all ends like to regard themselves as something of the 'market leaders' in violent escapades and style. This is perhaps

especially the case for young males from the London area who tend to argue, as a young West Ham fan did in 'Hooligan', that fans from the North might be wearing the same clothes as their London counterparts, but they would still look 'scruffy'.

22   Marsh *et al.*, *The Rules of Disorder*, p. 59.

Chapter Seven

FOOTBALL SPECTATOR BEHAVIOUR AS A EUROPEAN PROBLEM:
Some findings from a collaborative cross-cultural study of the 1988 European championships *

Although spectator problems had occurred at other major football championships, the 1988 European Football Championships were probably the first for which disorders between rival fan groups were actually *predicted* beforehand. Since 1985, English club sides and their supporters have, of course, been banned from European competition. However, the English national side continues to play abroad. Matches involving England in Sweden in 1986 and in Spain and West Germany (Dusseldorf) in 1987, all produced incidents of spectator disorder. In each case, right-wing groups were implicated in the disturbances and English fans were reported as victims of foreign hooliganism and not only as assailants (Williams *et al*, 1989). At the same time, throughout 1986 and 1987 problems of hooliganism were apparently escalating in a number of continental countries, notably in West Germany and Italy, but particularly in the Netherlands. Once again, right-wing organizations were regularly cited for their alleged involvement in promoting hooligan disturbances. There was also some evidence that the English remained the role models for hooligans abroad and that cross-national contacts were growing between hooligan ringleaders from different European nations (Van Limbergen and Walgrave, 1988; Williams *et al*, 1989). Newspaper reports in England just prior to the 1988 Championships described English hooligan 'generals' holding 'summit' meetings with their Dutch equivalents on trains *en route* to West Germany ('Yobs Plot War', *Daily Star*, 11 June 1988). Moreover, continental fans – as well as the English – now showed signs for the first time of *exporting* hooligan behaviour (Williams *et al*, 1989). In this context, the visit of Holland to Wembley in March 1988 was widely billed in the English press as a 'showdown' between Europe's most

*This chapter is based on research supported by the Council of Europe.

167

notorious football hooligans. According to Van Limbergen and Walgrave (1988), *Net Nieuwsblad* on 23 March 1988 described the meeting as promising 'Football War at Wembley'. In the event, few Dutch fans travelled to London for the match and the English fought only among themselves. Van der Brug and Meijs (1988) commented on the 'poor' Dutch turn-out by suggesting that, 'perhaps they [Dutch hooligans] were somewhat intimidated by the thought of meeting the English on their own ground'.

More widespread spectator problems at matches in continental Europe during the 1987–8 season did little to lessen speculation that the 1988 Championships would provide serious crowd-control problems. In England, even sections of the 'quality press' described the tournament as likely to be the context for the 'Hooligan Championship of Europe'. Tabloid newspapers also produced European League tables of hooliganism prior to the Championships, provocatively (for the English) establishing *the Dutch* as European football's worst hooligans (Williams *et al.*, 1989). In February 1988 *Het Volk* carried a report on how the 'hard core' from Feyenoord, Utrecht, Ajax and Den Haag were planning to join forces for the Championships with 'English football fans as the major enemy' (Van Limbergen and Walgrave 1988: 5). Stollenwerk and Sagurski also comment on how, several months prior to the meeting of England and Holland in Dusseldorf, West German TV broadcasts and newspapers began to disseminate 'horror news' on the conflicts to be expected. More generally, they suggest that in West Germany before the Championships, 'The organisers, the police and especially the media showed a distinct tendency to classify the fans of the participating teams according to their potential "dangerousness". The hooligans from England, followed by the Dutch football rowdies, were at the top of these "horror charts" ' (Stollenwerk and Sagurski 1989: 2).

According to more than a half of the sample of England fans whom we surveyed after they had attended the 1988 Championships, newspaper reports in England before the tournament were highly significant in contributing to the spectator disorders which occurred in West Germany (Williams *et al.*, 1988). The influence of the media in shaping expectations about spectator behaviour – and, thus, in shaping the behaviour itself – is also well illustrated by the very *positive* role of the media in Denmark in launching and sustaining the friendly 'roligan' image of Danish fans. The Danish newspapers, *BT* and *Ekstra Bladet*, have played a key role since the mid-1980s in reporting and promoting good behaviour among Danish fans, particularly those who travel abroad (Peitersen and Holm Kristensen 1988). Whilst it has been argued in countries like England that exporting hooliganism may be explained, at least in part, by national decline and associated economic and social problems, in Denmark, the image of the friendly roligan seems to act, instead, as a counterweight to deep-seated economic and social difficulties. In the words of *BT*, for example, 'If the Danes can't do anything else properly, they can at least be the best supporters in the world' (*BT*, 18 June 1988, quoted in Peitersen and Holm Kristensen 1988). It is probably also significant in this regard that Van der Brug and Meijs (1988) make reference to the 'peace offensive' launched by the media in the Netherlands prior to the Championships, a campaign which was designed to rid the Finals of some of their potential for violence.

To summarize: spectator problems involving rival groups of supporters were widely anticipated at the 1988 European Football Championships. They were predicted primarily because of:

1 the hooligan reputations of particular fan groups, especially those from England, but also those from the Netherlands and West Germany;
2 previous incidents of hooliganism at other Championships;
3 'increasing evidence from other countries, as well as from England, of *preparations* for involvement in hooliganism;
4 reported contacts between hooligan ringleaders from a number of European countries;
5 fears about the influence of extreme right-wing groups in orchestrating hooligan outbreaks; and
6 inflammatory newspaper and television coverage prior to the Finals on the likely scale of spectator violence in West Germany.

STADIA, TICKETING, TRAVEL AND ACCOMMODATION

All the stadia used for the 1988 Championships were of modern construction. All offered terracing as well as seated areas. And all were located in open 'green-field' sites which were well served by cheap public transport. Each location also provided more than ample car parking facilities. Major football stadia in West Germany – unlike, for example, most of their English counterparts – are local-authority owned and maintained. They provide facilities for a number of other sports as well as for football. Stadium improvements in preparation for the Championships were reported to have cost the city authorities in West Germany 950 million Belgian francs (£15 million) (Van Limbergen and Walgrave 1988). Although all the stadia used for the Finals had perimeter fencing, a simple pedal release system operated by stewards meant that in the event of an emergency the fences could be quickly removed, providing fans with easy access to the running track and playing surface. All the stadia provided for outer-wall and inner-wall security checks and had self-contained terraced and seated areas. In theory at least, these features should have provided for: the effective segregation of rival fans; precautions against fans attempting to take weapons or missiles into stadia; and the prevention of ticketless fans gaining access. To assist further with segregation, 5 per cent of the total ticket allocation for the Finals was withheld in order to provide some flexibility in ground management for the West German police and stewards. No alcohol was on sale inside any of the Championship stadia. Because of all these features and precautionary measures, we can agree with our research colleagues from Belgium that the 'German stadia gave a very safe feeling' during the Championships (Van Limbergen and Walgrave 1988: 21). It should also be reiterated in relation to this point that all the German stadia offered terracing as well as seated areas. Few problems relating to crowd safety or hooliganism occurred in, or immediately around, stadia during the Finals. This fact can be largely attributed to effective policing, the efficient segregation of rival fans and to the high quality and excellent locations of the stadia used for the 1988 Championships.

Out of 850,000 tickets available for the fifteen matches of the Finals, 240,000 were set aside for distribution through official channels to foreign fans. Some countries took very few tickets. The Soviet Union, for example, had only 145 'official' supporters in West Germany. By way of contrast, the Dutch FA was initially allocated 50,000 tickets for the Finals and eventually acquired 80,000 for distribution among the 420,000 Dutch fans who applied for tickets through the official channels. Fans who applied in this way were required to send in basic data about themselves which were fed into a central computer. This process of registration was disrupted, however, when additional tickets for the Championships began to be sold openly in Zeist (Van Limbergen and Walgrave 1988). Also, because tickets for most matches were easily available in Germany, a thriving 'black market' was always likely to undermine co-ordinated attempts at establishing a watertight registration system designed to exclude hooligans from the Finals.

Van der Brug and Meijs (1988) report that 53 per cent of their sample of Dutch fans bought their tickets from the KNVB (the Dutch FA), with up to a further quarter buying tickets in West Germany. The Dutch researchers confirm that some self-confessed Dutch hooligans did attend the Finals, but were no more likely to use non-official channels for tickets than were non-hooligan Dutch fans. Most estimates put the attendance of Dutch fans at the group matches at between 25,000 and 30,000 per match. There were fewer at the semi-final against West Germany in Hamburg – probably around 18,000, and, 'officially', 25,000 at the Final in Munich. However, many Dutch fans arrived in Munich ticketless, and a substantial proportion of the eighty Dutch arrests associated with the staging of the Final were for offences connected with illegal attempts to acquire match tickets.

Relatively few Dutch fans actually stayed in West Germany between matches. In the main, tickets in the Netherlands seem not to have been sold in association with travel and accommodation packages and the majority of Dutch fans came to the Finals in private cars and vans (55.3 per cent), or on buses hired by their clubs (26.5 per cent). Most of them returned to the Netherlands almost immediately after each match. Ease of access to and from West Germany and the staging of Holland's matches prior to the Final in the northern half of the country were obviously of considerable importance in this respect. By way of contrast, the vast majority of Danish fans (20,000) attended the Finals as part of package trips organized by the fifty-six travel agencies used by the Danish FA for the distribution of match tickets. With some Danish fans buying tickets in West Germany, estimates suggest that up to 30,000 roligans attended Denmark's first match (against Spain) in Hanover and that the numbers were only slightly lower for Denmark's other group matches (Peitersen and Holm Kristensen 1988). Some Danish fans camped or travelled and lived in West Germany in 'mobile homes', but the majority seemed to use hotel accommodation for their stay, with Cologne and the surrounding area serving as the main Danish base.

The English FA initially anticipated demand in England for 12,000 tickets for England's group matches, but scaled this down to a request for 8,500 tickets for the first-phase matches. Applicants for tickets were required, initially at least, to provide comprehensive data about themselves, including a reference, and information about their accommodation arrangements for West Germany. This process was designed to screen out hooligan offenders already on the FA blacklist and to guard against fans living out on the streets in West Germany. FA officials admitted, however, that, as the Finals came closer, it became impossible to check all applicants or to acquire reliable data about applicants' accommodation and travel arrangements. Another aim of the scheme was to limit the numbers of 'maverick' England fans who, on past experience, travel independently without pre-booked accommodation and who are likely to be at the centre of any serious hooligan outbreaks which occur. In the event, the FA sold around 6,000 tickets for each of England's group matches, including around 1,000 to British troops serving in West Germany and between 500 and 1,000 to people 'known' to the FA (county officials, administrators and so on). In addition to these travellers, an estimated further 1,000 'non-official' fans travelled to the Finals, many of whom had neither tickets nor pre-booked accommodation. Numbers in this group probably swelled for the game against Holland in Dusseldorf, when a considerable number of English fans made a 'one-off' trip simply to be present at what was billed as a major 'showdown' between Europe's two most notorious fan groups. English fans at the Championships, then, probably numbered between 7,000 and 8,000. Discounting the Soviet Union, England, along with Spain, probably had the fewest supporters at the Championships. Estimates suggest Irish support to have been around 12,000, with support for Italy judged to be between 20,000 and 25,000, though many fewer Italians obtained tickets for the opening match between their side and the hosts, West Germany.

According to the English FA, none of the thirty-five Englishmen who were charged with offences in West Germany had received their tickets through the official FA channels. The FA claim that none of their accredited fans were involved in hooligan incidents during the Championships, though, given the location and scale of the disturbances in West Germany, this seems unlikely. However, what is clear is that relatively few English fans – around 2,000 only – travelled to West Germany on pre-booked organized packages. Many more, even among the 'official' fans, made their own arrangements for accommodation, food and internal travel when they arrived for the Championships. Indeed, the survey of 'official' England fans suggests that up to 47 per cent of these 'organized' fans had no pre-booked accommodation. Thirty per cent of the sample spent at least one night during their stay for the Finals with no accommodation at all. A substantial minority of these fans spent more than one night 'out on the streets' or sleeping on trains, and one in ten fans in the sample spent three or more nights sleeping 'rough' (Williams *et al*, 1988). Clearly, some of these fans must have been among the hundreds of Englishmen who spent their nights in and around the railway stations of Frankfurt, Dusseldorf and Stuttgart. Others took advantage in Stuttgart of the 'fan camp' specially laid on by the local authorities to accommodate 'homeless' English and, to a lesser extent, Irish fans.

Among the foreign visitors to West Germany, the English alone provided substantial numbers of fans who planned to stay in that country without hotel or camping arrangements and with no real plans to seek out accommodation (although in Stuttgart a small number of young Irish fans did sleep 'rough' and 170 used the fan camp). The fan camp in Stuttgart was used by 630 Englishmen and, at the time of the match against Ireland, it was full to its 800-place capacity. On the evening of the USSR v. Italy semi-final in Stuttgart, when more than 20,000 Italian fans were in the city, only 150 fans used the camp, 'most of them English, Irish and German, together with a few Danes and Italians' (Stuttgart Youth Sports Council, 1989: 3). Many young Englishmen seemed content to drink heavily until the early hours of the morning before grouping together for safety in numbers and to sleep at the local railway station or even in shop doorways. It was by no means unusual to come across drunken young English fans in the early hours in Stuttgart or Dusseldorf who had 'no idea' where they were going to spend the night. Many of them had no sleeping bag or blankets, and cost was clearly a factor which limited the range of options available to them. As the organizers of the Stuttgart fan camp point out, 'The vast majority of English fans who stayed overnight in the camp were young people who, in many cases, came from a very poor background, had little money with them, and were more than content with the simple standard of accommodation in the camp' (Stuttgart Youth Sports Council, 1989: 4). However, it is also likely that at least some of the English fans who favoured the railway station for sleeping outdoors did so beause of the camaraderie and sense of excitement and adventure provided in sleeping out *en masse* in a potentially hostile foreign city. Certainly, their 'arrangements' for 'accommodation' provided a focal point for hooligan outbreaks throughout the English stay in West Germany, and such strategies – and their associated risks and potential for 'action' – have become part of the accepted way for many young working-class Englishmen to follow the national side abroad. That English fans of this sort may not have been looking too hard for accommodation is given some support by the fact that only 14 per cent of the sample of fans in the English survey thought lack of accommodation in West Germany to have been an important contributory factor to hooliganism at the Championships (Williams et al., 1988).

Because of the determination of some English fans to travel independently of contact with official channels and because of the belief which seems to exist among such supporters that ticketless English fans will always find ways into continental stadia, substantial numbers of Englishmen arrived in West Germany, not only with little money and no accommodation, but also with no tickets. The English FA agreed to allow the sale of tickets to such fans for the match in Stuttgart on the understanding that these 'maverick' Englishmen would temporarily surrender their passports and would be segregated from English fans in 'official' parties. No such guarantee was provided in Dusseldorf and, therefore, none of the unsold tickets from the original FA allocation was made available to ticketless fans for the match against Holland. As a consequence, a reported 500 English fans were refused entry to this high-risk game but no serious incidents occurred outside the stadium. In Frankfurt, West German police took the decision to allow the sale of tickets to ticketless English supporters for the 'low-risk' meeting between England and the USSR. Only 14 per cent of the fans involved in the English survey thought ticket arrangements contributed significantly to hooligan problems at the Finals (Williams et al., 1988).

English officials anticipated additional problems from British troops stationed in the Federal Republic. They were likely, it was felt, to purchase match tickets for unsegregated areas of stadia. In the event, a reported nineteen British soldiers were detained during the Championships, and there were no indications that segregation had seriously broken down at any of the three England matches. Our Belgian colleagues report on a number of 'hard-core' fans gaining admission to matches without tickets, and they also express concern about the way in which 'black-market' ticket dealings produced breakdowns in segregation (Van Limbergen and Walgrave 1988). We share their concern about the activities of ticket touts, but favour a more 'balanced' view on the issue of segregation. Many 'low-risk' matches (Spain v. Ireland; Denmark v. Italy; even Holland v. Ireland) were staged at the Championships, with few problems and *without* watertight segregation. Danish fans even vowed to 'take good care' of the 3,000 Spaniards who found themselves among roligans at the match in Hanover (Peitersen and Holm Kristensen 1988). It is probably both unrealistic and, at low-risk games at least, *undesirable* to expect to keep rival fans completely separated inside or outside stadia. In this respect, it is reasonable to agree with Wilhelm Hennes when he told *De Morgen* on 7 June 1988 that 'We can prepare for it, but it is utopian to assume that every form of violence (at the Finals) can be avoided' (quoted in Van Limbergen and Walgrave 1988: 24).

WHO WERE THE FANS AT THE FINALS?

The surveys conducted by our colleagues from the Netherlands were largely aimed at young fans, so it is relatively unsurprising that 83 per cent of the Dutch sample were aged between 17 and 33 years of age. Van der Brug and Meijs also make the point, however, that it was their impression that younger club supporters were under-represented among the Dutch in West Germany. Certainly, compared at least to the English contingent, the Dutch following at the Finals looked highly differentiated in terms of age and class background and, although no females were approached in the Dutch survey, women seemed to constitute at least 10 per cent of the 'Oranje' support. Respondents in the Dutch surveys came predominantly from the Hague, Utrecht, Den Bosch and Deventer and the surrounding area, and were drawn from all kinds of educational backgrounds. Just below half had attended Holland's home qualifying matches, but many fewer had travelled to see the Dutch team play in England. However, the self-confessed hooligans in the Dutch sample showed clear problems in relationships at school with teachers and fellow pupils and they also displayed a 'more relaxed' attitude to the prospects of being unemployed. The Dutch data also suggest that those who claim to be football hooligans are more likely to behave violently in other situations, and that the tendency to commit acts of football hooliganism is positively related to watching matches from the 'club stand' but is inversely related to the likelihood of being a member of a sports club (Van der Brug and Meijs 1988: 23–9).

Van der Brug and Meijs comment that 'Those who watched the matches at the European Championships will have been surprised at the ease with which the Dutch supporters could be identified' (1988: 12). Two out of three Dutch followers, according to the Dutch survey, could be identified by the wearing of orange caps, scarves or badges and/or by carrying 'Oranje' flags. Of those who were identifiable in this way, eight out of ten respondents wore distinctive orange caps, and many younger fans also used orange paint or dye on their faces and hair. The tendency of the Dutch to dress in this form of 'carnival' attire seemed to be increased at the Championship Final in Munich. As is the case with their English and West German counterparts, however, those claiming to be Dutch hooligans were much less identifiable by the trappings of 'Oranje' support. Some (19.5 per cent) were more identifiable as Dutch 'club' supporters, while others eschewed any obvious forms of identification in order, according to Van der Brug and Meijs, to avoid unwanted attention from the police (1988: 13). These Dutch fans, however, were swamped by the kind of support for Holland which, instead, celebrated the associations, songs and costumes of 'Oranje' enthusiasm and commitment.

In terms of the *style* of their support – and this is surprising given the media coverage of fans prior to the Championships – most Dutch supporters in West Germany seemed to have more in common with the Danes than they did with either the English or, indeed, the West Germans (though Van Limbergen and Walgrave (1988: 9) do refer to some provocation – by way of chants and banners – aimed by a number of young Dutch fans against the Germans). The costume and carnival atmosphere associated with 'Oranje' support was clearly echoed by elements of the Danish 'roligan' style. Roligans paid between Kr 6,000 and Kr 12,000 (£550–£1,100) for their 'summer holidays' trip to West Germany. Roligans were easily identified at the Championships by their painted faces, flags, scarves and various red and white hats. There is no mention in the Danish data of equivalents of the 'casuals' of England, Holland and West Germany being among Danish support at the Finals. According to the survey of Danish fans conducted by Peitersen and Holm Kristensen, 15 per cent of Danish support was female, though women make up 45 per cent of the official 'Roligan Association' (1988: 4). The average age of roligans who went to West Germany was 30 but almost one-fifth (19 per cent) of the Danish support was over 40 years of age and almost 3 per cent of the respondents in the Danish survey were 15 years of age or less (Peitersen and Holm Kristensen 1988). The Danish team also seemed to bring with them more female support, more very young supporters and more older supporters than any other visiting nation at the Championships.

The majority of the Danish roligans in West Germany were drawn from the skilled manual and clerical-worker sectors. According to Peitersen and Holm Kristensen (1988), 'The carrier of the roligan movement is the rather well educated fan, who is older, more educated and better trained than the typical hooligan fan'. Of roligans in West Germany 5 per cent were unemployed – a figure below the national average in Denmark – and the Danish data make no mention of hooligans among the official or non-official sectors of Danish support. To summarize the meaning of the roligan phenomenon we can, perhaps, best record the comments of one of Peitersen and Holm Kristensen's interviewees, a 25-year-old male fan who seems to capture much of the roligan philosophy. He observed that, 'A roligan means carnival. . . It's fun and a riot of colours. . . And cosy, I think, and if they [Denmark] win, then it's more fun.'

English support in West Germany was quite different in terms of general attitudes and appearance from that of the Dutch or the Danes. However, it was no less easy to identify, perhaps especially to English eyes. Many English fans sported Union Jack hats, tee-shirts and shorts, and a number brought with them Union Jack flags, often carrying the name of their own club or town. But many, too – perhaps particularly those on a non-official trip – eschewed any 'obvious' associations with England, save for the nuances of the English versions of the 'casual' style. Also prominent among some of the English support were provocative tee-shirts describing the threat posed by English fans to West Germany or, popular in Dusseldorf, those carrying 'matchstick' representations of English fans assaulting Dutch supporters. (A smaller number of Dutch fans wore shirts carrying messages expressing similar sentiments.)

Of those fans in the English survey who were identifiable by home location, 47.6 per cent came from the South-east of England (the London area and its surrounds). The North-west (the Greater Manchester and Merseyside area) provided 14.2 per cent of the sample; the Midlands, 11.0 per cent; and Yorkshire, 8.0 per cent. These data seem to confirm earlier findings on the predominance of fans from the South-east among England followers abroad (Williams et al. 1989). The youngest English fan in our survey was 17 years of age, providing confirmation for our observation that very few English fans in West Germany were in their early teens or younger. That the English contingent at the Finals had few of the gender and generational characteristics typically associated with 'family' support is also suggested by the facts that two-thirds (67.7 per cent) of the survey sample were single, 78.1 per cent were aged between 17 and 33 years (that is, the average age of the English was almost certainly less than the Dutch and Danish fan groups) and only 3.4 per cent of those

English fans who obtained tickets through official channels were females. Add to this the even fewer females and very young and older fans likely to travel 'unofficially', and one has a picture of the predominantly young, male support attracted to following England at the Championships.

Only 2.9 per cent of our English sample were unemployed – around one-half the national average – though unemployed England fans were, arguably, more likely to travel to West Germany 'unofficially'. Of those in work, the bulk (64 per cent) came from skilled manual and lower clerical occupational backgrounds, but 24 per cent of the sample came from social classes 1 and 2 as measured by occupation. These data seem broadly to support the available information on the occupational backgrounds of 'typical' football crowds in England (see Sir Norman Chester Centre for Football Research 1989), though it is important to make the simple methodological point that the unemployed and unskilled workers are likely to be under-represented in a postal survey of the kind undertaken for this research. Of our sample, 5.4 per cent claimed to have paid £100 or less for their entire trip to West Germany, and one-third (32.8 per cent) paid £250 or less for their stay at the Finals. These figures reflect the desire – perhaps the necessity – on the part of many English fans to attend the Finals 'on the cheap'. At the other end of the scale, 4 per cent of the sample paid £1,000 or more for the privilege of being at the Finals.

Finally, 26.7 per cent of our sample had had previous experience of watching the national side play abroad and, despite the ban on English club sides in European competitions, more than one-fifth (21.7 per cent) also claimed to have seen their favourite club side play abroad. Of those who had been abroad to watch football, 58.8 per cent claimed to have witnessed problems involving English fans, with 11 per cent of these specifying West Germany as a country in which they had previously witnessed spectator disorders (Wiliams *et al.* 1988).

Comparable details on the large number of 'unofficial' English fans at the Championships were, of course, extremely difficult to obtain. There is little doubt, however, that members of almost all the major hooligan gangs in England attended the Finals. This was confirmed by English police spotters and newspaper reports as well as by our own observations. At the same time, a number of police anti-hooligan undercover operations in England prior to the Championships probably helped to restrict attendance at the Finals of a number of the more prominent English hooligan 'ringleaders'. Even though cases against hooligan gangs in the London area collapsed prior to the Finals, our contacts suggested that at least some of the fans who had been pinpointed – but not convicted – by these strategies would choose to 'lie low' during the Finals. English security officials are satisfied that relatively few English 'super-hooligans' – some of whom have national reputations – were present in West Germany. One who did slip through the security net – Paul Scarrott, a Nottingham Forest fan – was soon identified by English officials and departed. Scarrott arguably has the sort of characteristics and background that are typical of English hooligan ringleaders in general. He is 32 and has 'Forest' tattooed on the inside of his lower lip. Although by no means unintelligent, he was an early school leaver who was academically unsuccessful. (He left school with no formal qualifications.) He has worked as a farm labourer, builder, skilled labourer and, most recently, as a cable layer. He is rarely unemployed, or in a job for long. He is quick-witted, physically imposing and clearly enjoys the prestige, the challenge and the excitement of being a well-known hooligan (he has thirteen football-related convictions). Scarrott describes himself as an 'English patriot, who would never trust any foreigner'. And he regards the Germans as the only other Europeans with 'any guts or standing' (*Sunday Telegraph*, 19 June 1988). He was arrested in the Old Ascot Bar in Stuttgart while reportedly 'Sieg Heiling' with other English fans under a Nazi flag.

For information on the characteristics of other fan groups in West Germany we must rely largely on press reports and our own impressions. Around 12,000 Irish fans were reported to have made the trip to the Finals – the first major football Finals for which the Ireland team has qualified. Like the Danes, the Irish were notable for the number of junior supporters in their ranks, for the number of older fans among their contingent and for the *family* emphasis in their support. Many of the Irish seemed to be using the occasion to combine a holiday with the opportunity to support the Irish team. Irish couples – sometimes with their children – were frequently seen attending West Germany's tourist attractions in between matches. For many young Englishmen, the Irish were simply 'Mickey Mouse' – that is not 'real' – football fans. The Italians were more identifiably *football* fans than the Irish. They brought fewer very young fans, and included more groups of young men who displayed a very high level of commitment to, and loyal enthusiasm for, the Italian team. However, it was not unusual to see significant numbers of accompanied women at Italy's matches, or to see considerable numbers of well-dressed, clearly affluent older Italian men supporting their country with almost as much intensity and verve as their younger counterparts. Significantly, too, perhaps, many of the Italian parties which grouped outside stadia for photographs under banners advertising the present of Italian 'Ultras' seemed very mixed in terms of the age and social class background of their constituents. Finally, unlike the English, Irish, Danes and Dutch, the Italians seemed little interested in heavy drinking either before or after matches. Nor are we aware of any reports at the Championships of Italian fans being the instigators of serious hooligan incidents. Indeed, after the meeting between Italy and Denmark in Cologne which attracted more than 40,000 visiting fans, the West German newspaper *Kölner Express*, reported on the 'brotherliness' of the rival supporters and that there was 'No thought of rioting or wild street fights, no trace of animosity between fans of the two teams. Instead it was the atmosphere of a public festival' (*Kölner Express*, 18 June 1988).

The same must also be said of the Spaniards who reportedly attended the Finals in much fewer numbers than the Italians, Danes, Dutch and Irish but who also displayed few of the hooligan traits now popularly thought to be associated with the game in Spain. Although West German police made 120 arrests in association with the West Germany v. Spain match in Munich, for example, as far as we can tell it was not *Spanish* fans who were identified as the main perpetrators of any of these incidents. Instead, the Spaniards and their ubiquitous drummer, Manolo, seemed to accept defeat and elimination with disappointment and dignity.

WHAT WERE THE MAIN 'CAUSES' OF THE HOOLIGANISM IN WEST GERMANY?

Perhaps we can begin to answer this question by looking, first of all, at the surprisingly *orderly* behaviour of Dutch fans at the Championships. Why did the Dutch not cause large-scale problems, as they were expected to? Van der Brug and Meijs show that Dutch hooligans did travel to the Championships; that some of them had intended to become involved in hooligan incidents; and that expectations among Dutch fans about the occurrence of hooliganism – particularly against the English and the Germans – were high (Van der Brug and Meijs 1988: 15–19). Van der Brug and Meijs conclude, however, that a number of factors were critical in restricting Dutch hooliganism. First, the KNVB (Dutch FA) launched a 'peace offensive' via the Dutch media prior to the Finals in order to promote a 'positive' attitude among Dutch fans. Second, ten plain-clothes Dutch police officers were sent to West Germany to help with the supervision of 'Oranje' fans at the Finals. Third, most Dutch fans travelled to West Germany in small groups and returned to the Netherlands immediately after matches. Thus, according to the Dutch researchers, Dutch hooligans lacked the cohesion, solidarity and organization of their German and English equivalents. Nor were many Dutch fans around late at night in city-centres when most of the serious disturbances took place. Fourth, Van der Brug and Meijs point to the deterrent effects of the fear among Dutch hooligans of missing important matches in the event of their arrest. Fifth, Dutch hooligans were concealed in, and submerged by, an enormous army of Dutch support which had quite different intentions from their own. In short, the sense of carnival promoted by 'Oranje' support swamped and effectively defused hooligan intent in the Dutch contingent. Finally, Van der Brug and Meijs also point to the 'calm and unprovocative' behaviour of police in Cologne, Dusseldorf and Gelsenkirchen which, in their view, 'undoubtedly had a pacifying effect' (Van der Brug and Meijs 1988: 36).

Van Limbergen and Walgrave (1988) offer the view that Dutch hooligan fans had spent too much time before matches searching for tickets to contemplate trouble-making, and that the success of Holland at the Finals deflected hooligans from the satisfactions that can be obtained from promoting disorders (for example, only ten arrests were made when the Dutch lost to the USSR in Cologne). The Belgian and UK researchers also point out that the Dutch were not entirely blameless during their stay at the Finals. A gang of around 150 Dutch hooligans arrived with clubs and stones, attacked English cars and vans in the stadium car park before the match in Dusseldorf, damaging twelve vehicles. Dutch fans were also involved in small-scale skirmishes with the English before and after the match in that city between their national sides. However, there were few reports of problems involving Dutch and German fans in 'high-risk' Gelsenkirchen (where Holland played Ireland). Nor, apart from small problems inside the stadium, did Dutch and German fans clash seriously before, during and after the highly charged Semi-final meeting in Hamburg. German attentions on that night turned instead to a violent 'political' demonstration against left-wing squatters living near the Hafenstrasse (see Van Limbergen and Walgrave 1988: 15–16). Nor did the thousands of Dutch fans who attended the Final in Munich embark on a 'celebratory riot' in that city. Although many fans remained to toast the triumph long into the night, the occasion was described by Peter Gauweiler of the Bavarian Ministry of the Interior as a 'totally peaceful football festival' (*Kölner Stadt-Anzeiger*, 27 June 1988).

According to Peitersen and Holm Kristensen, no Danish fans arrived in West Germany intent on hooliganism; quite the opposite. Danish fans seemed determined instead to add to the UNESCO fair play award they had won at the Championships in France 1984. In this sense, our Danish colleagues argue that the 'atmosphere' and sense of 'community' which foreign hooligans experience in their disorderly activities, is replaced for the Danes by forms of singing and yelling which signal the *rejection* of violence at matches involving Denmark (1988: 15). The determination to promote and sustain this *positive* image of Danish fans also involves a considerable amount of self-policing. As one 18-year-old male roligan commented:

> (C)learly there exists a form of keeping control inside the group among the supporters, because we could feel it. If anybody tried to kick up a row, then somebody said they should calm down. . . We have to keep up the image. In that way, it's nice to go to away matches.
>
> (Quoted in Peitersen and Holm Kristensen 1988: 10)

Nor was the behaviour of the Danes moved much to violence by drink. Along with the Irish and the English, the Danes were undoubtedly the biggest drinkers among the visiting contingents, some young roligans drinking themselves near to incapacity before matches. Although Van der Brug and Meijs found a positive relationship between drug and alcohol use and hooliganism among their sample of Dutch fans, there were few signs in West Germany of excess alcohol consumption producing violent disorder almong roligans or between Danish fans and rival supporters. As an older roligan told Peitersen and Holm Kristensen: 'A roligan is a guy who can drink fifteen beers and have fun, and we lose the match and then he continues having fun. That means fun all over' (male roligan, 45 years, quoted in Peitersen and Holm Kristensen 1988).

Broadly speaking, Irish fans in West Germany seemed to have a similar attitude to the Championships – and to drink – as the Danes. However, relations between the Irish and the English provided a 'political' sub-text lacking in relations between the Danes and supporters of other qualifying nations. This meant mutual provocation along the loyalist – republican axis which sometimes spilled over into 'trouble' in both Stuttgart and Cologne. It is probably fair to say, however, that most of the provocation which was intended to cause disorder was initiated by the English rather than the Irish. It is significant, for example, that the only serious problems involving the Irish in Cologne occurred when, according to the *Kölner Express*: 'For over one and half hours, the English rowdies laid into Irish fans and harmless tourists. They threw stones, hurled tables at windows and stabbed the defenceless Irish with knives. Twenty hooligans were arrested' (15 June 1988).

All the above arrests were English and, as far as we can tell, the only serious difficulties which took place between rival fans in Cologne occurred when *English* fans passed through the city. Englishmen also constituted the vast majority of those arrested during their stay, along with the numerically superior Irish, in Stuttgart. Away from the English, Irish fans showed a willingness to integrate with supporters from other countries and received an almost uniformly good press in West Germany. According to landlords in Cologne, for example, their Irish guests were 'very quiet and disciplined' resorting to unruliness rarely and only when 'English fans provoked their island neighbours' (*Köln Stadt-Anzeiger*, 15 June 1988).

The English, unlike the Danes or the Irish, were expected to be at the centre of hooligan problems in West Germany. Like the Danes, too, they largely fulfilled what was expected of them, but perhaps not in ways which were entirely predictable. In Stuttgart, save for one brief and small-scale missile attack by young Germans outside the main railway station, there was little potential fighting opposition for the English. There were 'political' attractions in confronting the Irish, but little evidence of large groups of young Irish fighters willing to take up the challenge. Instead, the weekend in Stuttgart involved routine (by English standards) damage and drunken excess, along with a number of random attacks by English fans on locals and Irishmen, plus a number of overtly right-wing and racist demonstrations linking loyalist politics with neo-fascist sympathies. Most of these exhibitions of extremism seemed to be orchestrated by English fans drawn from in and around the London area. Demonstrations of this kind could be found wherever the English appeared during the Finals, but they probably reached some sort of peak in Frankfurt when hundreds of English supporters appeared to be responding with fascist salutes to the national anthems at the match against the USSR. Despite these activities, however, only 12.4 per cent of our sample of English fans thought that the actions of political organizations were a significant factor in the spectator disturbances at the Finals. Many more (59.5 per cent) highlighted drink as a major ingredient in hooligan encounters (Williams *et al.* 1988).

Heavy but sensible policing, coupled with the accommodation provided at the fan camp which kept many young Englishmen off the streets in the early hours of the morning, helped to limit most of the disturbances in Stuttgart. Nevertheless, two nights in the city brought a reported 110 arrests, 85 of them of English fans. Most of the remainder were of young Germans who were involved in the railway station incident. The Stuttgart police declared themselves largely satisfied with their plans to curb damage and disorderliness (*Stuggart Zeitung*, 13 June 1988).

Many of the incidents which occurred at the Championships were undoubtedly unpleasant. However, they hardly merited headlines like 'World War III', which appeared on the front page of the English tabloid newspaper the *Sun* on Monday, 13 June. Indeed, many non-hooligan England fans in West Germany were already becoming enraged by English newspaper coverage of events at the Finals, as well as by the near-constant attentions of British and foreign film crews and journalists. Long before the end of the tournament, the latter were being physically attacked by English fans who claimed their reporting was biased and provocative. Some fans also claimed that journalists were trying to bribe the English into causing trouble in order to fill news space back in Britain (Willaims *et al.* 1988). Significantly, almost one-half (48.2 per cent) of our sample of England fans who were present at the Finals thought the behaviour of cameramen and journalists in West Germany were significant factors in causing hooligan problems during the Championships.

The English moved north to Cologne and Dusseldorf after the defeat by the Irish in Stuttgart. The problems of hooliganism associated with their stay in Germany moved with them and intensified. Lacking the provision of a fan camp, new arrivals in Dusseldorf gathered, for reasons of familiarity, safety and group strength, around the main railway station. At around 9 p.m. on the evening before the match against Holland, on 15 June, around 150 Germans, including right-wing skinheads from the extremist 'Gelsenszene' (Schalke) and the 'Borussiafront' (Dortmund), arrived unexpectedly from the peaceful

West Germany match against Denmark which had been played in Gelsenkirchen. This was clearly a premeditated arrangement involving two of West Germany's most notorious rival fan groups drawn from the tough industrial areas of the Ruhr. It was also one which seemed completely to outflank the West German police. Armed with stones, the Germans drove through the railway station smashing windows and furniture. English and German fans then fought a running battle from the railway station to Dusseldorf's Altstadt, smashing windows and seriously damaging or wrecking cars. In the Altstadt itself the violence and destruction escalated as more German fans arrived, returning by bus from Gelsenkirchen (Van Limbergen and Walgrave 1988: 12), and more Englishmen were drawn into the fight. Bars were wrecked as chairs and bricks were thrown through shop fronts and rival fans charged after one another through the crowded, narrow streets. By this time, the English had begun to get the upper hand and looting began to take place. As riot police took control of one street, problems quickly burst out elsewhere, and it was the early hours of the morning before the situation was finally brought under control. By this time, a reported 130 fans had been detained, 95 of them English. Estimates of the costs of the damage caused on the night ranged from £150,000 to £500,000.

Prior to the Championships, West German 'hooligan' magazines had been urging local fighters to 'Move actions to places where we are not playing. Hunt them [foreign hooligans] down throughout the country. We call upon all [German] rowdies to repel this invasion' (quoted in Van Limbergen and Walgrave 1988: 11). This temporary alliance between rival hooligan groups also mirrors patterns identified by research on hooliganism in England (Dunning *et al.* 1988). Van der Brug and Meijs report that interviews with German hooligans in Dusseldorf showed them to be 'hardly interested' in confrontations with their Dutch equivalents (1988: 18). Instead, German hooligans seemed almost totally absorbed by the prospects of testing their strength against the 'professionals' from England, and, in doing so, attempting to ensure that 'The world will finally know where West Germany lies' (from an interview with a West German hooligan in *Stern* magazine, quoted by Van Limbergen and Walgrave 1988: 9). Of our research sample of English fans, 69.3 per cent indicated that, for them, the *reputation* of the English was a highly significant factor in contributing to the hooligan disorders in West Germany. Almost three-quarters of the sample (74.3 per cent) also picked out 'provocation of the English by foreign fans' as being highly significant. (This was the most popular contributory factor of all for our sample.) However, 56.1 per cent of the sample also conceded that 'some English fans looking for trouble' was a very important factor in stimulating disturbances during the Finals. As a senior English security official put it, 'The "problem" with the English is that when they are provoked they don't run, they respond' (interview with the authors). There is little doubt that, although many of the problems in Dusseldorf may have been initially triggered by the actions of German fans, there were more than enough Englishmen present who were both willing and able to respond and, eventually, to escalate the disturbances to a level of considerable seriousness.

On the morning of the England v. Holland match in Dusseldorf, German police swamped the area around the main railway station and effectively sealed it off for local people. Most of the bars in the Altstadt were closed as proprietors cleared up the wreckage of what some of them were describing as a 'war' between rival fans. Most bars in the city closed at 1 p.m. by police order. Hundreds of English fans were hemmed in around the station by similar numbers of German police, some with dogs. Small, mixed groups of 'Oranje' fans arrived at the station, largely without incident. The arrival of groups of German 'casuals' however, provoked numerous disturbances in the streets around the station as pockets of Englishmen escaped the police cordon and attempted to fight with the new arrivals. These incidents were small-scale but covered a wide area. In fact, the vast majority of the 371 twenty-four-hour detentions made by the police on the day of the match involved the precautionary removal of large groups of young Germans from Cologne and the Ruhr area who were making their way, ticketless, to the Rheinstadion.

At the stadium itself, opportunities for confrontations between English and Dutch fans were rare. In fact, the main sentiment being expressed among members of the English 'firms' who wandered around the stadium after the match was that of frustration: first, because of the vast numbers of German police who were on the ground to maintain order; and, second, because of the 'disappointing' show by Dutch hooligans who were difficult to find and, apparently, uninterested in causing trouble.

Around the main station area in Dusseldorf after the match, there were more opportunities for clashes between downcast English fans and young Germans, some of whom continued to show themselves to be 'very game' (willing to fight). There were few signs of Dutch fans staying in Dusseldorf to toast their country's success. For Van Limbergen and Walgrave (1988: 13) the English and German fans involved in these incidents were sometimes indistinguishable because of their adoption of common elements of style. To English eyes, however, German 'casuals' were typically younger, wore their hair longer and their jeans shorter than their English equivalents. There were also few skinheads among the ranks of the English. Once again, fights spread over a wide area – some of them serious – as small groups of fans chased one another with the police usually in close pursuit. With bars in the Altstadt and elsewhere in the city closed, the police eventually re-established control over the station area. As the situation quietened, many English fans decided to catch trains to Frankfurt for the final group match against the USSR. Others, with the England team almost certainly eliminated from the Championships, headed for home. The centre of Dusseldorf could return, once again, to normality. 'It was bad,' concluded Bernard Abetz, an official responsible for public order, sport and transport in Dusseldorf, following the English departure from the city. 'But they [the media] gave the impression that Dusseldorf was burning, which was totally untrue. . . We have the same problem in Germany, and we expected worse from the Dutch fans' (quoted by the *Daily Telegraph*, 17 June 1988).

While the West German authorities seemed to be underplaying the obvious problems in Dusseldorf, sections of the British press and the British Government were continuing to recommend the withdrawal of the England team – and their violent followers – from the Finals. Meanwhile, in Frankfurt a (by now) familiar story was already beginning to unfold. Drunken Englishmen were involved in displays of extreme 'patriotism', spilling over into attacks on local people and on vehicles and bars in the 'red light' area of the city, near the railway station. On this occasion, members of the local skinhead neo-Nazi Adlerfront were reported to be trying to establish cordial contacts with their English 'colleagues'. Instead, they were reportedly greeted only with violence by West Ham and Chelsea fans (the *Guardian*, 18 June 1988). Van der Brug and Meijs were convinced that non-violent international contacts between hooligan ringleaders from different countries were of little or no importance as far as the European Championships were concerned (1988: 37). There is much to support this view though, given the recent evidence on the international spread of hooligan networks, it is perhaps a little too soon to agree totally with our Dutch colleagues that such contacts should be more generally regarded as unimportant. In any case, during a weekend of violent and destructive late-night disturbances in Frankfurt, police made a reported 170 detentions, most of them of Englishmen.

Statistical data on detentions and arrests during the Finals as a whole reveal an interesting and significant pattern. More than 1,200 fans were detained during the Championships, of whom 370 were English and more than 800 Germans. Many of these detentions were precautionary, and very few fans were charged with specific offences. In some cases, for example, large numbers of young Germans were removed from the streets (especially in Dusseldorf) simply to prevent them making contact with the English. This is one of the reasons why young German supporters dominate the list of detainees. This approach also meant that most of the English fans arrested or detained in Stuttgart, for example, were back on the streets again in Dusseldorf or Frankfurt. What is striking, though, is that approximately two-thirds of the detentions at the Championships were made in connection with incidents involving English fans. Moreover, although England provided only around 3 per cent of the ticket-holders for the Finals, English fans constituted over 30 per cent of the total number of detainees and, almost certainly, an even higher proportion of those actually arrested or detained for hooligan behaviour. Finally, although hooligan incidents *not* involving the English did occur in West Germany, we can find no example of a serious clash between fans from different countries which did *not* involve the English, either as targets or perpetrators.

One of the reasons why the English were so prominent in hooligan incidents in West Germany was undoubtedly because of the focus they provided for provocation by young Germans who wanted to challenge the position of the English as the 'hooligan champions' of Europe. At the same time, however, English hooliganism occurred – especially in Stuttgart, Frankfurt and Cologne – which was not provoked by German actions, and many other problems were prevented only by alert and very heavy policing. Indeed, rather than rely on a 'head count' of arrests and injuries as a means of measuring the relative 'hooligan performances' of the visiting fan groups, it is perhaps more helpful to contrast the often hostile, offensive and 'isolationist' demeanour of many – but not all – young Englishmen in bars and on the streets in West Germany, with the sense of carnival, cosmopolitanism and collective enjoyment which seemed much more characteristic of visiting contingents from other countries. This seems, at least in part, to reflect a specific form of patriotic association among the English fans which on many occasions made explicit links between 'good support' for one's own country and open hostility towards, or violent disregard for, supporters from other countries. Of the survey sample of English fans, 38.7 per cent thought 'English patriotism' to have been highly significant in causing disturbances in West Germany. A quotation from a young English fan – one who is clearly not typical 'hooligan fodder' – may serve to illustrate this general point more clearly. He commented:

> I would like to tell you exactly how I felt while on the trip to Germany. . . [W]hilst away representing my country, England, I had one of the biggest 'buzzes' of my life. I thought I was at war for them. The adrenaline that was pumping through my body, aching with the pride from the moment we landed, was something I have never experienced in my life before. . . It was better than sex or winning the pools.
>
> Within about an hour of leaving the station at Dusseldorf, about eight of us encountered about 15 Holland fans, all older and a lot bigger than us. They were singing that they were going to 'do' England (in very good English). In England, you wouldn't have fancied having a go [fighting] but because we were representing our 'queen and country' we ran straight at them and they were gone. . . Looking back, my friends and family would be ashamed of the things done in Germany.
>
> (26-year-old 'financial adviser', quoted in Williams *et al*.
> 1988: 3)

POLICING THE CHAMPIONSHIPS

Policing any major international football tournament these days is a costly affair. Especially given the predicted problems in West Germany, the 1988 European Championships were likely to be no exception. Costs for policing the Finals have been estimated as exceeding DM35 million or £11.5 million. (As a point of comparison, DM42 million, or £14 million, was raised from ticket sales at the Finals.) Some matches required extremely large police commitments. For example, a reported

3,800 officers of the Bavarian police and the Federal Border Guard policed the Championship Final in Munich. At least 2,500 were on duty on the streets for the 'problem' match of the Championships, England v. Holland in Dusseldorf. Many more were required inside the stadium. Extra police were also needed, of course, to cope with disturbances and misbehaviour *between* matches. In addition to these very large groups of local officers, a small number of policemen from the Netherlands and England travelled out with supporters from their respective countries to offer advice on policing and to provide channels of communication between fans and the authorities. In these activities they seemed to be reasonably successful.

In dealing with potentially troublesome fans, the German police were aided by laws which allow for the detention of persons for twenty-four hours without charge. This meant that potential confrontations, particularly between English and German fans, were sometimes avoided simply by removing one group of fans from an area. In addition to this, the so-called 'burring' approach to policing – that is, sticking to fan groups like a burr – was also effective in sometimes preventing noisy, drunken groups of (particularly English) fans from getting involved in serious hooligan activities. As Van Limbergen and Walgrave point out (1988: 18), the police strategy in between matches was to avoid creating the impression that many police were in attendance by having reinforcements standing close by but out of sight of potentially troublesome fan groups. The police motto was 'Keep in touch', which meant that large numbers of officers could be rushed to trouble spots very quickly with maximum impact but minimum provocative presence.

Van Limbergen and Walgrave also report that 'certain foreign police observers agreed that the German police pushed back limits of what was tolerable too far at certain points' (1988: 26). Arguably this judgement is too harsh. Certainly, Dutch fans at the Championships seemed to have had an extremely positive view of German policing. Most of the sample of supporters in the Dutch survey thought the German police had behaved better or as well as police in the Netherlands (Van der Brug and Meijs 1988: 22). Similarly, English fans, though not without complaints about policing, did not typically rate the behaviour of the German police as a significant factor in causing disturbances at the Championships (see Figure 3). On the whole, policing at the Finals seemed heavy but sensitive. With the exception of the lack of intelligence about German hooligans

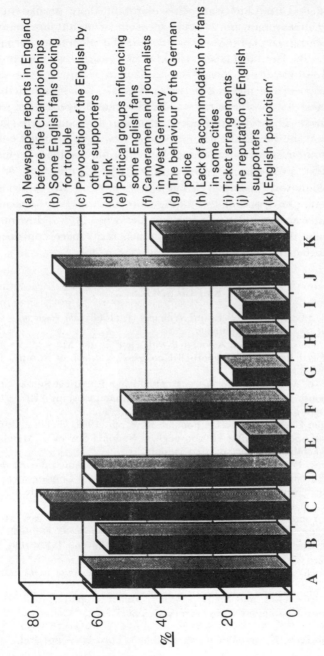

(a) Newspaper reports in England before the Championships
(b) Some English fans looking for trouble
(c) Provocation of the English by other supporters
(d) Drink
(e) Political groups influencing some English fans
(f) Cameramen and journalists in West Germany
(g) The behaviour of the German police
(h) Lack of accommodation for fans in some cities
(i) Ticket arrangements
(j) The reputation of English supporters
(k) English 'patriotism'

Figure 3 Factors rated by English fans as being highly significant in contributing to crowd problems in West Germany

travelling to Dusseldorf from Gelsenkirchen, there seemed to be no major mistakes in police deployment and communication. Nor did police strategies contribute to outbreaks of hooliganism. Perhaps, however, the German police might have anticipated earlier the political motivations of those German fans in Hamburg who used the occasion of the meeting between West Germany and Holland as a pretext for a violent riot in the city centre against left-wing sympathizers. These examples notwithstanding, the hooliganism which occurred at the Finals should not, in our view, be attributed either to inert or to over-zealous policing. Indeed, it may be more useful in this context to consider the words of *Der Spiegel* when it wrote on 20 June 1988 that in Dusseldorf '2,300 officers were on duty protecting the city; in the space of two days, more than 500 rowdies were temporarily arrested. No one has any idea what to do. How many police, how many truncheons, how much fan supervision does a European Championship require?'

REFERENCES

Dunning, E.G, Murphy, P.J. and Williams, J. (1988) *The Roots of Football Hooliganism*. Routledge.

Hahn, E. (1989) 'Violence Associated with Sport in the Mass Media and its Impact, Especially on Football Hooligans', Council of Europe, T-RV (89) 6.

Peitersen, B. and Holm Kristensen B. (1988) 'An Empirical Survey of the Danish Roligans during the European Championships "88"' , The Danish State Institute of Physical Education.

Sir Norman Chester Centre for Football Research (1989) 'Football and Football Spectators after Hillsborough: a National Survey of Members of the Football Supporters Association'.

Stollenwerk, H. and Sagurski, R. (1989) 'Spectator Conduct during the 1988 European Football Championships with Special Consideration of Pertinent News Coverage in the Printed Media', Paper for the Council of Europe.

Stuttgart Youth Sports Council (1989) 'Euro Fan Camp, Stuttgart, 10–13 June, 20–23 June 1988 on the Occasion of the European Football Championships in West Germany', Council of Europe T-RV (89) Misc 7.

UEFA (1988) *Report on the 6th European Football Championships in the Federal Republic of Germany, 1988*.

Van der Brug, H.H. and Meijs, J. (1988) 'Dutch Supporters at the European Championship in Germany', Paper for the Council of Europe.

Van Limbergen, K. and Walgrave, L. (1988) 'Euro '88: Fans and

Hooligans', Youth Criminology Research Group report commissioned by the Belgian Minister of the Interior.

Williams, J., Bucke, T. Dunning, E.G, and Murphy P.J. (1988) 'English Football Fans at the European Championships, 1988', Sir Norman Chester Centre for Football Research. Paper prepared for the Council of Europe.

Williams, J., Dunning, E.G. and Murphy, P.J. (1989) *Hooligans Abroad*. Second edition, Routledge.

Chapter Eight

WHY ARE THERE NO EQUIVALENTS OF SOCCER HOOLIGANISM IN THE UNITED STATES?

There is an idea which frequently surfaces in Britain and other European countries, especially when the subject of soccer hooliganism is being discussed. It is the idea that, even though the United States as a society is, according to most measures and in most respects, considerably more violent than its Western European counterparts,[1] it nevertheless has sports spectators who are almost uniformly orderly, well-behaved and peaceful. In Britain at least, this idea is sometimes mobilized to support the demand for all-seater stadia. American spectators are better behaved, it is argued, because most of them sit down. In other words, seated spectators are supposed to be less aggression-prone than those who stand or, as a slightly more sophisticated variant of the argument proposes, seated spectators are supposedly easier to control.[2] In either case, this rather simple-minded idea is exploded if it can be shown that American sports spectators are not as orderly and peaceable as they are often supposed by Europeans to be.

Not only are sports in the United States largely free from spectator violence, or so the argument runs, but America has never had a tradition of sports-spectator violence comparable to soccer hooliganism, a phenomenon which was once wrongly believed to be specific mainly to England but which is currently showing clear signs of developing as a pan-European phenomenon.[3] This chapter is devoted to an exploration of some of the problems that are posed by the attempt to analyze sports-spectator violence cross-culturally. We shall start by considering some theoretical issues. We shall then draw together the fragments of data that are currently available which permit the construction of a preliminary account of the structure and development of sports-crowd violence in the USA. It is hoped that this will yield

194

insights into the similarities and differences that exist between the generation of sports-crowd violence on either side of the Atlantic. It is hoped, too, that it will serve as a stimulus for more detailed and systematic cross-cultural research into such issues than has been undertaken hitherto. Moreover, with the 15th World Cup Finals scheduled to take place in the United States in 1994, such an analysis may perhaps be of some practical, policy relevance as well.

Apart from the pioneering work of Michael Smith[4] and that undertaken more recently by Kevin Young,[5] no one to our knowledge has yet attempted to carry out serious comparative research on sports and sports-crowd violence in Europe and the USA. The different forms, structures and organizational patterns of American and European sport may have acted as an inhibitory factor in this regard. So, too, may the tendency to see the nation-state as equivalent to 'society' or the 'social system' and, correspondingly, simply to explore problems that arise within the boundaries of one's own nation-state.[6] In other words, it seems that there is a failure at present to see the value or relevance of cross-national and/or cross-cultural comparisons. In suggesting this, we are not for one moment attempting to deny the very real difficulties that cross-national research is liable to encounter. We are, though, suggesting that such investigations are a potential source of new and fruitful insights, insights which may come simply by looking at familiar problems from a different angle. We are also suggesting that the need for studies of this kind appears to be especially urgent at the present time given the process of 'globalization' which is currently occurring. This urgency is, perhaps, especially acute regarding sports because globalization is conducive to the diffusion around the globe of different national sport forms and is thus likely to involve intense competition between their proponents.

The World Cup Finals of 1994 may well prove to be of considerable significance with regard to this competitive process. If, for example, they pass off peacefully, the cause of soccer in the USA is likely to receive a considerable boost. If, however, they provide a stage for the enactment – for the first time in the United States – of 'European-style' soccer hooliganism, then soccer in America may receive a serious set-back in its attempt to gain a more secure foothold in competition with such more deeply rooted native forms as the gridiron game.[7] This suggests that, if for no other reason, the comparative analysis of European and American patterns of sports-crowd violence is an issue of more than simply 'academic' interest. But let us look critically at what is, so far as we know, the only attempt that has been made so far to approach some of the issues involved theoretically; namely, the work on 'aggro' or 'ritual violence' of the psychologist Peter Marsh.[8]

SOME CRITICAL OBSERVATIONS ON THE THEORY OF 'RITUAL VIOLENCE'

As Marsh conceptualizes it, 'aggro' is a socio-cultural equivalent of the forms of ritualized intra-specific fighting observed by ethologists such as Lorenz[9] in many animal species.[10] However, whilst according to the ethologists such animal fights are instinctively restrained, human aggro in Marsh's view involves learned, socio-cultural restraints. Specifically regarding the United States, he argues that such rule-governed, ritualized and socially constructive forms of fighting have failed to develop. Here is how Marsh puts it:

> Looking for aggro in American history is like looking for the proverbial needle in an equally proverbial haystack. Even today, Americans find the concept difficult to handle. They have little experience of it and little in their past to give them any idea of the principles on which it is based. All of which might go some way towards explaining why the USA is in such a violent mess.[11]

Implicit in this argument is a possible explanation for the absence of equivalents to soccer hooliganism in the United States. That is the case because, according to Marsh, soccer hooliganism is one of Britain's principal forms of aggro. Given the absence of aggro traditions in the USA, or so it is reasonable to deduce from Marsh's arguments, it is unlikely that phenomena such as soccer hooliganism could or ever will develop there. In other words, contrary to the common American perception, soccer hooliganism in Britain and other European countries does not provide evidence of a 'counter-civilizing process', of some kind of 'de-civilizing' reversal. On the contrary, at least as March sees it, since they usually involve only violence of a ritualized and socially constructive kind, aggro in general and soccer hooliganism in particular are evidence of the more 'civilized' character of countries such as Britain. It is the United States which is *really* 'uncivilized' or which, in Marsh's words, is in a really 'violent mess'.

According to Marsh, with respect to violence America is unique. He sets forth his reasons for reaching this judgement in the following

words: 'The history of violence in America,' he says, 'is quite unlike
the history of violence elsewhere in the world. It reflects what can
happen when men set out to radically reshape their modes of living
and attempt to create new worlds from scratch.'[12]

The pioneers, Marsh continues, did not migrate to what became
the United States as tribes or communities but as individuals fired by
personal ambitions and Utopian dreams. As such, '[t]hey came without
social order and, from very early on, the order of nature was devalued
by the fact that guns were in the hand of every man and boy.'[13] In
that context, what Marsh calls 'unstructured mob violence' was
developed and the only means available for combating it was the almost
equally 'unstructured' vigilante tradition. In Marsh's words, once
more:

> The makeshift response to violence within the early American
> communities was to throw up various bands of vigilantes who were
> charged with the unenviable job of trying to introduce some sense
> of order and peace. But if anything, they probably made the situa-
> tion worse. In fact, Americans now suffer not only from the frontier
> tradition but also from the vigilante tradition which still finds its
> expression in the outrageous thuggery of groups such as the Ku
> Klux Klan.[14]

We are not entirely lacking in sympathy for this position. There
is reason for believing that attempts to create 'Utopias' can unintentionally have destructive consequences. There is also reason to believe
that attempts to purge human relations of violence entirely can unintentionally produce the opposite effect. That said, however, Marsh's
overall argument about violence in the USA seems to be the result
of over-generalization, first on the basis of what is on the whole a rather
inadequate theory, and second from data that are rather sketchy and
limited in scope. Where is his evidence, for example, that America
is *unique* regarding violence? Would one not expect it to display certain
similarities in this respect to other, originally colonial societies such
as Australia, Canada, New Zealand and South Africa? (We have
deliberately eschewed reference to Hispano-Catholic societies in this
connection in order to 'control' for culture and religion.) And is it
useful to compare the history of the United States since the seventeenth
century with the histories of European societies over exactly the
same stretch of time? Would it not be more appropriate from the
standpoint of comparative-developmental analysis, more a case of

comparing 'like with like', to compare US history since that century with European history over a longer period of time? If one does that even superficially, it becomes clear that the United States in the seventeenth, eighteenth and nineteenth centuries was a society at a stage of state formation in some ways comparable with that in Western Europe in the Middle Ages. There, too the state was weak and it was common for people to carry arms. Medieval Europe also experienced recurrent blood feuds and witnessed the regular formation of mobs and 'vigilante' gangs (for example, the English institution of the 'hue and cry'). Unlike the United States, however, the medieval societies of Western Europe were ruled by warriors and experienced frequent bloody wars.[15] By contrast, the United States has never been subject exclusively to military rule,[16] and the dominance there from early on of bourgeois groups helps to explain the 'hegemonic' force in America of *laissez-faire* values. That, in its turn, helps to explain why the American state has failed to penetrate as deeply into the social fabric as has been generally the case in Western Europe and why groups who campaign for the right of individuals to carry arms remain much more powerful than their European counterparts. However, perhaps the central weakness of this application of Marsh's theory is that he fails to consider the elements of 'aggro' that have been so amply documented in the behaviour of street-gangs in the United States. Perhaps the greater levels of violence they are known recurrently to engage in led him to fail to take them into account? Nor – and this is equally surprising – does he consider sport as a form of 'aggro'; that is, as an arena within which aggressive behaviour can, within certain limits, be canalized and expressed in a controlled and socially constructive way.

Let us sum up the argument so far. We have suggested that Marsh's application of an a priori theory is not very helpful for illuminating the similarities and differences between the forms and levels of sports-crowd violence in Europe and the United States. A critical examination of this application of his theory, though, does suggest that differences in the processes and trajectories of state formation on either side of the Atlantic may offer some useful clues in this regard. But let us become more empirical. Our first task in this connection is to provide a preliminary account of the structure, dynamics and history of sports-crowd violence in the USA.

THE STRUCTURE, DYNAMICS AND HISTORY OF SPORTS-CROWD VIOLENCE IN THE USA: A PRELIMINARY DIAGNOSIS

The account which follows is not based on systematic, primary research. Rather, it has been drawn together from a limited number of secondary sources and supplemented by reference to such newspaper material as has come to our attention. We shall start by recounting some comments of a rather general kind.

As late as 1968, Goodhart and Chataway were able to write that 'In America which is so often characterized as a land bubbling with violence, sporting hooliganism, apart from racial disturbances, seems to be largely unknown.'[17] The 'racial disturbances' they were referring to were evidently the fights between black and white youths which led to the banning of high-school 'night matches' in many parts of the USA.[18] Apart from these, they argued, crowd troubles at US sports events were few and far between. However, less than ten years after Goodhart and Chataway made their pronouncement, Andrew Yiannakis and a group of colleagues felt compelled to draw attention to the fact that sports-related violence in America was on the increase. More particularly, they wrote in 1976 that:

> During the past few years, crowd and player violence in sport has increased to such an extent that it has drawn the attention of the mass media, school officials and academicians and resulted in considerable debate regarding its antecedents and consequences. A specific type of violence, namely player violence, has even been taken up by American courts. This burgeoning of violence has also prompted the formation of special commissions at both local and national level to investigate its causes.[19]

Yiannakis *et al.* were not alone in articulating this belief. Peter S. Greenberg even went so far in 1977 as to claim that 'Fear and loathing in the stands is certainly not a new phenomenon, but mass recreational violence has never been so rampant in the sports arenas of America.'[20] Similarly, Edwards and Rackages suggested, also in 1977, that 'sports-related violence flourishes today in crisis proportions; . . . violence has indeed increased and become more malicious – particularly over the last three years.'[21] They were not writing simply of player violence but of crowd violence as well. Moreover, that none of these authors was referring simply to a temporary, short-

199

term trend restricted solely to the 1970s is suggested by Kevin Young, who wrote in 1988 of an 'emergent social problem' – namely, the 'evidence of a growing spectrum of forms and frequencies of sports crowd disorder in [the North American] context.'[22]

Young clearly regards this 'emergent social problem' as more the consequence of an actual increase in the incidence of sports-crowd violence than of an apparent increase that results from growing media and public sensitivity towards it. He also points out how the domestic problem tends to be downplayed by the North American media as 'trivial' in comparison with what is depicted as the much more serious problem of soccer hooliganism in Britain. Our own view on this issue is that the American media are probably largely right. Young seems to have accepted too uncritically the view of Marsh *et al.* that British soccer hooliganism mainly takes the form of relatively harmless 'aggro'. At any rate, the evidence available to us is not indicative of a soccer-style problem of crowd disorderliness having yet taken root in North America, at least not in a major spectator sport. Young also misses the fact that the judgement of American problems of sports-crowd violence as 'trivial' in comparison with soccer hooliganism is probably best understood, at least in part, by reference to the colonial history of North America, to the long-term dominance, especially in the United States, of WASPS,[23] and to the fact that, for a long time, an unreal image of the English as universally 'civilized' – an image derived largely from literary and cinematic depictions of the English upper classes – was widely held in the United States. Soccer hooliganism runs strongly counter to this image. However, it is not interpreted as evidence for the stereotypical – that is, over-generalized, over-simplified and unreal – character of the earlier image but as 'proof' of the 'decline' of English civilization.

However, let us push the analysis further by considering what the small amount of relevant secondary literature currently available to us has to say about the history of sports and sports-crowd violence in the USA. We shall look in this connection not only at the history of spectator violence but at that of player violence as well.

As one can see by reference to the arguments of Peter Marsh, the United States is widely regarded as one of the most violent societies in the 'developed' or urban-industrial world, if not, indeed, as *the* most violent. The popularity in America of sports such as gridiron football if often advanced as one element in this general characterization.

However, although neither the violence of American society nor the (usually controlled) violence of its football can be seriously denied, there is reason to believe that the present-day gridiron game has evolved out of beginnings that were considerably more violent. In the 1890s, for example, not only tackling and blocking but also 'slugging' – that is, the punching of opponents – were apparently accepted as legitimate parts of the game. 'Mostly [the players] stood bolt upright and fought it out hammer and tongs, tooth and nail, fist and feet', as a player of the time is reported to have said. He added that 'arguments followed almost every decision that the referee made.'[24] Methodically thought-out 'mass plays' such as the 'flying wedge' also formed part of the game at that stage. This was a tactic that involved two lines of players joined to form a V, each player except the foremost hanging on to the one in front and charging at full speed with the ball-carrier protected in their midst. Hapless opponents were supposed to bounce off the flying wedge when they tried to halt its progress. In 1905 alone, it seems, no fewer than eighteen college players were killed and a further 159 were seriously injured largely as a result of tactics of this kind. President Theodore Roosevelt was apparently so concerned that he convened a meeting of representatives from the universities of Yale, Princeton and Harvard, admonishing them that 'brutality and foul play should receive the same summary punishment as the man who cheats at cards.'[25] He also threatened to prohibit the game by federal decree.[26] The response to this presidential intervention and to the more general climate of growing concern was the legitimization of the foward pass, an innovation which marked a decisive break in the evolution of American football away from its roots in English rugby and which simultaneously opened up the game and eliminated what Gardner calls 'the ponderous bulldozing of the mass plays.'[27] It was also around this time, it seems, that players began to wear protective equipment, initiating the trend towards the fully armoured 'knights' of American football today. Such a line of development, of course, permitted the retention of a physically violent game while at the same time introducing the possibility of new forms of injury – for example, from the clash of helmeted heads.

Changes in inter-racial behaviour as black Americans have become increasingly integrated into major professional sports also seem broadly consistent with the view that a general decrease in the incidence of violent behaviour has taken place in American sports as the twentieth century has progressed. Take the case of boxing. When Jack Johnson defeated James Jeffries in Reno, Nevada, in July 1910 to become the first black heavyweight champion of the world, the response in many parts of the United States was violent in the extreme. As Allen Guttmann has described it:

> In Houston, Charles Williams openly celebrated Johnson's triumph, and a white man 'slashed his throat from ear to ear'; in Little Rock, two blacks were killed by a group of whites after an argument about the fight in a streetcar; in Roanoke, Virginia, a gang of white sailors injured several blacks; in Wilmington, Delaware, a group of blacks attacked a white and whites retaliated with a 'lynching bee'; in Atlanta a black ran amuck with a knife; in Washington . . . two whites were fatally stabbed by blacks; in New York, one black was beaten to death and scores were injured; in Pueblo, Colorado, thirty people were injured in a race riot; in Shreveport, Louisiana, three blacks were killed by white assailants. Other murders or injuries were reported in New Orleans, Baltimore, Cincinnati, St Joseph, Los Angeles, Chattanooga, and many other smaller cities and towns.[28]

Inter-racial violence – on the part of players – was also apparently common in the early history of baseball in the United States. For example, it seems that the practice of deliberately 'spiking' the legs of basemen with the 'feet first slide' was introduced in the late nineteenth century in an attempt to cripple black players as part of a more general campaign to exclude them from the game.[29] In the meantime, of course, as one might expect in a society in which racial inequality and racial prejudice remain deeply rooted, inter-racial violence has not disappeared from American sport. There were, for example, inter-racial disturbances in 1937 when Joe Louis became world heavyweight champion by defeating the German, Max Schmeling.[30] And, as we noted earlier, a spate of inter-racial fighting at high-school night matches accompanied the black push for greater equality in the 1960s, leading such matches to be banned up and down the country.[31] So far as we can tell, however, inter-racial violence has never recurred on the same scale, so concertedly or with such ferocity as in 1910, and it is reasonable to suppose that a greater number of white Americans are now able and willing to tolerate black supremacy in the sporting sphere and to countenance the individual and collective expression by blacks of pride in their sporting achievements without resorting to violence. But let us turn to the types of sports crowd violence that are observable in America today.

In 1975, Jerry Lewis collated the number of 'riots' at sports events reported in six newspapers in the USA in the years 1960–72. He discovered that a total of 312 'riots' (involving seventeen deaths) were reported in that period, an average of twenty-six per year. The sport-by-sport breakdown was as follows: baseball, 97; football, 66; basketball, 55; ice hockey, 39; boxing, 19; horse-racing, 11; motor-cyle and car racing, 10; golf, 4; soccer, 3; wrestling, 3; athletics, 2; tennis, 2; and air sports, 2.[32] Unfortunately, Lewis was not sufficiently clear in his definition of a 'riot' or in the criteria used in the construction of his table. One is, accordingly, unable to reach judgements regarding the scale and seriousness of the events he was reporting. Nor did Lewis cite lengthy descriptions, detailing what journalists perceived as having taken place in particular cases. However, that seriously violent crowd disturbances do take place at sports events in the United States is suggested by the following report of what happened at a gridiron football match at the Schaefer Stadium, Foxboro, Massachusetts, on 18 October 1977:

> The game started at 9 p.m . . . but the fans began drinking their dinners hours earlier, *en route* to Schaefer Stadium and in the parking lots outside the Foxboro, Massachusetts, sport complex. By game time, all the participants – the New England Patriots, the New York Jets, the ABC Monday Night Football Crew and the crowd – were primed for action. There was plenty of it. While the Patriots were routing the Jets, 41 – 7, the jubilant fans turned on each other, on the cops, and out onto the field. The game was interrupted half a dozen times as eleven rowdies, chased by security guards, tried out the Astro-Turf. Twenty one fans were arrested for disorderly conduct, eighteen were taken into protective custody for public intoxication, two were booked for throwing missiles, two for assault and battery and one for possession of a dangerous weapon. One fan stole another's wheelchair and was arrested for larceny. Thirty spectators were taken to hospital with cuts and bruises, one was stabbed and two died of heart attacks. Foxboro policeman, Tom Blaisdell, sustained a dislocated jaw and a concussion, and while a local sheriff was administering mouth-to-mouth resuscitation to a coronary victim in the stands, a drunken fan urinated on them both. 'It was a tough game,' said Foxboro police

chief, John Gaudett as he reviewed that night's blotter. 'But I've seen even worse.'[33]

It is, we think, not without significance that the police chief cited here claimed to have seen incidents that were 'even worse' than those which took place on that October night in 1976. Since, moreover, the behaviour of the disorderly fans in this case seems to have been related to the success and eventual victory of the local side on the field of play, it is probably safe to conclude that this was an example of what one might call a 'celebratory riot'. That such sports-related disorders in the United States do not take place solely in the immediate context of matches is suggested by the events described in the London *Times* as having taken place in Pittsburgh, Pennsylvania, in 1971, following the victory of the Pittsburgh Pirates in the final of that year's baseball 'World Series':

> An extraordinary orgy of destruction, looting and sexual excess took hold of Pittsburgh, Pennsylvania . . . following the unexpected victory of the Pittsburgh Pirates baseball team. . . During nearly 10 hours of wild, drunken celebrations around the city, men and women indulged in public love-making and nudity. More than 100 people were injured and about 100 others arrested. Some 30 shops were looted and another 30 damaged. Two incidents of sexual assault occurred in full view of hundreds of celebrating fans who, according to eye-witness reports, cheered the assailants and made no attempt to help the victims. There was scattered gunfire during the rampage and one of those admitted to hospital was a middle aged man suffering from a gunshot wound.[34]

A study of the 'Grey Cup Festivities' undertaken by Alan Listiak and his colleagues in Hamilton, Ontario, in 1976 sheds possible light on at least some aspects of the North American tradition of 'celebratory rioting'. The Grey Cup is played for between the winners of Canada's Western and Eastern Football Conferences and is the Canadian equivalent of the American 'Super Bowl'. Listiak and his co-workers compared the behaviour they observed in a number of middle-class 'lounges' with what they saw in several lower-class 'bars' in Hamilton when that city hosted the Grey Cup game. Listiak describes behaviour in the middle-class 'hostelries' as follows:

> The atmosphere of these establishments was super-charged with a high degree of gregarious behaviour and boisterous conduct,

and the level of this legitimate deviance continued to rise as the evening and the drinks flowed on. Spontaneous shouts and yells and horn-blowing emanated from various parts of the bar, competing with each other in . . . volume. . . Males engaged in spirited camaraderie and backslapping types of behaviour. Sporadically spirited fights would break out.[35]

By contrast, 'the whole lower class bar scene could be described as "business as usual".' That is to say, more serious 'fights broke out every hour or so'. Allen Guttmann comments on this difference as follows:

The fights that occurred in the lounge were unusual events associated with a special kind of celebration while the brawls in the bar were 'business as usual'. . . In plain terms, it is likely that the disadvantaged members of every society tend to express their frustrations in direct forms of deviance while the advantaged make greater use of the Saturnalia-like opportunities of the institutionalized 'time-out'. Since football combines primitive elements with a sophisticated complex of teamwork and strategy, it seems especially well suited for its dual function as a model of modern social organization and as an occasion for atavistic release.[36]

Because it avoids the contradiction involved in referring to deviance from norms as 'legitimate', the term 'tolerated deviance' is arguably more adequate for describing the form of middle-class behaviour discussed here by Listiak and Guttmann.[37] More importantly, these authors seemingly fail to see that, independently of social class, playing with, testing and in that sense deviating from social norms seems to be a common ingredient of many forms of leisure behaviour.[38] More importantly still, Guttmann's idea that deviance stems solely from frustration misses the fact that, again independently of social class, forms of pleasure-seeking – a hedonistic quest for enjoyable excitement – are often expressed in social deviance. That certainly appears to be the case as far as European or, at least, English soccer hooliganism is concerned. It is with a discussion of the complex issue of why no direct equivalent of soccer hooliganism appears to have arisen in the United States that we shall conclude this chapter.

WHY IS THERE NO DIRECT EQUIVALENT OF
SOCCER HOOLIGANISM IN THE USA?

Forms of crowd violence and disorderliness that stem basically from frustration are observable at soccer and in other sports contexts in Britain. Examples are disorders triggered by a team losing an important match or because fans are dissatisfied with the way in which their club is run. Celebratory riots are observable as well, though they are usually smaller in scale and less violent than some of those which apparently take place in the United States. In Britain, disorders of this kind do not usually involve much more than a 'pitch invasion'. However, British, and more particularly English, soccer hooliganism manifestly does not take either of these forms. Rather, it involves 'gangs' of adolescent and young adult males who have chosen soccer as a context in which to fight. For them, ability to fight, the expression of courage and physical prowess in a confrontation (usually) with similarly motivated fans who support the other side, together with the display of loyalty towards their 'mates' are sources of ego-enhancing prestige and hence enjoyable. As a result, they tend to seek out fights and to initiate them more frequently than other groups.

The generally macho climate of English soccer appears to be one of the reasons why such males have come to use the game as an arena for their 'war games', the violent masculinity rituals which they enjoy. Spice is added to the occasion by the element of risk involved in the confrontation with rival fans. It is also added by the fact that their activities are illegal and socially disapproved of and hence draw down the attentions of the police. The quest for and experience of pleasurable excitement and ego-enhancing prestige in a soccer context – such males receive positive pleasure and reinforcement from being defined by the media and other representatives of 'respectable' society as 'folk devils', as reviled and feared 'outsiders' – helps to explain why they are so committed to their hooligan activities at and in conjunction with football and why they are so difficult to dislodge. Fighting in soccer-related contexts is high up in their scale of values and acts for them as a stimulant.

Basic to the personality and values of these males is their attachment to what is perhaps best called an 'aggressive masculine style'. Although they are probably usually less seriously violent, their norms and values appear similar in many ways to those of the street gangs in the United States described in that rich sociological literature starting with Thrasher[39] and Whyte,[40] and added to more recently by scholars such as Cohen[41] and Suttles.[42] Indeed, the behaviour of the English soccer hooligans seems to conform closely in many ways to the present-centred hedonism described by Cohen. In short, soccer hooliganism can be understood in part as involving the usurpation of a major professional sport by street gangs. The government, those who own and control the clubs, and the people in charge of British soccer nationally have so far proved relatively unsuccessful in their attempts to resist the 'hooligan challenge'. They may have more or less succeeded, by means of a massive police presence at matches and a battery of stifling controls, in preventing hooligans from fighting inside stadia. However, they have totally failed to dislodge them from the game. In short, it is not stretching the point too far to say of English soccer hooliganism that it is as if the street gangs of Los Angeles, New York or Chicago had chosen, say, American football or baseball as a context in which to fight and usurped large sections of the physical and social space occupied by the game.

The currently available evidence does not suggest that American street gangs have chosen a major sport as a context in which to fight. That US gangs have nevertheless occasionally been involved in sports-related violence, however, is suggested by the public inquiry which took place into the riots that occurred in Detroit following the final of the 1984 World Series and which found that the trouble had been caused not by baseball fans but by 'street kids'.[43] Since the inquiry did not mention the 'street kids' as fighting opposing fans or as having attended the game itself, it seems that the Detroit riots of 1984 only resembled soccer hooliganism 'English-style' superficially. The 'street kids' were presumably simply taking advantage of a 'celebratory riot' in order to pilfer, loot and mug. But whatever is the case in this regard, it would seem safe to conclude that soccer hooligan-type spectator disorders have not yet emerged in the USA. It is worth enquiring why.

The United States has highly publicized mass spectator sports, some of which have a pronounced macho emphasis. It also has a long-established tradition of violent street gangs. Why, then, have such groups not been attracted to the sports context as an arena for engaging in their violent behaviour? Only systematic research could provide a definitive answer to this question. It is nevertheless possible to speculate about conceivable reasons. In fact, Listiak's Canadian research provides what are possibly some useful clues. Let us elaborate on this.

Listiak, it will be recalled, reported a highly charged and excited atmosphere in the middle-class bars in Hamilton that he studied on the occasion of the Grey Cup game. By contrast, the atmosphere he and his colleagues claim to have observed in their sample of lower-class bars was more low-key. This suggests a level of interest in the match among these lower-class Canadians that was lower than that among their middle-class counterparts. Perhaps it stretched as far as watching the game on the bar TV but not as far as actually attending the stadium? This, in its turn, suggests another possibility. Perhaps the lower classes in the United States and Canada (it is the former that we are primarily concerned with in this context), especially those sections to whom the term 'under-class' most literally and realistically applies, tend to be more excluded and self-excluding from national sports, particularly as spectators, than their counterparts in Britain? That would seem especially likely to be the case as far as those most heavily involved in 'the drugs scene' with all its associations of anomie and crime are concerned. The specifically *ethnic* dimensions of the under-class problem in the United States are also likely to be of significance in this regard. However, assuming that it can be empirically ascertained, such a pattern of exclusion may also have something to do with the peculiarities of the process of state formation in the USA. More particularly, the more highly developed 'welfare state' in Britain and the (pre-'Thatcherite') tradition of state intervention in order to smooth out and compensate for some of the vagaries of the 'free market' may have helped to integrate more sections of the working class more fully into the overall 'consensus', thereby incorporating more of them more fully into sports such as football. In the United States, by contrast, federal and state policies based to a greater degree on *laissez-faire* values may have resulted in a greater proportion of the lower classes being less incorporated into dominant values and, consequently, less integrated into sports. In its turn, a consequence of this may have been to insulate American sports to a greater degree from the lower-class pattern of gang fighting.

Possibly also working in the same direction may be the franchise system and the peculiar pattern of ownership of professional sports in the USA. That is to say, the fact that an owner can remove a club lock, stock and barrel from one town or city to another[44] may serve to inhibit the formation of long-term ties of communities with clubs. In its turn, that may facilitate the perception of matches more as sports contests pure and simple and less as 'battles' between rival communities. To the extent that that is so, of course, lower-class gangs are less likely to be attracted to matches as places 'where the action is'.

Maybe in North America, too, the high cost of tickets for major sports events acts as a deterrent to lower-class attendance, especially on the part of those lower-class youths who principally provide the membership of street gangs? Then again, the longer distances between clubs may inhibit travel to away matches. In any event, regular away-match travel does not seem to be such a central part of the culture of sports spectatorship in the United States as it is in Britain and many other European countries. As a result, opposing fans – a ready-made, highly visible, 'outsider' group, an easily identifiable 'enemy' or 'target' – are not so frequently in evidence at matches. In its turn, this may further reduce the incentive for regular match attendance by the members of street gangs. Finally, as Kevin Young has suggested,[45] the lack of a national press in the USA and the fact that only major crimes get regular coverage on national TV means that violent sports-related incidents tend to be given local treatment only, hence helping, on the one hand, to sustain a public perception of the sports context as largely trouble-free and, on the other, to 'devalue' sports (for the hooligans) as a potential site for exciting hooligan action.

This may change, of course. The siting of the World Cup Finals in the United States in 1994 may provide a stage for the English and other European hooligans. If their activities are widely publicized, perhaps they will act as role models for sections of American youth? Only time will tell. What is certainly the case is that cross-national research in this area is urgently needed in order to promote further understanding. Such understanding is not of mere 'academic' value or an 'end-in-itself'. It is a vital prerequisite for effective action; that is to say, for constructing a realistic policy designed to prevent soccer-style hooliganism from developing in or spreading to the United States. It is hoped that this chapter will act as a stimulus to the commissioning and implementation of such research. At the very least, it should help those in charge of policy-making for the 1994 Finals to avoid potentially tragic mistakes because their thinking is based on such patently false assumptions as that soccer hooliganism is a problem *only* with English fans.[46]

NOTES AND REFERENCES

1 See, e.g., Ted Robert Gurr (ed.) *Violence in America*, Vol. 1,

The History of Crime; vol. 2, *Protest, Rebellion, Reform*. London: Sage, 1989.

2 Such arguments are clear examples of the way in which forms of technological reductionism tend to dominate official thinking on these matters. It is easy to see why. Stadia can be made 'all-seater' in a more or less predictable time-period and at a more or less predictable cost. It is far harder, however, to assess the costs and the time likely to be required in order to effect a change in human behaviour. However, such changes are what is necessary in order to reduce the incidence of violence, whether in sports or elsewhere.

3 See Chapter 7 in the present volume, 'Soccer hooliganism as a European phenomenon'.

4 Michael D. Smith *Violence and Sport*. Toronto: Butterworths, 1983.

5 Kevin Young, 'Sports Crowd Disorder, Mass Media and Ideology'. Unpublished doctoral dissertation, McMaster University, Hamilton, Ontario, Canada, 1988.

6 This argument is based on that in Norbert Elias, *What is Sociology?* London: Hutchinson, 1978. A similar argument is proposed by Anthony Giddens in *The Nation-state and Violence*. Oxford: Polity Press. 1987.

7 This possibility has been recently envisaged by Paul Gardner. See his 'Should FIFA Ban England from USA '94?', *Soccer America*, 5 Oct. 1989: 12. Should trouble occur in 1994, suggests Gardner, 'it is unlikely that US soccer would survive in any meaningful form'. His analysis is in some ways persuasive but it contains one vital flaw: failure to recognize that soccer hooliganism is not restricted to England but a phenomenon of pan-European dimensions.

8 Peter Marsh, *Aggro: the Illusion of Violence*. London: Dent, 1979.

9 Konrad Lorenz, *On Aggression*. London: Methuen, 1967.

10 A more detailed and comprehensive critique of Marsh's theory can be found in our *The Roots of Football Hooliganism*. Routledge & Kegan Paul, 1988, pp. 19–23.

11 Marsh, *Aggro*, p. 81.

12 Marsh, *Aggro*, p. 82.

13 Ibid.

14 Ibid.

15 See especially, Norbert Elias, *The Civilizing Process: State Formation and Civilization*. Oxford: Blackwell, 1982.

16 C. Wright Mills, *The Power Elite*, New York: Oxford University Press, 1959, contains, in our view, what remains one of the best sociological analyses of the development of American society.

17 Philip Goodhart and Christopher Chataway, *War Without Weapons*, London: W.H. Allen, 1968, p. 144.

18 Allen Guttmann, *From Ritual to Record*. New York: Columbia University Press, 1978, p. 132.

19 Andrew Yiannakis, Thomas D. McIntyre, Merrill J. Melnick and Dale P. Hart, *Sport Sociology: Contemporary Themes*. Dubuque, IA: Kendall/Hunt, second edition, 1978, p. 216.

20 Peter S.Greenberg, 'Wild in the Stands', *New Times*, 9 (10): 25–7, 62–4, 11 Nov. 1977; reprinted in Yiannakis *et al. Sport Sociology*, pp. 217–21.

21 Harry Edwards and Van Rackages, 'The Dynamics of Violence in American Sport', *Journal of Sport and Social Issues*, 1977 7(2): 3–31; reprinted in Yiannakis, *et al.*, *Sport Sociology*, pp. 221–7.

22 Young, *Sports Crowd Disorder*, p. 383.

23 In the United States, the acronym 'WASP' means 'white Anglo-Saxon Protestant'. It is worth pointing out in this connection that much sports-crowd violence in the USA is probably trivial compared with some of the violent crimes that take place in that country, whereas, in England, football hooliganism stands out in the context of a wider society that is, on the whole, considerably more peaceful.

24 Paul Gardner, *Nice Guys Finish Last: Sport and American Life*. London: Allen Lane, 1974, p. 99.

25 Gardner, *Nice Guys Finish Last*, p. 100.

26 According to David Riesman and Reuel Denney, it was the photograph of a player injured in a Pennsylvania–Swarthmore match that led to Theodore Roosevelt's intervention. See their 'Football in America: a Study in Culture Diffusion', in Eric Dunning (ed.) *The Sociology of Sport*. London: Cass, 1971, p. 167.

27 Gardner, *Nice Guys Finish Last*, p. 100.

28 Allen Guttmann, *Sports Spectators*. New York: Columbia University Press, 1986, p. 119.

29 Robert H. Boyle, 'Negroes in Baseball', in Dunning (ed.) *The Sociology of Sport*, p. 261.

30 Guttmann, *Sports Spectators*, p. 132.

31 Guttman, *From Ritual to Record*, p. 132.

32 Guttman, *Sports Spectators*, p. 162.

33 Quoted by Peter S. Greenberg, in Yiannakis *et al.*, *Sport Sociology*, p. 217.

34 *The Times*, 19 Oct. 1971.

35 Alan Listiak, '"Legitimate Deviance" and Social Class', in Richard S. Gruneau and John G. Allinson (eds) *Canadian Sport*, Don Mills, Ontario, 1976, p. 416; quoted in Guttmann, *From Ritual to Record*, p. 135.

36 Guttmann, ibid.

37 See Eric Dunning, 'Der tolerierte Hooliganismus', in W. Hopf (ed.) *Fussball*, Bensheim: Pad-extra, 1979, pp. 191–2.

38 See Norbert Elias and Eric Dunning, 'Leisure in the Sparetime Spectrum', in their *Quest for Excitement*. Oxford: Blackwell, 1986, pp. 91–125.

39 F.M. Thrasher, *The Gang*. Chicago: University of Chicago Press, 1927.

40 W.F. Whyte, *Street Corner Society: the Social Structure of an Italian Slum*. Chicago: University of Chicago Press. 1955.

41 A.K. Cohen, *Delinquent Boys: the Culture of the Gang*. Glencoe, Ill: Free Press, 1955.

42 Gerald Suttles, *The Social Order of the Slum: Ethnicity and Territory in the Inner-City*. Chicago: University of Chicago Press, 1968; see also his *The Social Construction of Communities*. Chicago: University of Chicago Press. 1972.

43 Quoted by John Williams in his 'White Riots: the English Football Fan Abroad', in Alan Tomlinson and Gary Whannel (eds) *Off the Ball: the Football World Cup*. London: Pluto, 1986, p. 8.

44 A recent example is the transfer of the football Cardinals from St Louis to Phoenix, Arizona.

45 Young, *Sports Crowd Disorder*, p. 371.

46 See, again, Paul Gardner, 'Should FIFA Ban England from USA '94?', op. cit.

Chapter Nine

ENGLISH FOOTBALL AND THE HOOLIGAN CRISIS:
Prevailing policies and constructive alternatives

In *The Roots of Football Hooliganism*, we discussed a number of general policy issues particularly as they relate to the 'roots' and 'causes' of football hooliganism. By the nature of the case, that discussion was addressed primarily to central and local government and politicians. By contrast, most of the social policy recommendations in this final chapter of *Football on Trial* are aimed principally at officials and administrators in the English game. We decided on this focus because of the prominence recently given, largely as a result of the debates generated by the Government's plan to impose a compulsory system of identity cards on the professional game, to the 'community' and 'membership' functions of clubs. We are concerned here, accordingly, more with the limited options available to clubs for contributing to an amelioration – however slight – of the 'hooligan crisis' than we are with the sorts of longer-term measures that would be necessary to tackle that crisis in a more fundamental way. But let us become more specific.

In the minds of many people, hooliganism and football are inexorably intertwined. Indeed, some see the problems that beset the game as almost entirely attributable to the 'scourge of football hooliganism'. This view is not without some credibility. Hooliganism has reduced attendances by alienating many law-abiding supporters. The attendant safety and segregation measures have eaten into ground capacities. The costs of anti-hooligan strategies are a constant drain on the clubs and on bodies such as the Football Trust. Football hooliganism has besmirched the image of the English game. Since 1985, English clubs have been denied international competition. And, in all probability, untold numbers of commercial sponsors have been lost to the game. If anyone continued to harbour doubts about the magnitude of the threat facing English football, these must surely have been dispelled by

213

the comments of the Prime Minister in the wake of the disorders in West Germany in the summer of 1988 when she called into question the very future of the professional game as a spectator sport.[1]

Yet to lay all of football's troubles at the door of hooliganism is a gross over-simplification. Of no less significance is the structural capacity of the game's administration to deal with hooliganism and its other problems. Thus, although this chapter will primarily concern itself with responses to football hooliganism – both current and in prospect – and go on to propose the outline of an alternative programme for action, it will begin by focusing upon some aspects of the structure of the Football League.

Professional soccer in England and Wales is loosely organized. Notwithstanding the existence of a central administration, the predominant forces are centrifugal ones, a tendency which has long undermined the decision-making power of the League Management Committee. Shortly after his election in 1989, Bill Fox, the President of the Football League, gave clear expression to this tendency on a television programme dealing with the problems faced by the game.[2] On the one hand, he clearly wished to present himself as someone capable of bringing about the required changes. On the other hand, however, he continually harked back to the fact that the League consists of ninety-two self-governing entities: the clubs. His and the Management Committee's desire for change seems to be closely bound up with the recent appointment of a chief executive. It would, of course, be a mistake to think that the structure of the League could be changed solely by the qualities of a single individual. But if such an appointment were indicative of a recognition on the part of the constituent clubs that circumstances demand that they should relinquish some of their autonomy, then the scope for significant initiatives will begin to widen. Even so, to recognize the need for change in principle and even to facilitate the creation of the post of chief executive with a brief to enact radical measures is one thing; a willingness on the part of the clubs to accept the concrete consequences of the resultant policies is quite another.

In summary then, an effective leadership has to have at least two attributes. First, it has to be capable of determining the possibilities for movement – forced or otherwise – within the existing structure. Second, it has to assess the extent to which such changes will enhance the capacity of the organization to tackle the range of problems currently confronting it. Of course, it will also have to be open to the possibility that the existing structure of the League may be too ossified to address effectively the issues before it.

Another possibility is that outside bodies will intervene in such ways as to make at least aspects of the present structure of the League increasingly untenable. This pressure may come from a number of sources. For example, it is entirely possible that developments in other areas of the sports/leisure industry will further erode match attendances. More direct intervention will continue to come from television. In many ways, the ramifications of the television–football relationship have been unintended. They have been the result of the former pursuing its own objectives, and it cannot be said that these have to any great degree encompassed the long-term well-being of the game. Government interventions have taken a similar form. Concern about football hooliganism has led it to impose restraints and obligations on the game. In doing so, it has taken little regard of football's capacity to cope with these impositions. Perhaps in the longer term more concerted and constructive pressure for change will come from the growing involvement of local authorities with football clubs. Although the relationship between some clubs and their local authorities may be a fraught one, there is a range of interests that could be pursued to the mutual benefit of both parties. We have in mind such things as the enhancement of local identities; the pursuit of more egalitarian policies with respect to gender and ethnicity; a more rational use of sports-leisure facilities and the interchange of expertise. In fact, some local authorities own the grounds of League clubs. Many are increasingly involved in the community dimension of club affairs. Already, in some cases, this developing relationship might be more aptly described as a partnership. Furthermore, and notwithstanding the role of the proposed Football Licensing Authority, at the moment all local authorities have responsibility for issuing ground safety certificates. This leverage may enable local authorities, perhaps through such bodies as the Association of Metropolitan Authorities, to exert systematic pressure for change on football. Under these emerging conditions, it is certain that football will not be left 'to put its own house in order'.

The central concern of the above preamble has been to point to some of the limitations of the existing structure of the League and the implications these have for its ability to respond and innovate over a range of areas and issues. The focus will now become more specific, concentrating on the effects of these limitations on football's ability to handle the problem of football hooliganism.

FOOTBALL'S FINANCIAL CRISIS

From the outset, it should be recognized that the counter-hooligan strategies pursued over the past two decades have been, *on balance*, unsuccessful. Were this not so, the issue of football hooliganism would hardly figure as prominently as it still does on the political agenda. Nevertheless, this rather sweeping assertion requires some elaboration. It is undoubtedly the case that, as far as grounds are concerned, ordinary supporters are better insulated from the activities of hooligans than they were in the late 1960s and the 1970s. The 'pacification' of stadia has been achieved by the employment of such means as sophisticated policing techniques, segregation, penning and closed-circuit television. However, an unintended consequence of this policy of containment has been a tendency to compromise on the issue of spectator safety, together with the generation of enhanced levels of solidarity among certain hooligan groups and a commensurate expansion in their organizational abilities. These emerging features have found violent expression in other phases of match-days. This process of displacement seems to be an inevitable consequence of defining football hooliganism as a problem rooted specifically in football. To conceive of its antecedents in these narrow terms leads to the adoption of equally narrowly focused counter-strategies. The tragedy has been that, while the hooligans have adapted to and in many ways thrived upon the increased attention, the game itself and ordinary supporters have become increasingly enmeshed in the control measures. As we have already argued earlier in this book, the disaster at Hillsborough resulted, at least in part, from measures designed to prevent hooliganism. At the same time, it would still be unrealistic to think in terms of immediately dismantling the panoply of containment arrangements that at present characterise match-days. So how, then, is football to begin to extricate itself from this entrapment?

Clearly, its ability to do this is not advanced by the financial crisis that grips the game. At the moment, eighty of the ninety-two League clubs are said to be trading in the red. This is a state of affairs that the banking system would hardly tolerate in any other sector of the business world. But within this generally bleak picture, there are concentrations of wealth – specifically, in the hands of the 'big five' clubs. These concentrations have been facilitated by a series of processes, among them the abolition of the maximum wage, freedom of contract for players, retention of all the gate money for League matches by the home club and the increasingly skewed distribution of TV money. This concentration of resources gives this elite group a greater degree of autonomy and tends to make them less susceptible to the cold winds blowing around most clubs. Yet, even these assets are insufficient to protect them from international pressures. The present ban on English clubs competing in Europe has hit the big clubs particularly hard. It has denied them an important source of revenue and intensified the problem of retaining and attracting the more gifted players. These contingencies may have added a degree of urgency to the process whereby the big five have extended their control over the resources available to the domestic game. But this should not lead us to lose sight of the fact that this process has far deeper roots and more diverse sources of momentum than are traceable to the European ban alone. The likely long-term outcome is a European Super-League, even if the actions of hooligans decree that match attendance is limited to the fans of host clubs.

THE FOOTBALL SPECTATORS BILL AND MEMBERSHIP SCHEMES

The growing demands placed upon existing resources bring us to what is perhaps the most controversial issue of the moment (autumn 1989) – the Football Spectators Bill. The central objection of the clubs and the football authorities to the national identity card system is that such an approach will inevitably have a detrimental effect on their principal source of revenue – gate receipts. Perhaps understandably, the public debate on the issue of identity cards has been an emotional and heated affair, one dominated by invective as opposed to balanced argument. It would, therefore, profit us to take a calmer look at some of the developments that have taken place so far.

The first thing to establish is the range of options that are available. The central distinction to draw in this connection is that between the 'partial' and the 'total' approaches. The former allocates a portion of the ground to card-holding home supporters. The latter requires that every entrant be a card carrier. Both strategies can be geared to a single club or be national in scope. If the total approach is based on a single club, it can formally aim to exclude all away fans (as at Luton Town, for example) or it may allow entry of away fans who are members at their own clubs. If it is a national system, it can either allow any card-holder to enter any League ground or it can be so organized as to limit the right of admission to card-holding home supporters. It is, of course, possible to contrive variations on these themes, but in broad outline, these are the choices available. On this basis, let us now reflect upon some of the implications of these approaches by assessing the experiences of two pioneering clubs and then move on to a consideration of the proposed national scheme.

Five months prior to the Heysel tragedy, Leicester City launched its own partial membership scheme.[3] The principal reason for this unilateral action was the growing problem of a rowdy element entering the seated sections of the ground. As a result, many complaints were received from orderly fans. To retain their support, the club decided to convert one side of the ground into a membership area. The idea was to create a safe haven for those fans who prefer to watch their football under more orderly conditions.

Since this membership scheme is open to anyone to join, the desired atmosphere was actually brought about by a process of self-selection and self-exclusion. Those fans who wished to retain their traditional vantage point and those whose priority was to watch the game under more orderly circumstances took out membership. Conversely, those who were against membership in principle, those who preferred an alternative section and those who sought confrontation with visiting supporters opted not to join. Thus, as a result of these informal processes, the members' area at Leicester has been virtually trouble-free since its establishment in January 1985. This development has facilitated the almost complete withdrawal of the police from the members' section and the employment of low-profile security guards. Moreover, following Lord Justice Popplewell's report, the police sanctioned the dismantling of the perimeter fence in front of the members' stand as an alternative to embarking upon costly safety modifications. Another consequence of the success of the scheme is that police resources can now be concentrated in the potentially more troublesome areas of the ground. This, in combination with closed-circuit television (CCTV), has had the effect of generally subduing the hooligan element inside the stadium.

So the general conclusion must be that Leicester City's partial scheme has been a success within its own limited terms. Rightly, it was never conceived of as a total answer to hooliganism. Ideally, such schemes ought to be seen as elements in a broader strategy. But even with the success enjoyed by Leicester's approach, the club cannot afford to become complacent. For example, the seeds of future disorder may have been sown in the 1988–9 season. Leicester were drawn against their local rivals, Nottingham Forest, in the Littlewood's Cup. The demand for tickets was considerable. Sections of the crowd – including some of the rowdier elements – who perhaps had not previously contemplated joining the scheme applied for membership. Having taken the plunge and perhaps in flight from the heavy policing that characterizes their traditional sections, these fans seem now to have acquired a taste for the less controlled environment of the Members Stand. To date, their activities have largely been limited to a strong vocal presence, racist barracking and the stamping of feet. However, on the occasion of Chelsea's visit in the 1988–9 season, some of them exhibited an eagerness to join in the disturbances in the adjacent Double Decker stand. The implication seems to be that clubs have to monitor these schemes carefully and, if possible, react to changing patterns before they reach problem status.[4]

The Leicester scheme has received the minimum of national publicity. The same cannot be said of Luton Town's approach.[5] In April 1985, Kenilworth Road was the scene of a major disorder instigated largely by followers of Millwall. Crucially, it was captured on film by television cameras. The FA reacted by insisting that Luton install a perimeter fence in front of its Family Stand. However, rather than comply with this edict, the club took the radical step of introducing a home-fans-only membership scheme. This constituted the first systematic attempt by any club to exclude all away fans.

In general terms, this approach has had three major consequences. First, it has succeeded in making match-days in Luton virtually trouble-free. As such, the scheme has won the overwhelming support of the non-football-going public of Luton. Second, although the club has not managed, or even necessarily tried, to exclude all away supporters, it has substantially reduced their numbers. Third, the scheme has had the negative effect of reducing the gate. And, as David Evans, the ex-chairman of Luton has conceded, this decline has occurred in a period of unprecedented success for the club. But perhaps more important than the local impact of the scheme has been the influence it has had upon Government thinking and the support it is seen to provide for a national identity-card system. However, before generalizing the findings of the Luton experience, it is as well to recognize its distinctive character. First, Luton Town is a relatively small club. Because of its geographical location it had particular – though far from unique – crowd problems.[6] Second, because of its relative distance from other clubs, it has been able to draw a circle around its ground in order to establish a 'legitimate' catchment area for membership. Third, it should be recognized that part of the scheme's success has been due to the fact that it has been limited to a single club. In other words, it may not have been tested to the full because it is a specific rather than a general challenge to hooligans. Therefore, the questions to ask are these: 'How would the London clubs, for example, with their overlapping supporter markets, establish their catchment areas?' 'How would such a scheme deal with the fact that, on match-days in the capital, dozens of groups of fans with hooligan intentions are criss-crossing the city on the transport network?' Finally, if the Luton approach were generalized to all League clubs, how would the hooligan element react to the blanket ban on away fans?

Of course, for the time being, these questions have been placed on the back burner because the Football Spectators Bill, while partly inspired by the Luton approach, is likely to lead to an identity-card system which grants card-holders the right to enter all League grounds. The speed with which the Government was pursuing this type of scheme was slowed and deflected by the final report of Lord Justice Popplewell.[7] He came down in favour of the partial approach. And, after long and often acrimonious negotiations with the Government, the League Management Committee agreed to recommend the introduction of a 50 per cent membership scheme for all League clubs. These partial schemes were to be established and running by the beginning of the 1987-8 season.

Given our earlier comments on the structure of the League, it should come as no surprise to find that many clubs chose to modify the stipulated requirements. Some did so in conjunction with the police in order to meet local conditions. Others were simply intent on paying the minimal lip-service to the agreement. One club refused to comply in any way. So, before rushing in to judge a particular partial scheme, it is as well to take account of the enthusiasm, rigour and intelligence with which a club has planned and administered the project. Of course, it goes without saying that similar considerations should also apply to an appraisal of total schemes. The disparate nature of partial schemes, the unwillingness of many clubs to commit themselves to the possibility of their successful operation and the more general failure to recognize the limited objectives of this approach have meant that this experience has helped to force the issue of a national system back on the agenda. This process was simply brought to a head by the street disorders in West Germany in the summer of 1988,[8] In the wake of these disturbances, the Government announced its determination to see the establishment of a national system. Then, when the League representatives had to concede their inability to deliver the clubs' support for a self-imposed scheme, the Government embarked upon legislation.

Many of the pros and cons of a national identity-card system have been well aired, albeit selectively. But, of course, the eventual form taken by the scheme awaits the deliberations of the Football Membership Authority and the conclusions of Lord Justice Taylor's Final Report on the Hillsborough disaster. In anticipation of this, let us consider some of the issues that are likely to be central.

First of all, there is the question of civil liberties. Many people are opposed to identity cards in principle. It is said that these cards are at variance with British liberal tradition. Some people go so far as to argue that the imposition of ID cards on football supporters is but a stalking horse for their general introduction. Against this, others stress the civil rights of the non-football-going public – the residents in the vicinity of grounds and tradespeople whose lives and businesses have been regularly disrupted on match-days. While one can attempt to assess the consequences of the scheme on freedom of movement, weighing the respective interests of the various parties ultimately involves a value-judgement. The likelihood is that general perceptions of the system will depend very much upon the number of people who have negative experiences of its operation and the attendant media coverage.

Next, there is the technology itself. Is it vandal-proof? What is its level of reliability? Is it capable of performing the designated tasks? Is it able to process crowds under exacting conditions? Will the system be able to identify and exclude illegitimate card-holders without undue disruptions and delays? To what extent will the operation of the system be affected by the fact that it has been imposed on club officials and yet requires their active co-operation? Will the system increase or reduce police costs? And, very much connected with this issue, will its implementation further shift the focus of disorder away from grounds? How will the system affect attendances? Will crowds decline and, if so, will the majority of clubs be able to bear the losses? All that can be said at the moment is that the likely ramifications of the introduction of a national identity-card system will be more complex than most predictions allow.

Part II of the Football Spectators Bill is directed at the activities of English hooligans abroad. The proposal is to withdraw the identity card of anyone convicted of a football-related offence in the context of matches held at home or abroad. An additional requirement is that, for a stipulated period, they must report to a police station at the times when English teams are due to play abroad. However, it is important to note as far as offences committed abroad are concerned, that a card can only be withdrawn if the host nation is prepared to bring charges. As we saw, for example, with the disorders in Sweden in September 1989, while more than 100 English supporters were taken into custody, none was charged.[9] It should also be noted that some foreign police forces are highly sensitive to the threat posed by English hooligans and it is, therefore, conceivable that merely boisterous fans will be caught in a dragnet leading to conviction with inordinately punitive consequences.[10] The fact that there are now well-established hooligan groups in a number of European countries at least raises the possibility that orderly English supporters could be engulfed by a disturbance and, thus, run the attendant risks of arrest, conviction and black-listing.

Nevertheless, leaving aside the possibility that injustices could occur, this general strategy does hold out the promise of preventing regular offenders from travelling abroad for football and, possibly, for reducing the involvement of English fans in foreign disorders. However, if the legislation does not impose retrospective bans on convicted hooligans, and with the development of hooligan problems in Holland, West Germany and Italy, it is difficult to be sanguine about the prospects for the World Cup in 1990. If disorder occurs in the streets and stadia of Italy and if it centrally involves English supporters, then the ban on English clubs, far from being rescinded, could well be extended to include the national team. But, of course, as in the European Championships in West Germany in 1988, if disorders do occur, they are likely to feature hooligans from a number of countries. Should this occur, UEFA will have much more on its plate than the so-called 'English Disease'. The bleakest outcome might be that a significant number of European matches, at both club and national level, will be restricted to home fans only. This would be an ominous fanfare to '1992 and all that'.

MEMBERSHIP AND THE 'COMMUNITY' FUNCTIONS OF CLUBS

Returning to the domestic scene – if, as at least seems possible, the introduction of a national identity-card system triggers a marked decline in attendances, how are the majority of clubs going to cope? Some may decide to adopt the high-risk strategy of allowing the scheme to collapse around them. Given the precarious state of club finances and if a semblance of the present structure is to be preserved, a more effective course of action may be to attempt to get the strength of their supporters and their communities around them in other ways. If, or when, a national scheme comes into force, clubs may be better advised to try to turn it to their best advantage. It may be possible to transform it from being what is essentially a negative and defensive device into one which is more positive and forward-looking. In other words, the possibility may exist to transform it from being simply a means of identification and registration into a genuine system of membership and involvement. In this regard, they would do well to look at some of the clubs of continental Europe to draw upon their experience of alternative structures and different patterns of supporter involvement. [11] In addition, if a strategy of this kind is to be successful, clubs would be well advised to look beyond their current supporters to their wider communities. They might try, for example, to develop a network of ties with authorities, schools, youth clubs and other local groups and organizations. Such ties will ideally be characterized by permanent and reciprocal obligations. In a word, they should not simply involve regular contacts, but rather an institutionalized commitment. The means by which this general community approach can be pursued and extended are already in place in the form of the Professional Footballers Association-inspired and Manpower Services (now Training) Commission-financed 'Football and the Community' initiative which is at present operating at more than fifty clubs (October 1989). The Government deserves credit for supporting this programme. It would, however, deserve more if it were to make this initiative one of the central planks of its policy for football and, of course, if it were to provide the programme with commensurate funding. How much more productive such an approach would be, compared with the sterility of simply escalating the tired old containment and punitive policies, policies that have been found wanting over the years.

With the right sort of training and financial support, the PFA/TC schemes have great potential, but clubs will only reap the full benefits if they give them their whole-hearted backing. Conversely, if they simply view them as a means by which they can obtain additional resources from an external agency, they will be frittering away a golden opportunity – perhaps even the last opportunity for some clubs.

Research we have conducted into Preston North End's community project has provided the first substantive evidence that these schemes can actually have a positive impact on attendances.[12] So, while many Boards of Directors do not see themselves as being in the business of philanthropy, this happy coincidence of community activities and revolving turnstiles could prove to be the most persuasive argument of all.

The success of the Preston community project is partly based on the club's artificial pitch. Such surfaces are, of course, a contentious issue in football. We do not propose, in this context, to enter into the debate surrounding their playing properties apart from saying that the newer generation of such surfaces seem to be a considerable improvement on earlier versions. But what critics of the artificial surface should recognize is that community initiatives can be greatly facilitated by the possession of an artificial pitch. It is the means by which a club's principal asset, perhaps its only asset, can be transformed from one which is used for a few meagre hours a week – weather permitting – into one that is available for up to ninety hours a week. This creates the conditions whereby the stadium can become a vibrant focal point for the whole community and also another revenue-raising part of club activities. It is for this reason that the football authorities – and probably many football supporters – might be advised to reconsider their position on artificial playing surfaces, at least as far as Third and Fourth Division clubs are concerned.[13]

Consistent with this policy of encouraging greater community involvement is the aim of making football a thoroughly family game. There is much work to be done in this regard because, traditionally, football has been maintained as a predominantly 'male preserve'. The public position of many clubs is that they do indeed want to attract a family audience. But this aspiration rests rather uneasily alongside, for example, the general facilities on offer for female fans and the widespread ban on females entering board rooms. If it persists, such discrimination will testify to the shallowness of football's commitment to change and will surely epitomize an atrophying structure. Similarly, in contrast to the high profile of the women's game in many continental European countries, in England female soccer is still assigned Cinderella status – under-funded, under-publicized, with only a skeletal administration and given very little support, financial or otherwise from the male game or other outside sources. Opening the game up to females as participants, officials and spectators is likely to result in important changes. It will begin to undermine the image of football as a 'male preserve', a quality that the hooligans find so attractive. An influx of females also has the potential to change aspects of the atmosphere of stadia, the general demeanour of the crowd and the public's perception of the game. Football may be a particularly tough nut to crack in this respect but, in a range of social situations, it is empirically observable that the presence of females has a constraining, civilizing effect on the behaviour of males.

These proposals may be seen as too radical in certain quarters, but the reality is that some clubs already have associated women's teams – among them Millwall, Arsenal, Preston and Doncaster. Let us make our position on this issue crystal clear. We are not advocating the greater involvement of females in football simply as a means of curbing male aggression. We welcome their greater involvement as a valuable 'end in itself'. At the most fundamental sociological level, though, our point depends upon the socially produced balance of power between the sexes in society at large. It is only through an increment to the power of women relative to men that the sort of strategy we are advocating here can be made to work.

A recent indication of a growing willingness of clubs to move in the 'community' direction is the fact that fifty-seven of the ninety-two League clubs entered the 'Community Awards' Scheme, introduced by the Football Trust in 1988–9. This was a competition designed both to determine which clubs are in the forefront of this movement and to encourage others to emulate them. Had such a competition been held, say six years earlier, the chances of the vast majority of application forms ending up anywhere other than in the waste bins of club secretaries would have been remote. The broad community approach does not only provide clubs with the opportunity to make a significant contribution to the well-being of their local communities. Of perhaps equal importance in these image-conscious times, is that they will be seen to be doing so.

In advocating such an approach, it is important to make clear that our argument is not that this community/family/membership strategy will resolve the problem of hooliganism. As we have argued consistently in our publications, the roots of hooliganism lie primarily outside the game.[14] To expect football to resolve this age-old problem off its own bat is either a failure of the intellect or a particularly blatant piece of buck-passing.

Officialdom, both inside and outside the game, needs to face up to the fact that, on its own, the present strategy of containment underpinned by punitive measures has proved to be of only limited success. Its failings involve the fact that this approach, by its very nature, runs the risk of reinforcing the values and standards which are intrinsic to hooliganism. Of course, a custodial sentence removes a particular offender from circulation. But what is the probability that the experience will be a salutary/reforming one? The balance of evidence suggests that prisons operate as 'schools for crime' rather than as institutions for rehabilitation. More specifically, the hooligan is placed in a male preserve characterized by a formal and informal dominance hierarchy based, in large measure, on coercive control. As such, there is a certain congruity between prison and street culture. Prison life has the propensity to reinforce the brutalizing experience of the 'street'.[15] This is not to argue that custodial sentences have no place in the judicial system. Rather, it is a call for the reassessment of the nature and function of custodial establishments. Quite clearly, there is a need to protect the public from offenders who have been seriously violent in a football context or elsewhere. But, the use of custody in its current form as a general response to hooliganism has all the scientific credibility of the claim that alcohol is an effective cure for a hangover. It is, of course, also the case that the punitive approach aims at deterring others from enlisting in the hooligan ranks. There is, however, little in the history of the last few decades to indicate that football hooligan groups have encountered recruitment problems. In the short term, the authorities will be well advised to consider new forms of disposal for more 'marginal' football offenders as a means of breaking cycles of recidivism and releasing pressures on our already massively overcrowded prison system.[16] It is not our intention to sound glibly optimistic. We recognize that there are no easy solutions. But the shortcomings of traditional policies surely demand a willingness to consider other approaches.

Consider the record. Over the last thirty years, in response to football hooliganism, we have more or less run the gamut of social control measures. In the process, a relatively minor social problem has been transformed into one that commands a significant amount of parliamentary time. It has also damaged the international reputation particularly of England and now threatens the very future of the English professional game. Of course, the rise of football hooliganism has been a complex process and cannot be understood solely as a consequence of the social reaction to it. Nevertheless, the official response has been a central element in the developmental trajectory of the phenomenon. In light of these shortcomings, it should not be too difficult to improve upon this record.

The alternative strategy proposed here is based on the observation that one of the principal characteristics of twentieth-century British social history has been a process of incorporation – that is, a process whereby large sections of the working class have moved closer to the dominant standards and away from the traditional ones of street culture. We examined this process at some length in *The Roots of Football Hooliganism*.[17] Suffice to say in this context that it has been a partly planned, partly unintended process. History, it is sometimes said, is our only reliable guide to future action. And, this desire to derive lessons from history is presumably predicated on the wish to tip the balance of social development more in the direction of intentionality and control. It would also seem to follow that only central government, in co-operation with the local authorities, is in a position to initiate and co-ordinate policy programmes on the necessary scale. More specifically, these policies should not only be geared to a more equitable distribution of opportunities; they should also involve a recognition of the part played by the cultural transmission of disadvantage – that is to say, of the part played in the generation of hooligan values and standards by family life, the school, increasingly the media and the experience of the 'street', with its excitement and its alternative structures of power. Intervention at this level will necessarily involve a willingness to embrace policies which compensate for existing structural disadvantage. We concede that much work is required in order to hammer out the details of such a strategy and that, as part of this process, there is a need to pay constant attention to the compatibility of the elements of which the broader strategy is comprised.

In the present political climate, the likelihood is that these kinds of more general proposals – with their social planning and co-ordinated interventionist implications – will be dismissed either on ideological grounds or because of their lack of fit with what is held to be politically realistic. These are, however, essentially superficial judgements which take little heed of the underlying reality that anything as deeply historically and structurally rooted as hooliganism is unlikely to be amenable to policies conceived of on the hoof. So many prevailing social policies owe more to the imperatives of political expediency and ideology than they do to an understanding of the phenomena they purport to affect. If the guiding aim is to address in the longer term the roots of hooliganism, it is not our proposals that fail the relevancy test.

It should now be clear that none of the football-related proposals contained in this chapter are meant to be read as an attempt to remove primary responsibility from government. At the same time, it is not enough for football's representatives to parrot the statement, 'Football hooliganism is society's problem'. Football is a significant part of society and, as such, it is incumbent upon the game to shoulder its share of the responsibility. Football clubs are well placed to make a valuable contribution to the more general process of incorporation, and they can do so safe in the knowledge that they are also pursuing their own self-interests. It is almost certainly in their long-term interest, for example, to encourage the greater involvement of fans in the affairs of the club they support both financially and vocally. It is in their interest, too, to encourage the greater involvement of females who, if they attend matches at present, do so largely on male terms. They should encourage the greater involvement of the community which has traditionally been seen more as a catchment area than a partner. At the moment, few clubs have any real appreciation of the social composition of their crowd and, therefore, they have little knowledge of their potential market. Austere times require that clubs cultivate support by such means as opinion surveys, direct consultation and, yes – even though it may be anathema to exclusion-minded board members – by offering representation.

The policy 'We want their money but not their participation' is a failed one. It is no basis for developing ties of loyalty and commitment. Of course, money is a crucial ingredient of a secure future, but it is not the only source of strength. For all its troubles, football is still of immense cultural significance. Locally, clubs are the objects of great affection. The players are local heroes, albeit on occasions the fallen heroes of their fans. They are role-models for the young and as such they wield great influence. In these critical times, it is to this bountiful well of goodwill that clubs should be turning. If the exclusive and entrenched proprietorial view continues to hold sway, then the likelihood is that a number of clubs will go to the wall. If survival is the name of the game then the majority of clubs would seem to have little alternative but to pursue new approaches to their affairs. To wait complacently and compliantly for the elite clubs to decide their fate for them can only be seen as paralysis of the imagination. The proposals set forth here constitute a strategy for the future because they will not only widen the game's appeal; contact with schools and the community will also give the clubs a direct line to potential and nascent hooligans. Through these contacts, the clubs should be capable of presenting a different image of the game and, crucially, it will be an image of substance. Under these conditions, the tabloid-exploited picture of football as a male preserve ruled by 'hard men' can give way to one of football as a more integrating and non-discriminatory activity. To paraphrase Gordon Taylor, the aim should be to create an environment which is alien to hooliganism.[18] Who knows, perhaps the lasting paradox will be that hooliganism will come to be seen as the catalyst that helped to democratize the 'people's game'?

POSTSCRIPT: SOME COMMENTS
ON THE TAYLOR REPORT

This chapter on policy responses to soccer's long-standing and deep-rooted 'hooligan crisis' was mainly written in the autumn of 1989, several months before the publication of Lord Justice Taylor's final report on the disaster which took place at the Hillsborough Stadium, Sheffield, in April of that year. While writing the chapter, we could not be certain what the implications of the Taylor Report would be for the Government's plan to introduce a computerized national identity-card scheme for football. Nor could we know in advance how the Government would respond to the Lord Justice's recommendations. Accordingly, we felt it best to assume for purposes of writing that the Government's policy would be unaffected and comforted ourselves with the thought that, if the Taylor Report did come out strongly against the identity-card scheme and if the Government did decide to shelve it, we could always add a postscript bringing the analysis, at least to some extent, up to date.

In the event, the chapter has fallen foul of a problem one is always liable to encounter when dealing with up-to-the-minute issues: the onward march of events. The final Taylor Report *was* strongly critical of the Government's scheme. The Government *did* agree to put the scheme on ice, at least for the time being. Hence this short postscript. We hasten to add, however, that the diagnosis of the underlying problem presented in this chapter (and elsewhere in this book) has not, in our opinion, been fundamentally altered by these events. Nor, in large part, has the structurally conditioned capacity of football to respond to the 'hooligan crisis' been fundamentally enhanced. All that has happened is that a particular policy has been – perhaps only temporarily – partially withdrawn. Accordingly, the part of our analysis that deals specifically with this policy may have been rendered of historical interest only.

If we had sufficient time and space, we might, in this postscript, have essayed a full-scale sociological critique of the final Taylor Report. All that is possible in the present context, however, are a couple of comments. The first thing worthy of mention is the fact that the Lord Justice was surely right to be critical of the identity-card scheme on grounds of safety and practicality. Even so, whilst he may have been correct to reject this particular technological solution for what is a complex and deep-seated problem of human behaviour and relations, we are not so sure of two other aspects of the learned judge's case. In particular, we have doubts regarding his criticisms of the 'poor leadership' in British football. We also have a degree of scepticism regarding his advocacy of all-seater stadia as means for combating hooliganism and enhancing the safety of grounds.

Our doubts regarding the first of these two aspects of Lord Justice Taylor's case do not rest on the belief that the quality of British football's current leadership is high. Rather, they stem from the observation that such issues are questions of social structure and not just of the qualities of individuals. In this final chapter of *Football on Trial*, we have endeavoured to point to some aspects of British football's current structure which seem to us to militate against effective leadership and decisive unified action on a national scale.

Regarding the issue of all-seater stadia, it is, we feel, enough in the present context to say that, whilst such constructions may be desirable on grounds of comfort, their relevance to issues such as hooliganism and crowd safety is not so clear-cut. Thus, as we pointed out in an earlier report, seats did not prevent the occurrence of hooliganism at Coventry City.[19] Nor are they the answer to all potential problems faced by large crowds. They can obstruct egress in the case of fires, for example. In fact, similar to the faith of the Government and its supporters on this issue in the efficacy of computerised entry as a means for combating hooliganism, the Lord Justice and other advocates of all-seater stadia seem to place too much reliance on changing the built environment as a means of modifying behaviour. Sociologically, however, football hooliganism and crowd tragedies are both fundamentally problems of social structure and social behaviour. We hope that the essays in *Football on Trial* will help to persuade more people of the need for sociological research into and analysis of such issues. If we are right, only on that basis will it be possible to construct realistic policies which stand a chance of producing the intended results.

NOTES AND REFERENCES

1   See J. Williams, E. Dunning and P. Murphy, *Hooligans Abroad*. London: Routledge, 1989, Introduction to the second edition p. xlvi.
2   'Football Crazy', Channel 4, 19 Aug. 1989.
3   See P. Murphy, E. Dunning and J. Williams, 'House of Cards: the Development of the Leicester City Members Plan', Sir Norman Chester Centre for Football Research, Department of Sociology, University of Leicester, 1985.
4   In fact, early in the 1989–90 season, Leicester City officials cancelled the membership of four members of this group.
5   See J. Williams, E. Dunning and P. Murphy, 'The Luton Town Members Scheme: Final Report' (with new Postscript), Sir Norman Chester Centre for Football Research, Department of Sociology, University of Leicester, 1989.
6   The proximity of Luton to London and the nearness of the ground to the railway station and the city centre meant that the influx of rowdy fans caused considerable disruption to the commercial and residential life of the town. For a fuller account, see J. Williams *et al.*, 'The Luton Town Members Scheme'.
7   O. Popplewell, *Committee of Inquiry into Crowd Safety and Crowd Control at Sports Grounds: Final Report*. London: HMSO, 1986.
8   See J. Williams, E. Dunning and P. Murphy 'Hooliganism after Heysel: Crowd Behaviour in England and Europe, 1985–88', Sir Norman Chester Centre for Football Research, Department of Sociology, University of Leicester, 1988.
9   In fact, Swedish law explicitly allows for a cooling-off period in custody without charges being brought.
10 See, e.g. Williams *et al.*, *Hooligans Abroad*, pp. 87–91.
11 See, for example, *The Economist*, 31 May 1986.
12 See P. Murphy, E. Dunning and J. Williams, 'Preston North End Crowd Survey' (Preliminary report), Sir Norman Chester Centre for Football Research, Department of Sociology, University of Leicester, 1988.
13 The Football League have recently modified their position on plastic pitches. They have ordered the removal of all plastic pitches in the First and Second Divisions by the 1991–2 season. Clubs promoted to Division Two are to be given two years in which to comply with the above order. Clubs in the Third and Fourth Divisions can retain their plastic pitches. There is also the possibility that one additional artificial surface will be allowed per season in the two lower

divisions. See 'Commission of Inquiry into Playing Surfaces, Final Report', May 1989.

14 See E. Dunning, P. Murphy and J. Williams, *The Roots of Football Hooliganism: an Historical and Sociological Study*, London: Routledge, 1988.

15 See, e.g., HM Chief Inspector of Prisons, *Report on HM Prison and Remand Centre, Hull*, London: Home Office, 1989.

16 See, e.g., our comments on ideas for dealing with more 'marginal' football offenders in 'An Investigation of the Measures for Improving Spectator Behaviour Currently in Use at Seven English Football Clubs', Sir Norman Chester Centre for Football Research, Department of Sociology, University of Leicester, 1988, p. 18. The Government's White Paper of February 1990 recognizes that it 'is unrealistic to expect prisoners to emerge at the end of their sentence as reformed characters; imprisonment provides many opportunities to learn criminal skills from other inmates'. See *Crime, Justice and Protecting the Public. The Government's Proposals for Legislation*, London: HMSO, Cm.965, February 1990, p. 11.

17 See *The Roots of Football Hooliganism*, Ch. 6.

18 See the *Guardian*, 26 Aug. 1988.

19 See our *All-Seated Football Grounds and Hooliganism: The Coventry City Experience, 1981–84*, Sir Norman Chester Centre for Football Research, Department of Sociology, University of Leicester, 1984.

INDEX